take a hint from the heavens...

1986 is packed with promise. Make the most of it with the predictions, insights, clues and suggestions America's most popular astrologer, Sydney Omarr, has prepared for you!

Learn about the "geometry" of relationships—who you get along with, and why . . . pore over celebrity sun signs and personality profiles . . . discover how and why the movements of the zodiac affect men and women so differently . . . and much, much more. Whatever your desire, whatever your dilemma, let Sydney Omarr's time-tested wisdom guide you through 1986, and watch your dreams become exciting realities!

For Expanding Your Personal Knowledge of Astrology, SIGNET Brings to You

SYDNEY OMARR'S ASTROLOGICAL GUIDES FOR YOU IN 1986

- [ ] **ARIES** .... (136764—$2.75)*
- [ ] **TAURUS** .... (136772—$2.75)*
- [ ] **GEMINI** .... (136780—$2.75)*
- [ ] **CANCER** .... (136799—$2.75)*
- [ ] **LEO** .... (136802—$2.75)*
- [ ] **VIRGO** .... (136810—$2.75)*
- [ ] **LIBRA** .... (136829—$2.75)*
- [ ] **SCORPIO** .... (136837—$2.75)*
- [ ] **SAGITTARIUS** .... (136845—$2.75)*
- [ ] **CAPRICORN** .... (136853—$2.75)*
- [ ] **AQUARIUS** .... (136861—$2.75)*
- [ ] **PISCES** .... (136888—$2.75)*

*Price is $3.25 in Canada

Buy them at your local bookstore or use this convenient coupon for ordering.

NEW AMERICAN LIBRARY
P.O. Box 999, Bergenfield, New Jersey 07621

Please send me the books I have checked above. I am enclosing $_____
(please add $1.00 to this order to cover postage and handling). Send check or money order—no cash or C.O.D.'s. Prices and numbers are subject to change without notice.

Name_____

Address_____

City _____ State _____ Zip Code _____

Allow 4-6 weeks for delivery.
This offer is subject to withdrawal without notice.

SYDNEY OMARR'S
DAY-BY-DAY ASTROLOGICAL GUIDE FOR

Virgo (AUGUST 23–SEPTEMBER 22)

1986

A SIGNET BOOK

NEW AMERICAN LIBRARY

NAL BOOKS ARE AVAILABLE AT QUANTITY DISCOUNTS
WHEN USED TO PROMOTE PRODUCTS OR SERVICES.
FOR INFORMATION PLEASE WRITE TO PREMIUM MARKETING DIVISION,
NEW AMERICAN LIBRARY, 1633 BROADWAY,
NEW YORK, NEW YORK 10019.

Copyright © 1985 by Sydney Omarr

All rights reserved

Sydney Omarr is syndicated worldwide by Los Angeles Times Syndicate.

SIGNET TRADEMARK REG. U.S. PAT. OFF. AND FOREIGN COUNTRIES
REGISTERED TRADEMARK—MARCA REGISTRADA
HECHO EN CHICAGO, U.S.A.

SIGNET, SIGNET CLASSIC, MENTOR, PLUME, MERIDIAN and NAL BOOKS
are published by New American Library,
1633 Broadway, New York, New York 10019

First Printing, July 1985

1 2 3 4 5 6 7 8 9

PRINTED IN THE UNITED STATES OF AMERICA

CONTENTS

1 **Defining Terms** — 7
   - *Astrology* — 7
   - *The Zodiac* — 8
   - *Sun Sign* — 9
   - *Element* — 9
   - *Quality* — 11
   - *Element and Quality Together* — 12
   - *Planet* — 13
   - *House* — 15
   - *Rising Sign* — 16
   - *Horoscope* — 17
   - *Aspect* — 18
   - *Transiting Planet* — 19

2 **Your House of the Sun** — 21
   Your "Piece of the Pie"

3 **The Geometry of Relationships** — 32
   What Signs You Get Along with—and Why

4 **Twelve Places at the Table** — 35
   Personality Profiles of the Signs

5 **Moods of the Moon** — 44
   Day-by-Day Changes

6 **Venus and Mars** — 55
   Love and Sex . . . Peace and War . . .
   Cooperating and Competing

7	Venus Sign Position Chart 1910–1975	70
8	Mars Sign Position Chart 1910–1975	76
9	The Planets As "Stars" Astrological Cast of Characters	80
10	Astrotrivia—Rating Yourself in the Best Game in Town	95
	I Sun Signs of the Rich and Famous	95
	II More Celebrity Sun Sign Lore	97
	III Fascinating Facts About the Signs	99
	IV Where Do You Belong?	100
	V Which Animal Best Suits You?	102
11	Sun Sign Changes 1920–1975	105
12	VIRGO: The Big Picture	113
13	VIRGO: Objectives and Obstacles A Game Plan for Being the Most Successful VIRGO Under the Sun	116
14	Pairing Off with VIRGO Your Compatability with Other Signs of the Zodiac	121
15	The VIRGO Sex Role Dilemma	125
16	The VIRGO Female Child ... Young Woman ... Mate ... Mother	128
17	The VIRGO Male Child ... Young Man ... Mate ... Father	132
18	VIRGO Help Wanted Selecting a Career/Your On-the-Job Style	136
19	How "Pure" a VIRGO Are You? Your Moon Sign ... Your Rising Sign	139
20	Find Your Rising Sign	144
21	VIRGO Astro-Outlook for 1986	147
22	Fifteen Months of Day-by-Day Predictions	148

1

Defining Terms

What Are Those Astrologers Talking About?

Everyone knows it is more fun to visit another country if you know a bit of the language, and it's a lot easier to find your way around, too. The same idea applies to astrology, which is still foreign territory to many people. Astrology has its very own language, but it really isn't difficult to get a handle on it as long as you understand a few important terms. What follows is a kind of "Astrological Phrase Book," a brief compendium of the most basic words and concepts in the astrological language. Once you've learned them, you'll find you know a lot more about the why of your sun sign as well as information that will help you understand other astrological factors that make you what you are. Best of all, your new language can help you enjoy and explore one of the most exciting, underdeveloped territories under the sun—modern astrology!

Astrology Is an Ancient and Practical "Science"
The first definition of astrology in the standard dictionary is "astronomy," and at one time in history the two studies were synonymous. The word astrology derives from Greek and literally means "the science (or study) of the stars." However, even in earliest times astrology has had much less to do with the "fixed" stars, which appear to remain in one place, than the planets, which move. (The word "planet" means wanderer.) Early man noticed that, as these heavenly bodies moved, their movements coincided with certain earthly events—mainly the changing of the seasons. Gradually, the movement

of the planets was observed to coincide with other important worldly events, such as wars, and the science of "divination" (prediction) by the planets was born. Astronomy and astrology lived happily together until the Christian church banned the latter in about 1550, condemning it as mere superstition. Astrology bounced back in the 1700s, when it came into use as an indicator of human personality, as well as a way to foretell future events. However, this so-called modern astrology is based on the same premise the ancients set down thousands of years ago: "As above, so below." Simply put, what it means is that the positions of the planets, which represent the cosmic order, are related in a significant and observable way to both human behavior and events in human life.

The Zodiac Is a "Circle of Signs"
The zodiac ("circle of animals") is an invisible band in the sky which corresponds to the apparent yearly path of the sun, moon, and the major planets around the earth. It is the "apparent" path in the sense that it is what we *observe* from here on earth. Obviously we know that the earth and other planets revolve around the sun, but the study of astrology (and astronomy) takes earth as the reference point.

The 360-degree circle of the zodiac around the earth is divided into twelve thirty-degree segments—the twelve astrological signs. Throughout the year, as the sun appears to move, it passes through each of these segments in about thirty days. Zero degrees Aries, the vernal equinox or beginning of spring, is the beginning of the zodiac and the start of the seasonal year. It is at that point, on or about March 22, that the sun crosses or intersects with the *ecliptic*—another imaginary band that is (in the mind's eye) the extension of the earth's equator. Another major intersection of the sun's path and the ecliptic takes place at the fall equinox about September 22, the beginning of the seventh sign of the zodiac, Libra. (Equinox means equal days and nights, which is what we experience briefly in the early spring and early fall.) The zodiac "finishes" with the end of the twelfth sign Pisces, about March 21, then begins again with Aries.

Though the segments of the zodiac (the astrological signs) are *named* for the constellations of stars in the sky, they do not correspond with them. The constellations served as convenient visual markers for the ancient astrologer/priests, but the zodiac—and astrology—has always been based on the seasonal year, which never changes. The position of the constellations have changed with reference to our point of view here on earth, however, due to the slipping of the earth's axis. The constellations return a couple of degrees every year and have been doing so for centuries. That's why when the modern *astronomer* says "Aries," he is referring to a group of stars that is in a different position in the sky than the segment of the zodiac the *astrologer* calls "Aries."

Your Sun Sign is Determined by the Month and Day You Were Born

The twelve segments of the zodiac are the twelve astrological signs, from Aries through Pisces, and it takes the sun exactly one year to pass through all twelve signs. A person born when the sun is passing through a particular segment of the zodiac is said to be born under that sign, and it is his/her sun sign. For example, a person born October 14 is said to be born under the sign of Libra. Your sun sign is the most important component of your astrological personality, it is the "real you." However, there are nine other planets besides the sun, and at the moment of a person's birth, those planets are passing through certain segments of the zodiac, or signs, as well. You will learn about some of these lesser influences on your personality in this book later on.

An Element Is Part of a Sign

Obviously your sun sign is a lot more than simply a piece of the sky, or it wouldn't have any meaning. The meaning it has is based on two ancient astrological concepts, the *four elements* and the *three modes*. When these two factors are combined they form the basis of all astrological descriptions of human personality. You can't *see* an element or a quality; they are only to be understood in terms of analogy, but they are fundamental to everything else in astrology, so it is important to understand them.

The four elements, defined by ancient philosophers as the basic components of everything and everybody, are *fire, earth, air,* and *water*. It is doubtful that even in earliest times this breakdown was to be taken as a physical reality: The elements are really four different ways we experience both things and people. For instance, if a thing or a person was experienced as hot rather than cold, sharp rather than dull, active rather than passive, it was said to partake of the *fire* element. And it's easy to see the connection.

Later on, during the Renaissance, the four elements were called "humors," starting a whole new way of typing people. *Fire was the humor choler*, and people who were said to have too much of it were those angry, impatient types who are subject to modern-day diseases like high blood pressure and heart attacks. *The earth element was called black bile* and could cause extreme melancholia (depression) in a person who had too much of it. *Air was the sanguine or rosy humor* and meant a lighter personality. *The water element was the humor phlegm*, and people with too much of it had rather "soggy" personalities and tended to be fat, as well. If the relationship between the elements (or humors) and the signs of the zodiac is beginning to ring a bell, it should. Here's the way the twelve signs break down into elements:

Fire signs: Aries, Leo, Sagittarius
Earth signs: Taurus, Virgo, Capricorn
Air signs: Gemini, Libra, Aquarius
Water signs: Cancer, Scorpio, Pisces

The four elements as four primal types of being exist today in the way many psychologists categorize people's thought processes. Once again, the relationship to the ways in which the twelve astrological signs really do perceive and react to the world is uncannily correct:

The fire signs are instant reactors who put it all together very quickly; things rarely have to be spelled out for a fire sign. These types of people also see the future possibilities inherent in the present and want to bring them about *now*. Obviously, fire signs tend to be impatient, but they have strong wills. Fire is the principle of *action*.

The earth signs are more pragmatic and slower to react. If they can't literally see something or touch it, they have difficulty visualizing it. They operate out of *sense perceptions* and are the realists of the zodiac—the builders who provide stability and continuity. Earth is the principle of *sustenance*.

The air signs see everything as connected to everything else. They are sequential thinkers for whom there must be a beginning, a middle, and an end to everything. For the most part these people operate on *logic* and act only when they can see the sense of their actions. The air signs are endlessly curious and represent the principle of *connecting and reasoning*.

The water signs tend to feel their way through life. What is most real to them is what their emotions tell them; they do what their emotions tell them to do as well. They are imaginative thinkers, the poets and artists of the zodiac. The water principle is that of *caring, nurturing, and protecting*.

A Quality Is Part of a Sign

There are only four elements, but there are twelve signs. In astrological arithmetic, the *three qualities* which divide the *four elements* make up the difference. It isn't easy to grasp the concept of the elements, but the qualities (or "modes" as they are sometimes called) help a lot, because they make the elements a lot more tangible. Called *cardinal*, *fixed*, and *mutable*, the three modes can best be understood as *kinds of motion*.

Cardinal motion is start-up movement. It is the principle of bringing into being. Cardinal goes forward, so, the cardinal signs are *initiators*.

The four cardinal signs are those that start the four seasons:
    Aries (*spring*)
    Cancer (*summer*)

Libra (*fall*)
Capricorn (*Winter*)

Fixed motion means staying in place. Fixed things have come into being, and now simply are. The fixed signs represent stability, and are difficult to move. The four fixed signs represent the middle of each season:
Tarus (*spring*)
Leo (*summer*)
Scorpio (*fall*)
Aquarius (*winter*)

Mutable motion means flexible motion. Things that are mutable are changing, able to turn into something else. The mutable signs represent the *ability to adjust, and to accept change*. The four mutable signs are those that end the seasons:
Gemini (*spring*)
Virgo (*summer*)
Sagittarius (*fall*)
Pisces (*winter*)

Elements and Qualities Together Add Up to Signs

When you put elements and qualities together you begin to get a picture of what they add up to—the twelve astrological signs. Here is how each quality modifies each element.

Fire element/Cardinal quality = **Aries**
This get-up-and-go sign has all the flash and dash of fire plus an added dose of a pioneering spirit by virtue of its cardinal quality.

Fire element/Fixed quality = **Leo**
Leo burns with the ardor and enthusiasms of fire, but gives off very steady heat due to its fixed quality.

Fire element/Mutable quality = **Sagittarius**
Sagittarius represents the kind of fire that spreads, igniting everything and everybody in its path—which is rather erratic because of Sagittarius's mutable quality.

Earth element /Cardinal quality = **Capricorn**
Capricorn is the most active builder of the earth signs because of its cardinal quality. Capricorn's brand

of reality demands that something be brought into being.

Earth element/Fixed quality = **Taurus**
This strong sign stands and waits, holding things and people together. Taurus is the warmest and most nurturing of the earth signs, and is always "there."

Earth element/Mutable quality = **Virgo**
Virgo's practical sense knows that all things must change. This mutable sign represents the principle of stability with flux; that is, permanence in the face of change.

Air element/Cardinal quality = **Libra**
Libra's air nature moves forward, actively connecting people and things into partnerships via its cardinal quality of initiation.

Air element/Fixed quality = **Aquarius**
Aquarius is the most immovable of the air signs, representing the permanance of ideas and their practical application.

Air element/Mutable quality = **Gemini**
This very movable sign represents changing thoughts and opinions, the breaking up of static ideas so that new ones can come about.

Water element/Cardinal quality = **Cancer**
Cancer is the most initiating of the water signs because of the cardinal quality. Though shy, Cancer generally moves quietly but effectively to the forefront.

Water element/Fixed quality = **Scorpio**
Scorpio's powerful self-control comes from the emotional water element that is contained and compressed because of this sign's fixed quality.

Water element/Mutable quality = **Pisces**
Pisces extreme emotionalism—as well as this sign's creativity—comes from feelings that constantly change and move into new areas, creating new outlets.

Planets Are the Most Important Factor in Astrology
"Planet" is probably an even more important word in the astrological language than "sign." How can that be?

Because it is the placement of the planets in various signs which indicates personality and it is the movement of the planets through the zodiac that indicates events. In other words, without the planets the signs would have no application to people and what happens to them.

As early man noticed that the planets moved in fairly regular patterns, he began to associate certain characteristics with each of the planets, and each planet gradually took on a "personality." In a number of different cultures, certain planets were hooked up with certain gods, because it was the gods who really controlled life on earth. The moon was virtually always a female god—like Diana or Artemis. Jupiter, always a "good guy" planet, was known as Vishnu, the preserver, to the Hindus. Before he got his Roman name of Jupiter, the Greeks knew him as Zeus, a lusty fellow who had a heart of gold. (You'll get a complete rundown on each of the planets in Chapter p, "The Planets As Stars.")

From these planetary "personalities" came the idea that each planet caused a certain kind of behavior or event by virtue of its own nature. For instance, Mars, always the war god, is still regarded by modern astrologers as an indicator of strife and conflict. When predicting events, the astrologer looks at what sign and what house Mars will be passing through at a certain point in time to see what kind of influence it is most likely to bring into a person's life.

When looking at personality, the astrologer determines which sign a person's Mars is in at the time of the person's birth to see how that individual is most likely to assert him-/herself. The sun, the most important planet makes us what we are in totality according to which sign the sun is placed in at our birth; i.e., our sun sign's Venus is the planet of relationships, and its placement in a specific sign shows how a person is likely to relate to others.

In short, planets indicate *action*, and the signs in which the planets are placed indicate *the kind of action*.

Since ancient times, astrologers have recognized seven planets. The sun (which is really a star), the moon (which is really a satellite of our own planet, earth) Mercury, Venus, Mars, Jupiter, and Saturn.

With the development of the telescope, three more planets were discovered (although there is some evidence that early astrologer/priests divined their existence). Uranus was first spotted in 1781, Neptune in 1846, and Pluto as late as 1930. Some astrologers/astronomers anticipate that there are two more to be found, so that there would be twelve planets instead of the current ten.

A House Is an Area of Life—and a Planet's "Home"
Just as there is a great circle in the sky called the zodiac, and it is divided into twelve equal units of *space*, there is another circle which is based on units of *time*. As we all know, the earth makes one complete rotation on its own axis every twenty-four hours. Imagine yourself standing in one place during a twenty-four-hour period and making a mark on the sky every two hours while that sky appears to pass by you as the earth turns. At the end of twenty-four hours, you will have marked off twelve different units of sky. A "house" is simply one of those pieces of sky that has passed by during your day-long vigil. Toward the end of your day of skywatching, twelve houses will have gone by, and "house one" will be coming up again.

When an astrologer draws up a natal horoscope—which is simply a map of the sky when you were born—he/she does it by drawing a picture of the sky as it appeared from the exact place of birth, at the exact time of your birth. What happens is that the twelve houses are lined up in a very specific way—a very different way than if you had been born *in another place at the same time* or *at the same time in another place*.

What is most important about the particular lineup of the houses is that each house represents a different area of human life, and how those areas are positioned *for you* has a tremendous effect on your astrological makeup. For instance, the second house is the house of income and personal possessions and has a lot to do with attitude toward money and how easy or how difficult it will be to come by in your lifetime. The seventh house is the house of partnership and offers clues about who you are likely to marry. If you know the time of your birth within one hour or so, you can add a very important dimension to your astrological self-knowledge by reading the chapter "Your House of the Sun—Your 'Piece of the Pie,'" because the house of the horoscope into which the sun falls in your horoscope usually indicates what area of life will absorb you during your lifetime.

Your Rising Sign Is the One that Starts the First House

Your rising sign is sometimes called the ascendant, because it is the sign of the zodiac that was "ascending" on the eastern horizon at the time of your birth, no matter what time your birth occured. It is the "sunrise sign," corresponding to the nine o'clock position on the face of an ordinary clock. The astrologer's "clock" starts at this position and is read counter-clockwise around the circle of the face. If you were born around sundown, your rising sign will be the one 180 degrees *opposite* the sign you were born under. For instance, if you are an Aries born at sundown, your rising sign will be Libra. If you are an Aries born at sunrise, your rising sign is probably Aries as well.

Why is your rising sign so important? Because it starts the first house of personality, or your very individual way of presenting yourself to the world. No matter what your sun sign is, your rising sign will cover it to a greater or lesser degree (which is why it is so difficult to guess someone's Sun Sign when you first meet them). The rising sign has to do with appearances and can actually influence your physical looks.

If you don't know the time of day you were born, you can't determine your rising sign (although some astrologers can by doing what is called a "rectification," based on the events in your life so far). However, even those who do not know their rising sign can have their horoscopes read; what the astrologer does is put your sun sign on the first house, and do an analysis of what is called a solar horoscope. If you *do* know your birthtime within an hour or so, you can use the rising sign chart in this book to determine yours.

Planets in Signs in Houses Make Up a Horoscope

The whole basis of astrology is that anyone born in a particular moment in time partakes of the qualities of that moment in time. Actually, the same applies for things; for instance, a business that has its beginnings at a precise astrological moment also has a horoscope which can be read, and tells a lot about its potential for success or failure.

An astrologer looks at the particular moment in drawing up a horoscope—or "picture of the hour." A horoscope is basically a map of the sky, showing exactly where the planets were in relation to the signs and the houses, to each other, and from the particular reference point of your birthplace. It is also called a "natal chart" or "natal map."

Everyone's horoscope has ten planets and twelve houses. Those ten planets can be in a variety of signs, and in a variety of houses. Each planet means something different according to its own nature, how that nature operates in a particular sign, and what area of life the planet is most likely to affect by virtue of which house of the horoscope it falls into. Sound complicated? It is, and only a highly trained astrologer can interpret the many factors and put them together for you in a meaningful way. The most exciting part of astrology is the fact that *no two individuals are ever exactly alike*—not even twins, who are born a few minutes apart.

Although you can find out a lot about your astrological personality right in this book, many people like to take the next step and have a personalized horoscope drawn up for them and interpreted by a professional astrologer. There are a number of ways to find a good person to do this for you; in astrology, as in every other profession, there are variations in the level of competence. Two places you can start your search are:

National Astrological
  Society
62 West 39th St.
New York, NY 10018

American Federation of
  Astrologers
Tempe, AZ 85282

An Aspect Is the Distance Between Planets

Among the more sophisticated factors an astrologer looks for in your horoscope are the *aspects*. Within the 360-degree circle of the horoscope (and the zodiac), planets form certain aspects to each other by virtue of the distance between them. Some distances are considered harmonious, and some are inharmonious, in terms of how those two (or more) planets work together. It's all a matter of mathematics. The soft or harmonious aspects are the sextile (60 degrees apart) and the trine (120 degrees apart). The hard or inharmonious aspects are formed when planets are in square to each other (90 degrees apart) or in opposition, 180 degrees or exactly half a circle apart. These are only the major aspects, and there are lots and lots of minor ones between, but you can get a good picture of interplanetary relationships with only these few.

For example, if your sun sign is Aries, and at the time of your birth the planet Saturn was in the sign of Libra, or 180 degrees away from Aries, you are likely to have a more serious (Saturnine) disposition than the typical "happy" Aries. Depending on your point of view, this can be a positive note in your horoscope, because you will have greater powers of concentration than many an Aries—or a negative note, because you will be less happy-go-lucky. In another example, a person with a Capricorn sun sign may have a horoscope in which Jupiter, the planet of expansiveness, is 120 degrees away from the sun—either in the sign of Virgo or Taurus—and therefore in "trine" aspect to his/her sun. The result: a much more outgoing, giving Capricorn than the run-of-the-mill type. On the other hand, such an easy aspect could expand Capricorn's acquisitive nature too much, and make for a megalomaniac (someone who craves worldly goods and power).

The ancients separated aspects into "favorable" and "unfavorable," but psychologically-thinking modern astrologers know that it is not that simple; it all depends on the total horoscope, plus the individual's reactions to the particular vibrations of the planets in that horoscope.

A Transiting Planet Affects Your Life Now

When someone goes to an astrologer for the first time, he/she usually has *two* readings—separate, but interrelated. The first will be an interpretation of your natal chart or birth horoscope. This tells you about your given personality—the traits, problems, abilities, and advantages you are most likely to have by virtue of the placement of the planets in the sky at the time of your birth. The second reading will have to do with what you can expect in your life at the present time and the near future. Your birth horoscope always remains the same, but the planets in the sky keep changing their relationships to your birth horoscope throughout your lifetime. The astrologer will acquaint you with the current "transit"—or movements—of the planets and how you, the individual, can expect them to affect you. For instance, if an astrologer notes that Uranus, the "earthquake planet," is approaching your fourth house (the house of emotional security, the place where we really live), the astrologer might alert you to the fact that big changes are in the offing: even a total shaking of the foundations, or a pulling up of roots. This is a major transit, and many people change their residence, partners, or jobs when it occurs. Similarly, but on a less critical note, the astrologer may notice that the planet Venus is going to make a transit over the place in the zodiac occupied by Mars in your birthchart. This could indicate a firey romantic interlude or the rekindling of an old flame.

There are two important things to keep in mind about astrological predictions. The first is that your natal horoscope—your "birth imprint"—really determines how you will react to life's events. To put it even more strongly, your innate personality will really *create* the events of your life, because "character is destiny." There is no doubt that the planets create conditions, but we must take responsibility for how we cooperate with those conditions. The second thing is that *there are very few hard and fast rules*. There are guidelines, to be sure, and most of them have ancient roots; a lot of astrological prediction is based on the case history technique. However, since no two sets of conditions—

the one in the sky and the one in an individual birthchart—are ever *exactly* the same, it is virtually impossible for any astrologer to tell you specifically what is going to happen.

2

Your House of the Sun

Your "Piece of the Pie"

The prime symbol in the very symbolic language of astrology is the perfect circle; it represents the sky around us, the cosmic atmosphere into which we are all born. All astro-math is based on division of the 360-degree figure, which since ancient times has been regarded as having mystical qualities. When thinking about the houses of the horoscope, however, it helps to use a very down-to-earth analogy. Look at that circle as a great "pie in the sky," which is divided into twelve cosmic slices—each slice representing one house and a different facet of human experience.

Just as there are ten planets in everyone's horoscope, there are twelve houses. However, not all those houses may be occupied by a planet; it all depends on where the planets were in the sky at the moment of your birth. The placement of any planet in a specific house is a *very* important factor in your individual horoscope, but the most important is the placement of the sun. No matter what your sun sign, your House of the Sun has a lot to tell you about the life you've been "given" to live on this earth. As your sun sign is the prime indicator of *character and personality,* your house of the sun points to the *area of human affairs* that you are most likely to find yourself concentrating on in your lifetime.

In the sense that it helps define the boundaries of your life, your house of the sun is your "piece of the pie"—that slice of life within which you will live. Does your house of the sun totally box you in? In a way it does, but it is more productive to think of the dimensions of your house of the sun as *guidelines* about where you can most profitably focus your energies.

Here's the way it works:

- The *sun* is the most important planet in your horoscope. It is the planets that do the "acting," and the sun plays the leading role.
- Your sun sign determines *how* your sun (the real you) acts, i.e., the characteristics of the character you play.
- Your house of the sun is the "stage" on which you will play out your role.

For instance, if your sun sign is Scorpio (the great investigator) and your house of the sun is the twelfth (hidden things), you find yourself drawn to some kind of career in which you must "dig" to do your investigating. Ergo, you might make a good psychoanalyst, archeologist, or genetic researcher. Or, your greatest pleasure in life might be reading mystery novels or spy thrillers—or writing or editing them.

In order to figure out which piece of the pie you've been served, you have to know your birth-time within an hour or so. If you were born during Daylight Savings Time or War Time, you have to subtract one hour from your birth time to determine the "real sun time."

Each house is described here from three different angles:

- The matters or principles connected with it
- The people/places/things related to it
- The problems and the possibilities of having your sun in that house.

Birth time, 4 to 6 a.m.: **Sun in First House**

- *First house matters:* Exploration . . . use of the physical body . . . being on the scene . . . breaking new ground . . . independent action . . . emergencies . . . conquest . . . controversy . . . strategy . . . competition . . . being in the vanguard.

- *First house people/places/things:* Entrepreneurs ... acrobats ... cutting instruments ... rock music ... metals ... satire ... hardware ... the head and face ... opticians ... adrenalin ... new products ... commodities ... salesmen ... fighters ... firemen.
- *Problems and possibilities:* With your sun in the first house, your sun sign personality is quite strong. Regardless of what your sun sign is, you should be able to make clear-cut decisions and have a good sense of your own identity. If you are to gain control over your life, you are going to have to banish fear from it and develop both the moral and the physical courage that is available to you. Though your will should be strong, you will have to keep yourself from a tendency to tyrannize others. When you feel most defeated is the time your first house sun will come to your rescue. The one thing that could keep you from living out the very vivid life this house placement gives you is inflexibility and intolerance. Be willing to listen.

Birth time, 2 to 4 a.m.: **Sun in Second House**

- *Second house matters:* Calmness ... conservation ... ability to make grow ... eroticism ... collecting ... comforting ... administrating ... luxury ... stabilizing ... building up ... perpetuating ... patience ... using ... making stronger ... indulging.
- *Second house people/places/things:* Possessions ... money ... the voice ... landscape gardeners ... brokers and bankers ... love/passion ... personal adornment ... life-sustaining skills ... buying and selling ... security needs ... nurses ... food and shelter ... good music ... creature comforts.
- *Problems and possibilities:* You should be able to establish yourself firmly and securely in whatever you choose to do; self-adjustment should come easily to you. Your economic life could be relatively worry-free but you must resist valuing money and

possessions for their own sake and becoming overly materialistic. You must develop the will that is given you and turn it into willpower, or you could lose self-respect. You are a good manager, but if you allow yourself to become too settled, you will fear to take the necessary risks to make your life less limited. Though things come to you fairly easily, do not let yourself over-indulge in any of them, including rich food.

Birth time midnight to 2 a.m.: **Sun in Third House**

- *Third house matters:* Connecting ... associating ... verbalizing ... dexterity ... inquisitiveness ... distribution ... novelty ... thinking and reasoning ... cause and effect ... exchanging ... bringing the news ... being responsive ... "here today, gone tomorrow."
- *Third house people/places/things:* Short journeys ... realatives (especially siblings) ... speech/languages ... high school teachers ... role-playing/entertaining ... computers ... graphic arts ... handwork ... transportation ... the nervous system ... handwriting .. repair men ... gossip ... comedy ... ventriloquists.
- *Problems and possibilities:* You should be an excellent communicator who reports things clearly and accurately. In your desire for information, however, you could become rather superficial and a bit of a talebearer. If you don't focus your mental energies carefully, you may waste the gift of curiosity your third house sun gives you. You must also learn to live with uncertainty, and to keep your opinions flexible. If life scares you, you are likely to become very defensive and locked in to your ideas. Develop your capacity for listening as well as your talent for talking.

Birth time 10 p.m. to 12 a.m.: **Sun in Fourth House**

- *Fourth house matters:* Adaptability ... change ... instinctiveness ... fluctuation ... protecting ...

imagination ... softness ... the subconscious ... survival ... enveloping ... integrating ... fertility ... mothering.

- *Fourth house people/places/things:* Dreams ... the past ... roots ... home and family ... physical sensation ... museums ... caterers ... water and other liquid ... introverts ... obstetrics ... boats ... domestics ... imagination.
- *Problems and possibilities:* Via your fourth house sun, you are given the possibility of understanding yourself and your motivations quite thoroughly. If you handle your life in a mature way, you will establish a warm and comfortable home for you and your family. However, you must strive for real self-knowledge if you are not to become simply self-absorbed and self-centered. Your imagination is considerable, and you could be highly creative; the down side is that you could develop irrational fears that verge on paranoia. Work to see the world clearly at all times and try to conquer your tendency to play the introvert. No mater what your sun sign, the placement of that sun in the fourth house will make you instinctively avoid the limelight. Get out there and shine!

Birth time 8 to 10 p.m.: **Sun in Fifth House**

- *Fifth house matters:* Being at the heart of things ... pleasures ... power ... ambition ... generosity/giving ... "gilding the lily" ... showmanship ... stability ... management ... territorial rights ... self-expression ... autocracy ... organization.
- *Fifth house people/places/things:* Philanthropy ... corporations ... impresarios ... holidays and vacations ... romantic love ... children ... gamblers ... gold ... circuses ... nursery teachers ... fashion and fashion designers ... public life.
- *Problems and possibilities:* Even if you have a "shy" sun sign, your fifth house placement of the sun will force you into some form of self-expression that is possibly very creative. You also have a capability

for approaching life with a joyful, expectant manner; however, your pursuit of pleasure and play could become extreme. Consciously avoid any pleasure that threatens to get out of control. Your affairs of the heart could be many, but it is important to keep alert for anything that smacks of an abusive partner; it's possible you could enjoy the drama of an unhappy situation. Develop your capacity for warmly accepting others.

Birth time 6 to 8 p.m.: **Sun in Sixth House**

- *Sixth house matters:* Competence/skill ... specialization ... refining ... categorizing ... analyzing ... obedience ... realism ... responsibility ... purifying ... invention ... making things work ... ministering ... discriminating.
- *Sixth house people/places/things:* Service ... critics ... crafts ... libraries ... closets ... public health ... the harvest ... small animals ... dependents ... dental hygienists ... research ... diagnosing ... numbers work ... chemists.
- *Problems and possibilities:* With your sun in the sixth house you have the potential of becoming a true master at something; however, if you allow yourself to get bogged down in life's details, you could possibly end up being a wage slave. No matter what your sun sign, your instincts tell you to be of service to others. While you are capable of great self-sacrifice, you must avoid the temptation to be overly humble and to assume the servant role. You are mentally very keen, and can break things and jobs down into smaller parts in order to accomplish them. Do not let the state of your own health become an obsession. With the sun is the sixth house, your basic constitution should be quite strong. Don't worry!

Birth time 4 to 6 p.m.: **Sun in Seventh House**

- *Seventh house matters:* Sharing ... comparing ... give-and-take ... peacemaking ... negotiation ...

making things beautiful ... creating balance ... fairness ... sociability ... gratification ... advocacy ... diplomacy ... aestheticism.
- *Seventh house people/places/things:* Divorce lawyers ... love poetry ... marriage brokers ... the kidneys and lower back ... illustration ... resort managers ... public relations ... fine arts ... receptionists ... boutiques ... jugglers ... tailors ... pianos.
- Possibilities and problems: You have a great need to identify with others, and can create a wonderful rapport with them easily. However, your need for a life partner could make you overly dependent. If you have an independent sun sign, this could create a serious life conflict. With this placement, you are able to adjust to new people and new situations easily, but you must avoid a tendency not to stick with a position when you really believe in it. You have the potential of forming very warm, balanced and intimate relationships; however, if you do not handle this gift in a mature manner, you could develop a fear of intimacy, and shy away from it or become an outrageous and insincere flirt.

Birth time 2 to 4 p.m.: **Sun in Eighth House**

- *Eighth house matters:* Release of blockages ... probing ... anonymity ... procreation ... rejuvenation ... willpower ... endurance ... controlling ... investigation ... aloneness ... demolishing and rebuilding ... crisis ... elimination.
- *Eighth house people/places/things:* Puzzles ... generals ... political parties ... labor lawyers ... the healing arts ... death and dying ... taxes ... spies ... superathletes ... crime detection ... statesmen ... sex symbols ... geologists ... explorers ... mating instinct ... sanitation engineers.
- *Problems and possibilities:* A light sun sign (like Gemini or Libra), the placement of the sun in this house will add depth to your character. You will feel compelled to investigate things that are hidden or

even dangerous. While it is good to probe, you must beware of a tendency to concentrate on what is morbid. All things being equal, you will be highly sexed; however, with insufficient self-knowledge, your healthy sexual instincts could turn into obsession with the subject—or a total advoidance of it. Learn to live with your dynamic physical body and you will live with others quite happily. Also, encourage your religious or mystical feelings, which are quite real. You have the potential of totally transforming your life at one point or another.

Birth time noon to 2 p.m.: **Sun in Ninth House**

- *Ninth house matters:* Anticipating ... aspiring ... moving around ... expanding things ... speculating ... idealism ... advising ... unpredictability ... search for truth ... search for opportunity ... taking aim ... magnanimity ... excess.
- *Ninth house people/places/things* Casinos ... ambassadors ... passport offices ... luck ... international transportation ... trading/high finance ... dancers ... aristocrats ... large animals ... higher studies ... lawmaking ... profiteers ... veterinarians.
- *Problems and possibilities:* Even if you have a routine-loving sun sign (like Virgo), this placement of the sun will give you the desire and the ability to constantly renew your life, and to adapt to new patterns of behavior. You will feel strongly about one religious or ethical system or another, or at least have a very strong personal philosophy. However, you could become rather dogmatic and rigid in your opinions. Your adaptability is admirable, but a desire for the new and novel could be the "downside" of your openness to new experience. Exercise control. With certain sun signs, there may be a tendency toward inner battles between opportunity-seeking and a firm set of principles. You are a spender—of both your money and your physical resources.

Birth time 10 a.m. to 12 a.m.: **Sun in Tenth House**

- *Tenth house matters:* Realism ... structure ... ambition ... rigidity ... integrating ... limitation ... disciplining ... reputation ... social position ... creating the useful ... contraction ... coolness ... convention.
- *Tenth house people/places/things:* Figures ... fame ... common sense ... property ... correctional systems and facilities ... ceramics ... money lenders ... efficiency experts ... the bones ... the elderly ... sculptors ... watches and clocks.
- *Problems and possibilities:* You have the capacity of becoming a respected member of whatever group you move in, because your public image is very important to you. If you play your cards right, you can arrive at a sense that you are fulfilling your destiny. However, if you become obsessed with power and appearances, you could end up living a shallow, meaningless life behind your strong facade. It is most important with this placement of the sun to find the right outlet for you to express yourself and get positive feedback from others. You won't be happy starving in a garret, because both money and recognition are too important to you. This position of the sun often brings fame.

Birth time 8 to 10 a.m.: **Sun in Eleventh House**

- *Eleventh house matters:* Helping ... experimentation ... humanitarianism ... association ... liberalism .. freedom ... suddenness ... awakenings ... combining ... freethinking ... rationality ... caring ... breaking through ... observing coolly ... predicting.
- *Eleventh house people/places/things:* Paradoxes ... stunt men ... electricity ... zealots ... divorce ... fireworks ... the social sciences ... reform ... geniuses ... aviation ... weathermen ... brotherly love ... magnetism ... groups ... friends ... causes.
- *Problems and possibilities:* If you are a very personal

sun sign (like Cancer), you will gain a lot of objectivity with the placement of the sun in this house. You should have very high aims and goals, and some of them will undoubtedly involve helping the less fortunate in some way or another. Though this is admirable, if you don't set yourself on a definite path in life and stick to a definite plan, you could simply drift along, with only vague ideas about where you can shine. It is important to be quite realistic with the sun in this house. Your own crowd is important to you, but you must avoid becoming such a part of the group that you lose a sense of your own individuality—which is potentially very great. Some people with the sun in the 11th house are downright wacky, but often very achieving people.

Birth Time 6 to 8 a.m.: **Sun in Twelfth House**

- *Twelfth house matters:* Dissolving ... ambiguity ... disguising ... retreating ... sensualism ... enchantment ... paying dues ... healing spiritually ... insubstantiality ... confinement ... persuading ... comprehending the incomprehensible ... merging ... pretending.
- *Twelfth house people/places/things:* Makeup ... escapism ... alcohol and drugs ... drama and dramatic actors ... films ... advertising ... pastoral work ... fishing ... astrophysics ... con men ... magicians ... hospitals ... alibis ... myths ... prisons.
- *Problems and possibilities:* Yours is not an easy house of the sun to have—especially if you are a very self-expressive sun sign type like Leo. You may feel that life is confining you in some way or another; what you are really sensing is your gift of the ability to transcend self to a much higher spiritual level. You should be an expert at coping with intangibles and sensing the nuances of any situation. In a sense, you have a kind of ESP which can be developed for life success. However, the real down side of the twelfth house sun is that it

can lead to a very confused, unfocussed attitude toward life. It is essential that you give yourself a definite structure to work within if you are to free yourself from the worries and cares of life. By all means avoid any form of escapism that is dangerous.

3

The Geometry of Relationships

What Signs You Get Along with—and Why

The first thing most people want to know about their sun sign is what other signs they are compatible with. It's a natural question, and a good one to ask an astrologer, because one aspect of astrology, called "synastry" (literally, "stars together") concentrates on the subject of relationships. When practising synastry, the astrologer compares the two birth charts of the two people involved to find what connections there are between them. It is a complicated process, but it provides excellent clues about how two people will relate to each other. What chart comparison does is *describe the nature of the relationship*. Actually, to an astrologer there are no "bad" or "good" relationships; there are just a lot of different kinds and each has a special character. Of course it is true that some relationships end up on the rocks, sometimes devastating one or both parties involved. But, even in such cases, the astrologer looks at it as a "karmic" relationship—one in which people *had* to come together in order to learn some life lessons.

While comparing two complete horoscopes is the ideal way to look at a relationship, there is a very simple method of looking at two sun signs, and coming up with an overall prediction of how two people will relate to each other. This method goes back to the great circle of the zodiac and to the division of the twelve signs into four elements: fire, earth, air, and water.

Here's the lineup of signs in each element:

Fire: Aries, Leo, Sagittarius

Earth: Taurus, Virgo, Capricorn
Air: Gemini, Libra, Aquarius
Water: Cancer, Scorpio, Pisces

The general rules of thumb for element-mixing are as follows:

Great	Good	Semi-tough or Difficult
Fire and air	Fire and fire	Fire and water
Water and earth	Earth and earth	Earth and air
	Air and air	Fire and earth
	Water and water	Air and water

Here's the way it looks mathmatically:
   If you divide the 360-degree circle of the zodiac by the twelve signs, you find that each sign is 30 degrees away from the next.
- Signs that are 30 degrees apart—or next to each other—are semi-tough.
- Signs that are 60 degrees (two signs) or 180 degrees (six signs) away from each other are the best combinations. (The latter, 180 degrees away from each other, makes these signs polar opposites, and in astrology polar opposites attract.)
- Signs that are 120 degrees apart—four signs away from each other—are in the same element, and their relationship is good, but far from perfect.
- Signs that are 90 degrees or three signs away from each other have the most difficult relationships of all. They are said to be in "square aspect" to each other.

When you look at the four elements in terms of what they signify in the physical world, you get a good idea why some elements get along more easily.

Fire turns water into steam (hot air).
Water puts fire out.
Fire scorches earth.

Earth smothers fire.
Air fans fire and makes it brighter.
Fire warms up cool air.
Water softens up hard earth.
Earth makes water keep its shape.
Water and air do nothing (unless you add heat).
Air blows earth around.

What about combinations of the same element, such as fire with fire? In effect, they tend to neutralize or cancel each other out. Or, they can simply be too much of one element for comfort.

- Two fire signs together could experience "burn out" fairly quickly.
- Two air signs might analyze each other to the death of the relationship.
- Two earth signs could depress each other a lot.
- Two water signs could make for an overly "heavy" relationship.

4

Twelve Places at the Table

A Mini Astrodrama in Which the Twelve Signs Play Themselves

No matter how accurate or colorful any description of a zodiac sign may be, it is still a description—not the real thing. A sign is simply an abstract concept until it takes form in a living, breathing human being. There are obviously as many different types of people as there are individual horoscopes, and no two are exactly alike. However, the twelve signs of the zodiac are still the best guidelines we have for sorting out human behavior into broad but meaningful categories. There are even fiction writers who use the zodiac signs as prototypes for characters they create because it makes them more realistic, i.e., more like people you are likely to meet.

What follows is fiction, but it gets closer to the truth about each zodiacal sign than a general description ever can. The twelve characters in this docudrama are obviously caricatures, because their behavior is highly exaggerated. But it is exaggeration for emphasis, and for the purpose of bringing to life the twelve signs of the zodiac, which don't really exist except as real people. Like real people, these twelve characters have foibles; but they have fine points too. As you read this drama, you may find yourself drawn to some signs and put off by others. Make mental notes of which signs you find yourself most sympathetic with and check out your findings in the parts of this book about astrological compatibility. It could prove very interesting—

and very revealing. As each sign of the zodiac has a sex or gender, they are portrayed here as male or female accordingly. But the basic behavior pattern is applicable to both sexes.

The twelve signs of the zodiac are invited to dinner at that great dining room in the sky. When they arrive, they find that their host (who shall remain signless) has slipped up, and there are only eleven places set at the table. Since it is a fancy affair, each sign is trying to be on his/her best behavior. However, the situation is a bit unsettling, so in the course of trying to resolve it, they all relapse into their natural zodiacal characteristics.

Aries An energetic young man, he comes bounding into the room, almost tripping on an untied shoelace. He is dressed rather casually for the occasion, and looks as if he got dressed rather quickly. When he realizes what the situation is, there's no doubt in his mind how to handle it.

"Only eleven places? Don't worry; Pisces will probably never show anyway. But, I got here before anybody else (the doorman will prove it) so I should definitely get a seat. In fact, I should sit down *first*. No, I don't need to wash my hands or anything. I'm *starved*, so I hope you aren't having anything like the gooey mess with the French name you had before. A hamburger will do just fine. And don't serve it cold like you did the last time. Hey, there's a great-looking dish over there, ha ha! Seat me next to her, will you Cancer? Well, she looks like a nice warm type, so I think I'll go let her warm me up. By the way, I'm organizing a sky-diving club. Want to join? Seriously, if you can't afford the membership fee, I'll put it up for you, because I'd love to have you join. Oh, you're doing okay now? Glad to hear you're off the rack. Got any pretzels?"

Taurus An attractive young woman with faint dimples in her roundish cheeks and a slightly unruly but pretty mass of curly hair comes sauntering into the room. She is dressed in a soft and pretty outfit that looks expensive, and has her handbag clutched tightly under her arm. She looks around the room with moderate curiosity. As the host walks up to her, she gives him a warm smile; when she speaks, her voice is low and melodious—but firm.

"Only eleven places? You mean, only eleven *chairs*. All you have to do is set another place and give me a pillow to sit on. I don't mind, as long as I'm comfortable. And I smell something wonderful, so I know the food is going to be delicious. To be honest with you, that's really why I came. I don't like to go out much, you know. What I really like is curling up in my warm and comfy bed—with someone warm and comfy, of course. (Are you busy later on?) But, now that I'm *here*, there's no way I'm not going to eat. What's for dessert? Who's that nervous-looking lady over there? Virgo? I'll go try to make her feel comfortable."

Gemini It's hard to tell just how old this fellow is as he springs in the door; he could be any age, though he looks about eighteen. He is dressed in the very latest style, though nothing he has on is really extreme. His eyes dart all over the room, and he is carrying a notebook under his arm. When the host tells him about the eleven places, he is so busy listening to another conversation, he almost misses it. When he reacts, it is in a typically casual way.

"Don't worry about me; I don't need a place. I'll just float around the room, because what I really came here for is the conversation. I'm writing a book, you know— it's called *1001 Opening Conversational Gambits* and tonight I'm researching. I see you've got some really fascinating types here. How did you make up the guest list? Are they all married? Why did they come alone? What's the menu? Who's the chef? Can I see the wine list? Who's that blowsy-looking type over there? Taurus? I'll bet *she's* got a story. Where's the telephone? I've got to make a call."

Cancer A sexy, voluptuous woman of indeterminate age pauses at the door; she seems shy, but conscious of the impression she is making. Her clothes are a bit unusual, and some things are from the thrift shop. However, her antique jewelry is genuine, and the whole effect is glamorous. When she discovers there are only eleven places, she is visibly upset, and there is a touch of a whine in her voice as she speaks.

"I wish I'd known; I could have stayed home with the children. They have colds, you know. If you want, I'll simply leave; but I really don't want to go home by myself; I'll get scared and have bad dreams. Upset? Yes, I am upset, and when I get upset I can't eat. Unless it's really soothing and nourishing. Did you know that a touch of heavy cream in mashed potatoes is simply heavenly? Chicken soup? I make it by the gallon. Say, you look as if you could stand a little fattening up. Well, all right. I *guess* I'll stay—unless I change my mind, of course."

Leo This is a fine figure of a man—fairly tall, rather muscular, and with a thick crop of curly hair that is somewhere between blond and red. He is elegantly dressed and his gold cufflinks probably put a real drain on Fort Knox. His grand entrance is smooth and practised, and his handshake is hearty and warm. When his host tells him the news, he takes it very personally.

"Well, let me tell you, this is embarrassing! I mean, all these people here to see me, and I may have to stand? I've given bigger parties than this, and they've always gone off without a hitch. Let me handle things for you the next time. For now, just get that chair over there and squeeze someone in—Virgo won't mind. No, *here*; not *there!* While we're all waiting I guess I can entertain everyone with my tantrum act. What? No, I'm only kidding—though I am mad. I'll do my Hamlet number instead. Like my cufflinks? They match my Gold Card. I've ordered another pair with sapphires, too."

Virgo A rather prim woman stands quietly at the door looking as if she would like to blend into the woodwork. She is dressed very neatly, but conservatively, with flat-heeled sensible shoes. In her handbag she carries a surgical mask to wear in case any of the other guests has a cold. Her reaction to the news that there are only eleven places is swift and shrill.

"Well, it certainly isn't *my* fault. I answered the invitation the minute I got it. I *always* do! Why didn't you check on things more carefully? If you had, this wouldn't have happened, and you wouldn't have all these people standing around thinking terrible things about you. I don't mind for myself, you understand, I don't eat much anyway; you never know what you're going to get. I'll stay in the kitchen and help the cook clean up. You can't be too careful about these things, you know. You wouldn't believe the sanitary conditions I've found in *some* kitchens. Not mentioning any names, of course. Oh, *why* did you mess things up this way; you are simply impossible. . . ."

Intermission: Our host walks away as Virgo continues to complain. As he checks on the guests, he discovers that Libra has just arrived. Sagittarius and Pisces are nowhere to be found, but Scorpio, Capricorn, and Aquarius are waiting to greet him. Because he looks like he's a bit uncomfortable, the host talks to Libra first.

Libra A very attractive male, wearing all the right things, walks tentatively into the room, looking as if he is searching for someone. He is visibly uncomfortable alone. His gaze scans the room, quietly appraising everything and everybody in it. He seems to approve, but in his nervousness, he approaches the table, and starts rearranging one of the settings, then rearranging it again. All this is done very tactfully and gracefully. In fact, he looks as if he couldn't make an awkward gesture if he tried. His host approaches him and breaks the news. Libra's reaction is smooth and unruffled.

"Oh, how *clever* of you to arrange this little puzzle for us. It will make things so much more fun. Of course, we've got to make things absolutely fair; we wouldn't want to hurt anyone's feelings. I could leave if it would help, but . . . Oh, how nice of you to tell me I'll definitely have a place; it makes me feel a lot less awkward. I rarely go places alone, you know. Who would I like to sit next to? Well, the Capricorn lady looks like a sturdy and sensible type. But on the other hand, Scorpio is a *knockout*. Is she attached? Hmmm, Taurus looks like she'd like to chat, but oh, that Cancer! Decisions, decisions; I'll make up my mind later on. Where did you get that *great* painting?

Scorpio A slim and sexy woman dressed totally in black comes slinking into the room. Her style and movement are absolutely magnetic, and every eye turns to look at her. But she gives no visible response that she is aware of it. She doesn't seem to be feeling anything at all, but when her host approaches and tells her what is going on, she is seething with quiet rage.

"Do you really think you are going to get away with this? I suspected something when I got that weird invitation. Who in the world would ever come as they are and let everybody else know what they're really like? No matter how many times you tell me it was an innocent mistake to set only eleven places, I'll never believe it. Nothing in this world is innocent. And when it comes to drawing straws, just remember you owe me one from the last time. You know, the *last* time! Who's that wimpy looking guy over there? Gemini? Maybe I'll amuse myself with him for a while. I need a new conquest; I'm getting out of practice."

Sagittarius While Scorpio has been talking with the host, a tall rather rangy male has come loping into the room carrying a suitcase. He is a bit disheveled because his flight was late. He throws the suitcase in a corner and starts putting himself back together—a bit absentmindedly because he is looking around the room with a big smile and a lot of anticipation. He moves toward the host and gives a slap on his back that is almost *too* hearty.

"Only eleven places? Why worry? We'll work it out somehow. Life's too short to get uptight anyway. Had the greatest trip, and I'm turning right around tomorrow and going to the Orient so I can practice my Chinese. Say, are you serving Chinese food? I love Chinese food—and a good beer to go with it. At least I hope you're serving better wine than you did last time. You're looking a little pale . . . been partying too much lately? Ha ha, only kidding. Who's that guy over there with the flashy cufflinks? And the mouse with the sensible shoes? Think I'll see if I can loosen her up a bit. Did you hear I'm going to win the lottery again? What do you mean, how do I know? I just *know*. And I've got a great idea for an international fast food chain I'm going to bankroll with my winnings. I'm gonna call it 'The Great Gobler' and serve only turkey sandwiches. Hey, I'm thirsty. Where's the bar?"

Aquarius An intellectual-looking gentleman—sort of an absentminded professor type—has been standing in the doorway quietly puffing his pipe and scrutinizing the crowd. His jacket and pants don't match, but he isn't aware of it. An even stranger—but typical—sartorial note is his electric blue tie with orange stripes. He's got his earphones with him; if things get too dull, he'll listen to some hard rock or electronic music and be in seventh heaven. When he finds out about the missing place, he gives a thoughtful answer and makes an impractical suggestion.

"Oh, well, rather than make anyone feel left out, we could cancel the whole dinner and bring the food to the local shelter for the homeless. Ah, you don't care for that idea. Too bad; I'm becoming more and more concerned about poverty in our own backyard. Of course, I'm no bleeding heart like Pisces, but fair's fair. Want to hear about a new invention I'm working on? It's an electronic stamp sorter that will revolutionize the whole philatelic world. Huh? Oh, that's stamp collecting. Glad you asked me to come alone, since I'm free as a bird now. My last attachment got so *sticky!* I've sworn off. At least off those emotional types who want you to get so involved. No, I never get lonely—I've got too many friends for that. By the way, I can just sit on the floor in the lotus position, and get some meditating in at the same time."

Capricorn A rather handsome, perfectly put together woman has been quietly observing the crowd and the room, mentally putting a price tag on everything. What she has on is very expensive, but understated and in excellent taste. In her handbag she carries a petition with her name on it. She wants to run for local office, and is hoping to pick up some supporters tonight. If they are "her kind of people," that is. Her reaction to the host's situation is sober but logical.

"Well, it's obvious someone will have to go, but I

trust your judgment to decide who is most important—if you know what I mean. Your appointments are in excellent taste; I see you like Tiffany as much as I do. Who's that rather tacky looking type over there? Cancer? Where *does* she get her clothes? I have little sympathy for people who can't get their act together and run their lives successfully. She's probably a poet. Ah, well, different strokes for different folks; fantasy has no place in *my* life, you know. By the way, I have some excellent ideas about how to shape things up in the community; will you sign my petition? At dinner, are we going to discuss great books? I just bought a whole series . . . all leather-bound, of course. They look smashing in my living room."

Pisces Meanwhile, a rather wispy but very pretty woman has been wandering in and out of the doorway, looking as if she isn't quite sure she is in the right place. She is dressed in a misty fabric of very pale colors; there doesn't seem to be a clear-cut edge anywhere. In fact, if you don't rub your eyes, you might think you are seeing an apparition. The host knows it's Pisces and catches her just as she's about to drift out the door again. He doesn't bother telling her about the missing place, because he knows she wouldn't understand why that was important.

"Late? Am I late? I lost my watch two weeks ago. Or was it three? Oh well, what's time anyway in the larger scheme of things? Hungry? Not really, though I can't remember the last time I ate. *Love*—it's *love* that's food for the soul, and that's what I care about nourishing. I wonder if any of these people have had any *real* soul food lately. No, don't worry, I won't try to convert anyone tonight. I'm too, too drained because of my current work. What kind? Well, it really isn't a job-job, I mean where you make money, and all. I've started a shelter for homeless animals in my apartment; I cry so much when I see a stray that I can't stand it. Who? Ho, he left some time ago. Something about there being 'other fish in the sea.' What in the world do you suppose he meant by that? By the way, I'm a little short of cash. Do you think you could lend me . . .?"

At this point, things are at a stalemate, but the situation will quickly resolve itself in one of twelve ways. Take your pick: This time *you* can choose the ending you like—and the one you think makes best astrological sense.

A. Aries gets in a fight with Leo and has to go to the emergency room.
B. Taurus gets really tired and hungry and decides to go home, cook a hamburger, and go to bed early.
C. Gemini runs out of note paper and gets laryngitis at the same time.
D. Cancer gets a call from the babysitter and is so worried she goes home to take care of her children.
E. Leo gets so irritated that no one is paying attention to the bruises Aries gave him that he leaves in a huff.
F. Virgo gets a stomach ache and decides to leave. Besides, it's time for her mineral bath.
G. Libra isn't able to make up his mind and gets a headache in the process.
H. Scorpio decides it's definitely a plot to humiliate her, and bows out less than graciously.
I. Sagittarius gets a little drunk and leaves early to get the plane.
J. Capricorn leaves as soon as she gets her petition filled up because there isn't anyone there *really* worth knowing.
K. Aquarius decides to go teach people at the shelter to use his stamp-sorting machine so they can get jobs.
L. Pisces remembers she has a date with her spiritual advisor and that she forgot to feed the animals.

5

Moods of the Moon

How to Successfully Navigate Its Day-by-Day Changes

Never underestimate the power of the moon. It is the closest planet to earth, and the only one whose effect on human life can actually be measured. Even the most skeptical antiastrology person has to admit that the moon rules the tides. If you stand on the beach for even a half hour or so, you can literally *see* how the moon works its magic as the water flows higher or lower, according to the time of day. There are places in the world where the tide rises as much as forty feet from its lowest to its highest point—that's *power*. If you think about the fact that humans are about 98 percent water in our chemical makeup, it's much easier to accept the fact that the moon has the same powerful effect on us as it does on the tides.

Like the "female" she symbolically is, the moon also changes her mind—or her sign—more quickly than any other planet. If you look at the day-by-day predictions in this book, which gives the position of the moon for every day, you will see that this changeable planet moves into a different sign about every two days.

As it moves from sign to sign, the moon brings a different kind of energy to the earth's atmosphere. Those who are particularly sensitive—like Cancers—feel it most strongly. But even the most stolid types are often moved by the effect of the particular sign the moon occupies on any given day, though they may not want to admit it.

Are we then slaves to the moods of the moon? Not if we understand its energies and cooperate with them. If you work *with* the moon and not against her, you can actually make life a lot easier for yourself. For instance, there are certain activities that go more smoothly when the moon is in a particular sign, just as other activities are more difficult to accomplish. Scheduling things accordingly could prevent a lot of frustration. You don't have to become a complete "lunatic" (ancient meaning, "one ruled by the moon") to benefit from its positive vibes, but simply go with the flow. Keep in mind, however, that the moon's effect will be *modified* by your sun sign, so be sure to check out your individual daily prediction. For instance, for *any* sun sign, the days when the moon is in that sign should bring a surge of energy. Whether you handle that energy positively or negatively is up to you.

Here's a rundown of the moods of the moon and the human activities that go with them.

When the Moon Is in Aries There is a very *physical* tone to this day. People may be throwing their weight around in more ways than one. Impatience, independent action, and quick tempers can sprout up all over the place. The good news is that most people will be feeling rather decisive, so some things can be completed. The bad news is that decisions may be totally unilateral; what *you* want may be exactly what someone else *doesn't* want. Similarly, people may be invading each other's territories; "keep off the grass" signs won't mean much today. Rule-breaking is the order of the day, and so are the consequences that go along with it. However, if there's a big mountain to scale, today's the day to begin the climb. If there's a formidable task that requires a lot of get-up-and-go to accomplish, today's the day to plunge in with both feet. If there's something you've been hesitating to tell someone, today you'll get the nerve to say it, but it may be difficult to be tactful. Try, anyway. On the up side, people will be feeling in the mood for some fun and frolic—practical jokes are very "moon in Aries." Even the boss may get in the spirit of things. It's a good day to:

Make a sale
Do heavy housework
Do some baking
Start a diet
Buy a lottery ticket
Get a haircut
Have your eyes checked

Sharpen knives
Stop worrying
Make a clean break
Start an exercise class
Do something on your own
Try a new recipe
Throw a last-minute party

When the Moon Is in Taurus Today, the amber light goes on, and people start to proceed with more caution. Rather than being adventurous, most people will feel like sticking with routine tasks. It is not a good day to try something new. In this more conservative mood, people will tend to hold on to what they have; don't try to borrow money from a friend today. Concentrate on making your own money grow, instead. Speaking of increase, this is an excellent day to "make your garden grow" in every sense of the phrase. Along with a quieter mood of the day, you may feel like pampering yourself a bit; allow yourself at least one luxury. Chocoholics, beware, however; this is a day for food binges and all forms of dietary excess. Creature comforts are a lot on everyone's mind; in fact, it may be difficult to crawl out of that comfortable bed in the morning. And more than a few people will be crawling back into it fairly early—with their favorite person. Sexual cravings are high on the list of "moon moods" today. Enjoy!

It's a good day to:

Put something off until tomorrow
Buy clothes or jewelry
Get your teeth filled
Start a savings account
Stick to your guns
Buy candy
Stay home and watch television

Put up preserves
Have a massage
Start singing lessons
Sell high on the market
Buy a plant
Buy real estate
Hug somebody

When the Moon Is in Gemini There's a touch more energy in the air today, and people will begin moving around a lot more. For some, there will be a lot of nervous energy and the scattery feeling that goes along with it; don't force yourself to concentrate if you can avoid it. It's a day to make connections—call, write, or bump into both new and old friends. Wits are generally sharp today, and people could be cracking jokes all around you. On the other hand, they may also be spilling some secrets. Gossip is easy to start today, and it could spread like wildfire. Mind your mouth! Anything requiring manual dexterity can easily get done today; even those who are usually clumsy may find they have nimble fingers. The tendency today is to do things quickly, if a bit superficially. If there are a couple of things that require a once-over-lightly treatment, get them out of the way now. If you haven't been invited to a party, give your own—or at least plan to get together with some buddies for a little socializing; the time is definitely right.

It's a good day to:

Get your hair cut	Use your hands
Join a club	Pay bills
Have a tooth pulled	Eat out
Sign up for a new course	Take a walk/drive
Send a letter	Call your brother/sister
Try something new	Tell a fib
Learn a language	Do two things at once

When the Moon Is in Cancer In Cancer, the moon is in her very own sign—and you'll know it. All those "moon" characteristics—like changeableness, sensitivity, and the desire for security—will be heightened. Cancers, of course, will feel it most strongly; and the other water signs, Scorpio and Pisces, may be even moodier than usual. The general tendency today is to do things that make you feel comfortable and feel good. For some, that means eating a lot of food; for others, it could be hitting the bottle a bit. People tend to feel a bit sorry for themselves during the transit of the moon through Cancer. When two people who live together are both feeling that way, the result can be a rather touchy day—and evening. As much as you want the comfort of others, you are better off on your own and working off those anxious feelings by yourself. Not for safety, but for comfort's sake, the best place to go today is no farther than your own backyard. You'll probably be feeling very stay-at-home anyway. However, it's an excellent day for memories. Reminisce with somebody you love, or get out that old photo album by yourself. You might find yourself shedding a tear or two, but it's all in a good cause.

It's a good day to:

Bake something delicious	Hug your children
Buy something old	Take care of somebody
Put up preserves	Go without makeup
Buy property	Call your mother
Start a habit	Buy something for the house
Plant something	Entertain at home
Pamper yourself	Give your hair a treatment

When the Moon Is in Leo Today, everyone feels like "coming out of the woodwork." Just as Cancer moon makes you want to hide, Leo moon makes you want to get out there and be seen. Nothing but the best will do on this day, so it could be a rather expensive one. Most people will be more generous than usual—both with their money and their affections; many a new romance has started under a Leo moon. Leo is also one of the more playful signs, so a lot of you will be in the mood for fun and games. Eating out is very Leo moon—and so is picking up the check. Today, you may have to fight for it. However, the boss may be a lot stricter than usual, and even those with nobody to "boss" will try to push somebody around. If you've got children, today you will appreciate them very much—no matter what they do. Most people find themselves reaching for the newest thing in the closet under this transit of the moon. If they don't have anything new to wear, they'll probably go out and buy it—on credit. No matter what time of the year it is, you'll be looking for a little sunshine or at least a warm place. On the beaches or by the fireplaces are where most people would like to be today—wishing life were one long vacation.

It's a good day to:

Borrow money	Buy jewelry
Get a new hairstyle	Invest in the market
Start building something	Do something creative

Follow a hunch
Steal the spotlight
Be brave
Be waited on
Prepare a gourmet meal
Dress up
Kiss somebody new

When the Moon Is in Virgo Now it's back to work, and back to reality. There's a sharp distinction between the Virgo moon mood and what precedes it, so you may shock yourself. Perhaps by deciding it's really time to get organized and then actually *doing* it. On the home front it's a great day to rearrange all those sloppy closets and cupboards On the job, you couldn't pick a better time to wrestle with that nasty detail work you've been avoiding. However, all is not good news under Virgo moon. For one thing, by contrast to Leo moon's generosity, people will be positively stingy today—both with their money and their love. Even the best of situations could deteriorate today when one or the other of the involved parties decides to point out the other's flaws. Your best course under the Virgo moon is to check that impulse to criticize. People can become highly self-critical during this transit, too. One extreme example of the going-over some people can give themselves during a Virgo moon is to develop mysterious maladies or to discover aches and pains they never felt before. Not to worry; they'll be all better by the time the moon moves into the next sign. Virgo moon is also inspection time, so the boss may be particularly sensitive to messy desks today and sloppiness in general. Keep things buttoned up and tidy for best results.

It's a good time to:

Start a diet
Get a physical
Bake bread
Quit smoking
Buy a pet
Try to do without something
Buy health food
Start a new job
Sew or mend something
Read a good book
Get a complete makeover
Call your maiden aunt
Feel like a martyr
Do a puzzle

When the Moon Is in Libra Now it's time to kiss and make up. Any relationships that suffered from the ragged nerves of Virgo moon time can be nicely patched up today. Pleasantries should be easy for one and all. In fact, even people who are normally rather gruff should smile a bit more today. Libra moon is one of the most social of moon periods; meeting and greeting should be prevalent activities. Most people will want to put their best foot forward, too, so the impulse to dress up and look your best may come upon you. You may feel rather self-indulgent as well; hard work is not as compatible with the Libra moon period as rest and relaxation are. It's definitely a time of togetherness, so even habitual loners may be looking for company. Most people will feel they need people—possibly one special person. Romance blossoms under the Libra moon in its purest form. It's not so much sex people want now as romantic love and companionship. No one's actually made a count, but it's a fair bet that more flowers get sent under the Libra moon than at any other time. Physical beauty is also highly important, so Libra moon is a great one under which to get yourself a whole new look or to redo anything that needs it. Something that's off-balance will bother you more at this time.

It's a good day to:

Be tactful	Forgive and forget
Redecorate	Add color to your life
Give a party	Luxuriate
Fall in love	Sign up for a dance class
Join a singing group	Buy a stereo
Buy something beautiful	Buy a down comforter
Try a new makeup	Learn about wine

When the Moon Is in Scorpio Things could easily get heavy today, and the tendency will be to go to extremes. Haters will hate more; lovers will love more passionately and physically. The sex drive is stimulated in many people during this transit of the moon. With all those intense emotions flying around, it's not surprising that people easily get hot under the collar—and/or imagine that somebody is out to get them. However, there is an up side to the Scorpio moon, and that is the extra jot of will power it gives the most weak-willed people. If you've got to dig in your heels and clench your teeth to get something done, today's the day you will be able to do it. People *endure* a lot under the Scorpio moon. The only problem is that they may develop some resentment toward those they believe should be enduring with them. However, the tendency is to keep silent. In spite of the intense emotionalism of the Scorpio moon, there isn't a lot of outright complaining. People will let the pressure build up inside of them and then burst out into violent rages. If your temper isn't good under the best of circumstances, control it during the Scorpio moon, by all means. It's also a time when people tend to feel a bit claustrophobic; a good walk in the fresh air can work wonders at this time.

It's a good day to:

See a psychiatrist	Have good sex
Buy a house	Face up to a crisis
Open a secret bank account	Read a good mystery
Make a firm decision	Take body-building
Do your taxes	Get a prescription filled
Throw away what you don't need	Buy life insurance
Do some strenuous exercise	Change your life

When the Moon Is in Sagittarius Things definitely lighten up when the moon moves into Sagittarius—and people loosen up, too. In fact, one danger under this moon is getting too relaxed—with your diet, your money, or your generous spirits. Moderation is not the mood of the day, so you may have to force it on yourself. It is not a good time to try to stop smoking—or to stop doing anything self-indulgent. There's definitely a "live and let live" attitude in the air when the moon is in Sagittarius, so bad relations should be easily improved. A spirit of good will is pervasive, as well as a lighthearted attitude. One thing that means is that even normally conservative people will be willing to take chances; those for whom a more liberal outlook is a natural state of affairs could really go too far out on a limb. If you gamble, bet *only* what you can afford to lose today. The place everyone will want to be today is outdoors. In fact, more than one person will simply disappear from the scene to do something either adventurous or relaxing. It's an excellent day to think big, but you may find the follow-through a bit difficult. The big picture is what's easiest to see right now; leave the fine brush strokes for another time. Enjoy the spirit of fun and generosity that should be in the air.

It's a good day to:

Make a long-distance call
Plan a trip
Buy a dog (or a horse)
Contribute to a wildlife-
 foundation
Try a new approach
Sell anything to anybody
Try your luck/feel lucky
Go to church
Enjoy a hobby
Learn a new language
Do something charitable
Borrow money
Run away from it all
Get a bigger place

When the Moon Is in Capricorn In sharp contrast to the "easy come, easy go" feeling of the Sagittarius moon, the moon in Capricorn brings on a much more serious mood. You could call it the "workaholic's moon," and even those whose work style is less intense will find themselves wanting to get a lot done. It's important to *accomplish something* when the moon is in Capricorn, if you are to feel comfortable. Most people want to tread only on solid ground at this time, so there could be a bit of distrust in the air. No one wants to waste time—and least of all on things or people from whom they are not likely to derive some kind of benefit. Another curious facet of the Capricorn moon mood is a tendency to feel older and more serious; some lighter types dislike the feeling so much they will go out of their way to look young. It's the kind of day that matronly secretary in the office is likely to appear in something rather frilly. People can really handle things under the Capricorn moon too; endurance is *very* Capricorn. That means those who exercise will work out harder and longer; those who normally do not push themselves will do at least a little self-prodding. A good image is paramount to many people when the moon is in this sign, and the tendency is for people to be quite status conscious. Self-control is the order of the day, in every respect.

It's a good day to:

Start a new job
Buy antiques

Make a list
Keep your money

Buy anything for investment	Go to the dentist
Wear anything with a good label on it	Start a diet
	Work late
Bet on a favorite	Ask for repayment of a debt
Go to the chiropractor	
Buy insurance	Clean house

When the Moon Is in Aquarius When the moon moves into the sign of Aquarius from the sign of Capricorn, it's as if somebody took the cork out of the bottle. Suddenly, the rather repressed mood bursts into a desire for change—a *need* for change. This is one of those days when people tend to make rash moves like quit a dull job, call it quits with a clinging person, throw out everything in their closet and start all over again. Reaching this point is easy to do under the Aquarian moon. However, it's usually very positive. What's important at this time is to try something new, not just get rid of something old. Some people decide to experiment with a new recipe, a new lover, or a new hair style. It's the kind of day when a woman with long hair will decide to get a crew cut. On the relationship side, the mood now is one of brotherly love and friendship rather than highly charged sexual encounters. Wanting to be with friends and feeling like part of a group is what's important now. No one is a stranger under the Aquarian moon, and talking to people on the street is very common. The thing to be careful of under this moon is doing something irreparable—like finally telling the boss what you really think of him. He/she could easily decide that it's time for a change of personnel.

It's a good day to:

Do something kinky	Buy/wear something crazy
Try a new food	Color your hair
Do something friendly	Contribute to a charity
Start flying lessons	Move to a new place
Do something impulsive	Buy a television/stereo
Join a club	Make a new friend
Make a speculative investment	Be fair

When the Moon Is in Pisces This is a time when people wear their hearts on their sleeves and feel *very* vulnerable. There's a lot of ultrasensitivity under the Pisces moon, and a lot of crying on shoulders—if you can find one that isn't already occupied. Mixed in with the emotionalism is a real feeling of empathy with others; now's the time people feel that everyone is in the same boat. However, it may be a bit difficult to keep things afloat today, because there isn't a lot of firm direction from anyone or anything. It's confusion time, and even the clearest of messages can get a little garbled. Indecisiveness will spread like the plague, so don't expect to get any clear-cut answers today. Creative people get more creative under the Pisces moon, and anyone could feel just a bit poetic. Romantic relationships are heavenly under the Pisces moon as long as they don't get out of control. Keeping certain other things under control—like drinking and other forms of escapism—is a wise precaution, too. The most satisfying and least dangerous escape is to hold hands with someone you love while you watch a real tearjerker movie. Lots of people call in sick under the Pisces moon, and there's a good reason: Most people don't like to cry in public.

It's a good day to:

Put on weight
Fall in love
Develop ESP
Find God
Buy flowers or perfume
Swear off something
Get hooked on something

Write a poem
Take in a stray dog or cat
Visit the sick
See a therapist
Stay home and read
Pamper yourself
Buy a camera

6

Venus and Mars

Love and Sex
Peace and War
Cooperating and Competing

Next to your sun sign, your moon sign, and your rising sign, the positions of Venus and Mars in your horoscope are probably the most important indicators of your personal psychology. This is because Venus shows your affectional nature and Mars shows your sexual nature. To put it another way, *Venus shows your wants and needs in romantic love while Mars shows your sexual style and your manner of expressing it.*

In a broader sense, Venus and Mars are the principles of peace and war. Venus wants to cooperate and relate to others, to share life experiences. Mars is totally concerned with self and getting what you want. Everybody's got a Venus and Mars in their horoscope because every human being has to both live with others and assert him-/herself. It's all a matter of degree. If you want to, you can think of Venus as the "higher" side of human relationships; Mars the "lower." However, you've got to keep in mind that—like all other opposites in the universe—both *cooperating* and competing are necessary if the world is to continue going round.

Because Venus has to do with the need to share, the sign in which it is placed will tell a lot about how you attract people you want to share with. It will also show what attracts you to others. Beyond the love arena, the position of Venus in your horoscope shows your attitudes toward money and personal possessions, creature comforts, and things of beauty. Venus is "feminine" in nature, and women tend to relate to their Venus sign more than men. But for *both* sexes, it is an available energy.

The good side of Venus is:
Sharing, beautifying, peacemaking
The bad side is:
acquisitiveness, self-indulgence, laziness

Because the position of Mars shows how you go about getting what you want, it will tell a lot about your personal drive—how *much* you want what you want. It is the desire principle, and will indicate just how passionate your passions are. Ambition, assertiveness, and anger are just a few steps away from each other, so Mars will also reveal what makes you angry or what gets you going. The planet Mars is "masculine" in nature—highly so—and men will find it easier to get in touch with their Mars energy. However, every woman's got a Mars too, and sooner or later a woman's Mars energy will present itself.

The "good" side of Mars is:
Dynamic energy, courage, sexual drive
The "bad" side is:
manipulation, cowardice, sexual abuse

No matter what area of life you are relating these planets to, it is useful to think of them in sexual terms, and of our human sexual organs. Venus is open and receptive; Mars thrusts forward and penetrates. Because we normally attract someone or are attracted to someone before we get sexually involved, Venus energy precedes Mars energy. In other words, Venus shows how *receptive* you are; Mars shows how *active* you are. Venus also has a lot to do with our ideas and images of romance, our romantic fantasies, while Mars is an indicator of sexual fantasies—which may or may not be acted out, depending on the individual's degree of inhibition.

Just as some combinations of people can coexist in constant harmony while others are in constant conflict,

Venus and Mars in an individual person can work well together, or at cross-purposes. When your Venus doesn't get along well with your Mars, you've got a problem. Sometimes a sexual problem, but always an inner conflict. How can you tell if your Venus and Mars are "friends" or "foes"? First, by looking up the positions of your personal Mars and Venus in the charts provided at the end of this chapter, reading the descriptions of those planets in the signs they fall in for you. But, just to make things a bit clearer, here's a rundown of easy Mars/Venus relationships and difficult ones. (By the way, you can also apply this principle in comparing your Venus/Mars positions to those of someone else, as well.)

Venus and Mars are "at war" when:

- One is in a fire sign, and one is in an earth sign. Here you've got a conflict between the practical and the experimental sides of yourself.
- One is in a fire sign and one is in a water sign. One part of you says "let's do it"; the other side says, "I might get hurt," so you might be stalled.
- One is in an earth sign and one is in an air sign. Air likes to think about things a little; earth needs to know it will work. Once again, it may hold you back.
- One is in an air sign and one is in a water sign. Yours is a conflict between the mental relationship and the emotional one; you may find it hard to decide what you want.

Venus and Mars are on good terms when:

- One is in a fire sign, one is in an air sign.
- One is in an earth sign and one is in a water sign.
- Both are in the same element.

Venus and Mars in The Signs

Venus in Aries (fire element)

While this position of Venus in a man or a woman indicates the kind of person who falls in love impulsively, both sexes want to be conquered, when they have Venus in Aries. They may be outrageously flirtatious, but can lead others on a merry chase before they give in. There is a tendency to look for trouble when Venus is in ths position; actually, it is excitement Venus in Aries people crave. Their personal likes and dislikes will be quite clearly defined, and they will be vocal about them. In matters of taste, there is less refinement than when Venus is in a softer sign. Both the males and the females may play up their sexuality in the way they dress; they like very loud things like rock music and bright colors. There is also an impish charm in these people and a tendency to play love games. The *real* goal is to be swept away by a romantic lover who lives up to a mediaeval code of chivalry and/or chastity.

Mars in Aries (fire element)

This is a highly competitive position for Mars; people with Mars in Aries leave no doubt about the fact that they want it, and they want it *now*—whatever "it" is. Mars in Aries can cut through a lot of life's red tape. When it comes to courtship, Mars in Aries people are equally able to disregard the small talk and get right down to business. However, this position of Mars often makes for a rather selfish lover—one who is so concerned with getting that he/she doesn't do an awful lot of giving. Mars in Aries people are likely to turn off as quickly as they turn on. Passion burns brightly, but is often short-lived. They are highly independent and likely to leave if a romantic partner gets too possessive or demanding. Mars in Aries is also always ready for a fight, so relationships are a bit stormy.

Venus in Taurus (earth element)

This is a highly sensual position for Venus to be in. People with Venus in Taurus are turned on by sweet words and soft music—and any form of touching. They like all kinds of nice and beautiful things, and will be attracted by someone who dresses well and has expensive taste. Venus in Taurus people can be a little self-indulgent, but in the main their desire is to make the object of their affection comfortable. And they will do it in very tangible ways; Venus in Taurus people of both sexes like to do things for others. When someone with Venus in Taurus is attracted, he/she is loyal. Love does not come in a flash, as it does with Venus in Aries people, but when it comes, it usually stays. At least as far as the person with Venus in Taurus is concerned. These people are generally so devoted that a breakup is extremely unsettling. You can always make a Venus in Taurus person happy with candy or flowers. The best kind of love feels good, tastes good, looks good, and smells good.

Mars in Taurus (earth element)

This Mars can express itself as ambition with a definite direction—or as controlled sexuality. Mars in Taurus people of both sexes can appear rather lazy, but actually their slow movements are usually on a deliberate course. Some people with Mars in Taurus are really looking for a safe position in a job or with a partner. Their manner of sexuality is highly sensual though they may be slow to get aroused. When a Mars in Taurus person enters into an affair, however, there is usually the intention to make it a long and serious one. These people are certainly capable of quick affairs, but they generally prefer a comfortable relationship where they do not constantly have to keep proving their love. There is a certain giving quality to Mars in Taurus, and the men are exceptionally considerate lovers. The women are fairly passive, but passionate and giving when they get going.

Venus in Gemini

Venus in Gemini people of both sexes tend to be turned on more by *talk* than by physical stimulation. Relationships have to have a mental dimension in order for them to get involved. In fact, Venus in Gemini people are likely to make better friends than lovers. When their affections *are* engaged, the connection is likely to be a little tenuous, and the Venus in Gemini's feelings may not run as deep as his/her partner's. Fickleness is a reality with these people— they like a lot of changes, and that goes for people as well as environments. Job-hopping is a trait of Venus in Gemini, and so is a constant changing of the guard in their romantic lives. However, Venus in Gemini people make wonderful romantic partners, because they are really *interested* in the people they get involved with. Never tell a Venus in Gemini person to "shut up and make love"; he/she will be very likely to shut the door on the relationship.

Mars in Gemini

Mars in Gemini people assert themselves rather erratically; there isn't a lot of staying power, in jobs or in relationships. The "alternating current" of Mars in Gemini energy makes for a rather on again, off again sexual life. People with Mars in this position are capable of having a number of purely mental relationships in between their sexual ones. These are the kind of people who talk their way into things, including a job and someone's bed. Their approach is a bit on the delicate side, and one may wonder when the Mars in Gemini person is really going to get started. However, once their passion is aroused, Mars in Gemini people like a lot of variety; sex can get quite original with these people. The tendency to bore easily goes both for their attitudes toward their sexual partners and the manner in which they have sex. Both sexes are real charmers, however, and sometimes get their way in a rather devious manner.

Venus in Cancer (water element)

The overriding thing that people with Venus in Cancer want is *security*, really the emotional kind, but since a secure home base goes along with their needs, the material kind is important too. Venus in Cancer people can be highly traditional in their romantic values—home, mother, and apple pie are symbols of the things that turn these people on. If you want to engage the emotions of a Venus in Cancer person, all you have to do is look as if you *need* somebody—preferably a mother. Venus in Cancer people need to be needed, but sometimes can go overboard by totally taking over the other person's life. With Venus in this sign, people respond strongly to all kinds of romantic things, from the card that says "I love you" to a little token of affection for no special occasion. However, Venus in Cancer people are highly self-protective, so you first have to break down their natural reserve and fear of getting hurt. Once you do, you won't find a more faithful lover. Except perhaps Taurus.

Mars in Cancer (water element)

Mars in Cancer people can sneak up on you when they've decided they want you; their approach is a bit sideways, like the locomotion of the crab that is the Cancer symbol. They are soft and subtle lovers and said by some to be among the best sexual partners in the zodiac. However, as sensitive and understanding as they tend to be in the sexual area, they can be overly possessive with people they love, and even turn rather cruel when they are rejected. Cancer is a water sign, and it is as if that water starts boiling—invisibly—then the lid totally pops off when the explosion comes. Mars in Cancer people tend to be a little blind to their sexual/ambition drive and can even pretend to themselves that it doesn't exist. For this reason, they make formidable enemies, because while they look as if they are asking for peace they are really preparing for battle.

Venus in Leo (fire element)

There's a pretty simple way to get a Venus in Leo person to like you. Give him/her a lot of attention—*positive* attention. Venus in Leo people do want love, but they want admiration and adulation to come along with it. A bit like Venus in Aries, Venus in Leo wants a *courtly* lover—someone who will swear absolute loyalty. When it's a Leo sun sign person who also has Venus in Leo, you've got the absolute monarch of them all. Venus in Leo also goes only for the best, and is attracted to what looks expensive or rewarding—in both jobs and people. Venus in Leo expects you to dress and look your best, no matter what the circumstances. It is not a "casual" Venus. Demonstrations of love are very important, too. Words are great, of course, and so is a lot of hugging and the rest of the physical love spectrum. However, candy—or some other tangible token of affection—is expected. Venus in Leo has fierce pride, so if you even slip once and appear not to *respect* this person, he/she is likely to brush you off—with a very grand gesture of course.

Mars in Leo (fire element)

Speaking of grand gestures, Mars in Leo wrote the book. This kind of person is the one who will lavish the object of his/her affection with all kinds of luxurious things. Mars in Leo is a real showy person and expects to be appreciated for it. Both the males and the females are aggressive about going after what they want, and once they are happily ensconced—with a lover or a job—they are loyal and steady. However, the down side of the Mars in Leo position is a violent temper: a *really* violent temper. Both sexes can get quite physical in expressing anger. This is the position of the female who throws plates and the man who slaps his faithless lover on the cheek. Mars in Leo is unrelentingly honest— and will expect you to be too. One devious move, and it's over

Venus in Virgo (earth element)

Venus in Virgo wants a love that *works*. Pure sex or romance may appeal to Virgo's desire for the unadulterated, but there's got to be an element of the practical in it too. People with Venus in Virgo often actually fall in love with their jobs faster than they do with people. When Venus is in the sign, you often find the dedicated, loyal, "number two" person who spends a lifetime catering to the needs of a powerful boss. He/she is likely to be just a little bit in love with that boss too. As for sex, the Venus in Virgo person has a very healthy attitude toward it—possibly too healthy in the sense that it is sometimes regarded as an excellent form of exercise. Venus in Virgo people are not really cold—in fact, when they love someone they can't do enough for them, particularly in attending to their physical comfort. The problem is that this position of Venus makes a person overly analytical in determining what he/she wants. If the Venus in Virgo person keeps his/her mouth shut, and doesn't openly criticize, there is a much better possibility that he/she will make good, solid relationships.

Mars in Virgo (earth element)

Virgo's inventive sexuality is one of the best-kept secrets in the zodiac; Mars in Virgo turns out some of the most experimental and skillful lovers of all. That is, if you can attract one of these people in the first place. Mars in Virgo people are far from promiscuous; in fact, their standards are likely to be a bit too high. They are constantly questioning their *own* desires and drives, picking them apart instead of acting upon them. Mars in Virgo is ideal for success in just about any job or profession. With any sun sign, it adds to the ability to cooly analyze problems and solve them with a reasonable amount of dispatch. When it comes to romantic involvement, this is not one of the more "romantic" Mars positions (unless the sun sign is Libra). You may feel as if your Mars in Virgo lover is checking you over first for anything that might turn him/her off. This is the sign that usually says "let's shower together" before he/she says "let's go to bed."

Venus in Libra (air element)

First off, remember that when the planet Venus is in Libra, it's in its "home sign." When it comes to beauty, harmony, and balance, Venus in Libra people want it all. When Venus is in Libra, the most attractive things in life are the *nicest*—people, places, jobs, clothes, you name it. Venus in Libra people want it nice, but they also want it *easy*. In fact, this sometimes "cold" position of Venus can make for a person who marries for status or money. If you look comfortable in every sense of the word, you've got a shot at attracting that Venus in Libra person who catches your eye. And he/she will, because this position of Venus usually confers a great-looking body. Even if the Venus in Libra person loves or marries for convenience, he/she gives an awful lot in return. Once you've engaged his/her love the Venus in Libra person considers you the best, the most beautiful/handsome, and the brightest person in the universe and will treat you accordingly.

Mars in Libra (air element)

This position of Mars often makes for a passive/aggressive type of individual—a specific psychological pattern. The Mars in Libra person rarely goes directly after what he/she wants, but more or less lingers in front of it, waiting for the other person to make the right move. Mars in Libra people don't get hired as quickly as other types because they don't seem to *care* enough about whether or not they get the job. When it comes to love, Mars in Libra can be quite frustrating. You really don't know what's going on here—does or doesn't he/she want to get involved? This is also a rather "refined" position for brash Mars. Mars in Libra people usually have excellent manners, and never appear to get ruffled. They will just sit and smile while you rant and rave. Suddenly, however, they can turn on their heel and walk out the door. The technique Mars in Libra people use to go about making their subtle conquests is *talk*—but it can easily fool you because it seems so casual.

Venus in Scorpio (water element)

A lot of people with sun sign Scorpio have Venus in Scorpio too; (one's Venus sign is often one's sun sign because Venus is so close to the sun in the solar system). These double-whammy Scorpios are extraordinarily intense in all their emotional needs, but anyone with Venus in Scorpio is going to be touched by the madness of this intense sign. The curious paradox is that Venus in Scorpio people are either totally *turned on* by someone or something—or totally *turned off*. There are very few halfway deals in their lives. Venus in Scorpio can also be highly manipulative, adjusting his/her emotions to suit other needs—like money. When Venus is in Scorpio, people are attracted to what seems mysterious, dangerous, or hard-to-get. They love puzzles, and can be a bit of a puzzle themselves to prospective romantic partners. When they do get involved, however, they have a great deal of staying power—emotionally at least. They can fairly easily separate their physical *actions* from their mental states, however.

Mars in Scorpio (water element)

People with Mars in Scorpio have a very strong "energy field" surrounding them; you can almost see it and feel it. What they want, they want passionately—and will seek in no uncertain terms. They are equally positive about what they *don't* want—so you will know whether you've got a shot with them right away. No waiting with *this* aggressive sign. The legendary super-sexuality of Scorpio is real with Mars in Scorpio people. However, they may use their sexual power to control other people and situations. And, if they are rejected against their will (which doesn't happen too often) they are capable of the worst kind of venomous reactions. Jealous lovers who are violent to their former partners are a parody of the Mars in Scorpio type of intensity. One way Mars in Scorpio people can hurt or simply tease others is by withholding their love—and their physical passion. They have great powers of self-control.

Venus in Sagittarius (fire element)

People with Venus in the restless, mobile sign of the Centaur often get the reputation for being fickle, and there is more than a grain of truth in that label. But the reason a Venus in Sagittarius person may move around or not become committed is that he/she is so vulnerable to deceit and dishonesty. As the saying goes, "once burned, twice shy," and openhearted, friendly Sagittarius is likely to get burned very early in life. When Venus in Sagittarius people do get involved, they are absolutely delightful to love. Broadminded, unpossessive, full of fun, they really want to enjoy romance. Sagittarius is also a very intellectual sign, so in order to get Venus in Sagittarius people to stick with you for a while, you've got to keep them interested. Sex is great, but sex with talk is even greater for these people. Venus in Sagittarius is also highly idealistic, so you've got to be a higher type to appeal to someone with Venus in this sign. Love is gallantry and honor and all those things that are so hard to find in life.

Mars in Sagittarius (fire element)

Sagittarius is a sign that thinks in global terms, so when Mars is in the sign of Sagittarius, you find a person who wants it all—and often has to be satisfied with nothing. People with Mars in Sagittarius assert themselves bluntly and get right to the point. However, they tend to be so optimistic in their expectations that they may just as quickly decide they have made a mistake. Better luck next love. Mars in Sagittarius doesn't deliberately hurt people; this sign is kind to all—both animals and humans. Their sexual nature can also be rather "animalistic" because this is a lusty sign, and so fond of all outdoor sports that they often want to do it anywhere, anytime. One way Mars in Sagittarius people get to your heart is through your sense of humor; they really know how to make people laugh. It is a powerful weapon in their professional lives too; it's hard to fire someone who is such a delight to have around—even if he/she isn't around that much. The big problem with Mars in Sagittarius people is that they sometimes don't want to take responsibility for their own actions, and lay things on other people. Even if Mars in Sagittarius is the one to break things up, he/she will somehow or other get you to believe that it's *your* fault.

Venus in Capricorn (earth element)

Appearances count a lot to Venus in Capricorn people—in every sense of the word. In order to appeal to them, you've got to look solid and substantial—and fairly rich as well. Because there is a natural reserve to Capricorn, people with Venus in this sign will dislike public displays of affection; the cooler you are in your approach, the better. Their public image and their private one are not too far apart, either. Not that Venus in Capricorn isn't normal; he/she can be quite passionate in bed. But very, very *serious*, too. If you mistake this sign's sober approach to life for coldness, you will not be the first person who has. Once again, like those with Venus in Virgo, Venus in Capricorn is attracted to *practical* people—people who can really work for them in one way or another. While some do actually consciously go after a financially comfortable marital situation, what the vast majority will settle for is someone who is willing to help handle a lot of the more serious aspects of life. Male or female, Venus in Capricorn people want you to be *useful*. Unfortunately, some people with Venus in this sign have such a low sense of self-worth, that they will try to buy love—or sell it—because they don't feel anyone will accept them for what they are.

Mars in Capricorn (earth element)

Mars in Capricorn people always want to know the rules before they enter the game; they assert themselves with extreme caution. However, when they *know* what they want, they have incredible powers to help them get it. One is patience; Mars in Capricorn can wait very well. Another thing they have going for them is self-control; their timing is excellent because they can hold themselves back when they want to. All this makes for a rather sexually confusing type, and sometimes one who is sexually confused. Mars in Capricorn people can go without sex for amazing lengths of time if nothing seems worth the effort. When they do go for it, their approach can be extremely lusty and earthy, as befits the earth element of Capricorn. Even more than someone with Mars in Scorpio, the person with Mars in Capricorn can be a user. In love or business, he/she can easily fake it to get the carrot on the end of the stick. Then, before you know it, the person who seemed so hot for you has now turned stone cold. Sad, but true.

Venus in Aquarius (air element)

The best way to attract someone with Venus in Aquarius is to be a bit unconventional; these people love anyone or anything that is off-beat. However, you may find that you are considered a specimen rather than a romantic partner—or at least that's how it's likely to feel. People with Venus in Aquarius seem to have a real problem with deep involvement; often they really *want* it, but somehow or other their deepest wells of emotion are very difficult to tap.

Their habitual reaction to love is often "easy come, easy go." Are they cruel people? Generally not, and often Venus in Aquarius people suffer a lot from their difficulty with feeling. They will rarely tell you, however, because there is a real need for distance there. And distance is what they seek in one-on-one relationships. If you become possessive with, or jealous of a person with Venus in Aquarius, you will lose him/her very quickly. As with some of the other mental signs like Gemini and Libra, you have got to keep the affair or the marriage *interesting* in one way or another. This is a Venus position that often likes kinky sex, porno movies, and other forms of artificial stimulation. However, they usually don't care enough about sex-for-the-sake-of-sex to be unfaithful.

Mars in Aquarius (air element)

When Mars is in this erratic sign, people tend to go through periods of feast and famine, largely because they can fluctuate between being extremely assertive and sure about what they want or totally inactive. During the latter periods you could actually call the Mars in Aquarius person lazy. In love, the Mars in Aquarius person tends to go after the unusual or difficult; involvements with people who are already attached are quite common. In many cases it is because the Mars in Aquarius person really is terribly afraid of deep involvement. There is a detachment about Mars in Aquarius people that sometimes works against permanent attachment to people or professional situations. Mars in Aquarius really prefers to go it alone. Perhaps the reason is that they always want to be free to experiment with the new. In sex, the Mars in Aquarius person is hung up on technique; he/she likes intelligent sex, and sometimes wants to prove how clever he/she is via this rather bizarre route.

Venus in Pisces (water element)

For people with Venus in Pisces, what's attractive is often bound up with some kind of sacrifice. This is the position of Venus that leads to martyrdom of all kinds. Some Venus in Pisces people find it impossible to get involved with anything or anyone normal and healthy; their instinctive need is to care for the lame and needy. Therefore, many Venus in Pisces people are rather easily taken advantage of by unscrupulous types who use them or take them for all they're worth. By the same token, Venus in Pisces people can put a real *drain* on the object of their affections—demanding more and more proofs of undying love, soulful demonstrations, sometimes even more tangible support. However, in the broadest, most universal sense of the word, Pisces is the "best" position for Venus as it represents the principle of *true love*. True love is totally unselfish, totally self-sacrificing. Though few normal mortals are capable of such "divine" love, Venus in Pisces people come closest to being able to make it. On the more mundane side, people wth Venus in Pisces are attracted by all kinds of sentimental and often impractical things. They will love you most if you spend your last penny on a bouquet of violets rather than bread for the table. So what? You'll just live on love.

Mars in Pisces (water element)

Mars in Pisces people can easily lose their way; the sign of Pisces is not stable enough for the aggressive energy of Mars, so Mars in Pisces people tend to scatter their energies in too many places. On the other hand, they are the most subtle and devious people in the zodiac when it comes to going after what they really *do* want. Their come-on is usually to be rather weak and helpless. Both the males and the females snare you by making you think they really *need* you. There's a lot of poetry to Mars in Pisces people, so the start of an affair is likely to be all moonlight and roses. However, you may find that once you are entangled, you can't get yourself out when you want out. Mars in Pisces people have a way of snarling you up in their webs of erratic energy. Just when they've agreed that you should go, they'll become helpless again and make you feel you have to stay. However, Mars in Pisces people do offer a very wonderful kind of love—soft, sensitive, and caring. The object of their desires is often someone similar or someone involved with art or music in some way. However, Pisces types are best off hooking up with a strong partner—someone who can keep their Mars energy on a straight and even course. The best part of Mars in Pisces people is that they are rarely, if ever, cold.

VENUS SIGN 1910–1975

	Aries	Taurus	Gemini	Cancer	Leo	Virgo
1910	5/7-6/3	6/4-6/29	6/30-7/24	7/25-8/18	8/19-9/12	9/13-10/6
1911	2/28-3/23	3/24-4/17	4/18-5/12	5/13-6/8	6/9-7/7	7/8-11/8
1912	4/13-5/6	5/7-5/31	6/1-6/24	6/24-7/18	7/19-8/12	8/13-9/5
1913	2/3-3/6	3/7-5/1	7/8-8/5	8/6-8/31	9/1-9/26	9/27-10/20
	5/2-5/30	5/31-7/7				
1914	3/14-4/6	4/7-5/1	5/2-5/25	5/26-6/19	6/20-7/15	7/16-8/10
1915	4/27-5/21	5/22-6/15	6/16-7/10	7/11-8/3	8/4-8/28	8/29-9/21
1916	2/14-3/9	3/10-4/5	4/6-5/5	5/6-9/8	9/9-10/7	10/8-11/2
1917	3/29-4/21	4/22-5/15	5/16-6/9	6/10-7/3	7/4-7/28	7/29-8/21
1918	5/7-6/2	6/3-6/28	6/29-7/24	7/25-8/18	8/19-9/11	9/12-10/5
1919	2/27-3/22	3/23-4/16	4/17-5/12	5/13-6/7	6/8-7/7	7/8-11/8
1920	4/12-5/6	5/7-5/30	5/31-6/23	6/24-7/18	7/19-8/11	8/12-9/4
1921	2/3-3/6	3/7-4/25	7/8-8/5	8/6-8/31	9/1-9/25	9/26-10/20
	4/26-6/1	6/2-7/7				
1922	3/13-4/6	4/7-4/30	5/1-5/25	5/26-6/19	6/20-7/14	7/15-8/9
1923	4/27-5/21	5/22-6/14	6/15-7/9	7/10-8/3	8/4-8/27	8/28-9/20
1924	2/13-3/8	3/9-4/4	4/5-5/5	5/6-9/8	9/9-10/7	10/8-11/12
1925	3/28-4/20	4/21-5/15	5/16-6/8	6/9-7/3	7/4-7/27	7/28-8/21
1926	5/7-6/2	6/3-6/28	6/29-7/23	7/24-8/17	8/18-9/11	9/12-10/5
1927	2/27-3/22	3/23-4/16	4/17-5/11	5/12-6/7	6/8-7/7	7/8-11/9
1928	4/12-5/5	5/6-5/29	5/30-6/23	6/24-7/17	7/18-8/11	8/12-9/4
1929	2/3-3/7	3/8-4/19	7/8-8/4	8/5-8/30	8/31-9/25	9/26-10/19
	4/20-6/2	6/3-7/7				
1930	3/13-4/5	4/6-4/30	5/1-5/24	5/25-6/18	6/19-7/14	7/15-8/9
1931	4/26-5/20	5/21-6/13	6/14-7/8	7/9-8/2	8/3-8/26	8/27-9/19

VENUS SIGN 1910–1975

Libra	Scorpio	Sagittarius	Capricorn	Aquarius	Pisces
10/7-10/30	10/31-11/23	11/24-12/17	12/18-12/31	1/1-1/15	1/16-1/28
				1/29-4/4	4/5-5/6
11/19-12/8	12/9-12/31		1/1-1/10	1/11-2/2	2/3-2/27
9/6-9/30	1/1-1/4	1/5-1/29	1/30-2/23	2/24-3/18	3/19-4/12
	10/1-10/24	10/25-11/17	11/18-12/12	12/13-12/31	
10/21-11/13	11/14-12/7	12/8-12/31		1/1-1/6	1/7-2/2
8/11-9/6	9/7-10/9	10/10-12/5	1/1-1/24	1/25-2/17	2/18-3/13
	12-6/12-30	12/31			
9/22-10/15	10/16-11/8	1/1-2/6	2/7-3/6	3/7-4/1	4/2-4/26
		11/9-12/2	12/3-12/26	12/27-12/31	
11/3-11/27	11/28-12/21	12/22-12/31		1/1-1/19	1/20-2/13
8/22-9/16	9/17-10/11	1/1-1/14	1/15-2/7	2/8-3/4	3/5-3/28
		10/12-11/6	11/7-12/5	12/6-12/31	
10/6-10/29	10/30-11/22	11/23-12/16	12/17-12/31	1/1-4/5	4/6-5/6
11/9-12/8	12/9-12/31		1/1-1/9	1/10-2/2	2/3-2/26
9/5-9/30	1/1-1/3	1/4-1/28	1/29-2/22	2/23-3/18	3/19-4/11
	9/31-10/23	10/24-11/17	11/18-12/11	12/12-12/31	
10/21-11/13	11/14-12/7	12/8-12/31		1/1-1/6	1/7-2/2
8/10-9/6	9/7-10/10	10/11-11/28	1/1-1/24	1/25-2/16	2/17-3/12
	11/29-12/31				
9/21-10/14	1/1	1/2-2/6	2/7-3/5	3/6-3/31	4/1-4/26
	10/15-11/7	11/8-12/1	12/2-12/25	12/26-12/31	
11/3-11/26	11/27-12/21	12/22-12/31		1/1-1/19	1/20-2/12
8/22-9/15	9/16-10/11	1/1-1/14	1/15-2/7	2/8-3/3	3/4-3/27
		10-12/11-6	11/7-12/5	12/6-12/31	
10/6-10/29	10/30-11/22	11/23-12/16	12/17-12/31	1/1-4/5	4/6-5/6
11/10-12/8	12/9-12/31	1/1-1/7	1/8	1/9-2/1	2/2-2/26
9/5-9/28	1/1-1/3	1/4-1/28	1/29-2/22	2/23-3/17	3/18-4/11
	9/29-10/23	10/24-11/16	11/17-12/11	12/12-12/31	
10/20-11/12	11/13-12/6	12/7-12/30	12/31	1/1-1/5	1/6-2/2
8/10-9/6	9/7-10/11	10/12-11/21	1/1-1/23	1/24-2/16	2/17-3/12
	11/22-12/31				
9/20-10/13	1/1-1/3	1/4-2/6	2/7-3/4	3/5-3/31	4/1-4/25
	10/14-11/6	11/7-11/30	12/1-12/24	12/25-12/31	

VENUS SIGN 1910–1975

	Aries	Taurus	Gemini	Cancer	Leo	Virgo
1932	2/12-3/8	3/9-4/3	4/4-5/5 7/13-7/27	5/6-7/12 7/28-9/8	9/9-10/6	10/7-11/1
1933	3/27-4/19	4/20-5/28	5/29-6/8	6/9-7/2	7/3-7/26	7/27-8/20
1934	5/6-6/1	6/2-6/27	6/28-7/22	7/23-8/16	8/17-9/10	9/11-10/4
1935	2/26-3/21	3/22-4/15	4/16-5/10	5/11-6/6	6/7-7/6	7/7-11/8
1936	4/11-5/4	5/5-5/28	5/29-6/22	6/23-7/16	7/17-8/10	8/11-9/4
1937	2/2-3/8 4/14-6/3	3/9-4/17 6/4-7/6	7/7-8/3	8/4-8/29	8/30-9/24	9/25-10/18
1938	3/12-4/4	4/5-4/28	4/29-5/23	5/24-6/18	6/19-7/13	7/14-8/8
1939	4-25/5/19	5/20-6/13	6/14-7/8	7/9-8/1	8/2-8/25	8/26-9/19
1940	2/12-3/7	3/8-4/3	4/4-5/5 7/5-7/31	5/6-7/4 8/1-9/8	9/9-10/5	10/6-10/31
1941	3/27-4/19	4/20-5/13	5/14-6/6	6/7-6/1	7/2-7/26	7/27-8/20
1942	5/6-6/1	6/2-6/26	6/27-7/22	7/23-8/16	8/17-9/9	9/10-10/3
1943	2/25-3/20	3/21-4/14	4/15-5/10	5/11-6/6	6/7-7/6	7/7-11/8
1944	4-10/5-3	5/4-5/28	5/29-6/21	6/22-7/16	7/17-8/9	8/10-9/2
1945	2/2-3/10 4/7-6/3	3/11-4/6 6/4-7/6	7/7-8/3	8/4-8/29	8/30-9/23	9/24-10/18
1946	3/11-4/4	4/5-4/28	4/29-5/23	5/24-6/17	6/18-7/12	7/13-8/8
1947	4/25-5/19	5/20-6/12	6/13-7/7	7/8-8/1	8/2-8/25	8/26-9/18
1948	2/11-3/7	3/8-4/3	4/4-5/6 6/29-8/2	5/7-6/28 8/3-9/7	9/8-10/5	10/6-10/31
1949	3/26-4/19	4/20-5/13	5/14-6/6	6/7-6/30	7/1-7/25	7/26-8/19
1950	5/5-5/31	6/1-6/26	6/27-7/21	7/22-8/15	8/16-9/9	9/10-10/3
1951	2/25-3/21	3/22-4/15	4/16-5/10	5/11-6/6	6/7-7/7	7/8-11/9
1952	4/10-5/4	5/5-5/28	5/29-6/21	6/22-7/16	7/17-8/9	8/10-9/3
1953	2/2-3/13 4/1-6/5	3/4-3/31 6/6-7/7	7/8-8/3	8/4-8/29	8/30-9/24	9/25-10/18

VENUS SIGN 1910–1975

Libra	Scorpio	Sagittarius	Capricorn	Aquarius	Pisces
11/2-11/25	11/26-12/20	12/21-12/31		1/1-1/18	1/19-2/11
8/21-9/14	9/15-10/10	1/1-1/13	1/14-2/6	2/7-3/2	3/3-3/26
		10/11-11/5	11/6-12/4	12/5-12/31	
10/5-10/28	10/29-11/21	11/22-12/15	12/16-12/31	1/1-4/5	4/6-5/5
11/9-12/7	12/8-12/31		1/1-1/7	1/8-1/31	2/1-2/25
9/5-9/27	1/1-1/2	1/3-1/27	1/28-2/21	2/22-3/16	3/17-4/10
	9/28-10/22	10/23-11/15	11/16-12/10	12/11-12/31	
10/19-11/11	11/12-12/5	12/6-12/29	12/30-12/31	1/1-1/5	1/6-2/1
8/9-9/6	9/7-10/13	10/14-11/14	1/1-1/22	1/23-2/15	2/16-3/11
	11/15-12/31				
9/20-10/13	1/1-1/3	1/4-2/5	2/6-3/4	3/5-3/30	3/31-4/24
	10/14-11/6	11/7-11/30	12/1-12/24	12/25-12/31	
11/1-11/25	11/26-12/19	12/20-12/31		1/1-1/18	1/19-2/11
8/21-9/14	9/15-10/9	1/1-1/12	1/13-2/5	2/6-3/1	3/2-3/26
		10/10-11/5	11/6-12/4	12/5-12/31	
10/4-10/27	10/28-11/20	11/21-12/14	12/15-12/31	1/1-4/4	4/6-5/5
11/9-12/7	12/8-12/31		1/1-1/7	1/8-1/31	2/1-2/24
9/3-9/27	1/1-1/2	1/3-1/27	1/28-2/20	2/21-3/16	3/17-4/9
	9/28-10/21	10/22-11/15	11/16-12/10	12/11-12/31	
10/19-11/11	11/12-12/5	12/6-12/29	12/30-12/31	1/1-1/4	1/5-2/1
8/9-9/6	9/7-10/15	10/16-11/7	1/1-1/21	1/22-2/14	2/15-3/10
	11/8-12/31				
9/19-10/12	1/1-1/4	1/5-2/5	2/6-3/4	3/5-3/29	3/30-4/24
	10/13-11/5	11/6-11/29	11/30-12/23	12/24-12/31	
11/1-1/25	11/26-12/19	12/20-12/31		1/1-1/17	1/18-2/10
8/20-9/14	9/15-10/9	1/1-1/12	1/13-2/5	2/6-3/1	3/2-3/25
		10/10-11/5	11/6-12/5	12/6-12/31	
10/4-10/27	10/28-11/20	11/21-12/13	12/14-12/31	1/1-4/5	4/6-5/4
11/10-12/7	12/8-12/31		1/1-1/7	1/8-1/31	2/1-2/24
9/4-9/27	1/1-1/2	1/3-1/27	1/28-2/20	2/21-3/16	3/17-4/9
	9/28-10/21	10/22-11/15	11/16-12/10	12/11-12/31	
10/19-11/11	11/12-12/5	12/6-12/29	12/30-12/31	1/1-1/5	1/6-2/1

VENUS SIGN 1910–1975

	Aries	Taurus	Gemini	Cancer	Leo	Virgo
1954	3/12-4/4	4/5-4/28	4/29-5/23	5/24-6/17	6/18-7/13	7/14-8/8
1955	4/25-5/19	5/20-6/13	6/14-7/7	7/8-8/1	8/2-8/25	8/26-9/18
1956	2/12-3/7	3/8-4/4	4/5-5/7 6:24-8/4	5/8-6/23 8/5-9/8	9/9-10/5	10/6-10/31
1957	3-26/4-19	4/20-5/13	5/14-6/6	6/7-7/1	7/2-7/26	7/27-8/19
1958	5-6/5-31	6/1-6/26	6/27-7/22	7/23-8/15	8/16-9/9	9/10-10/3
1959	2-25/3-20	3/21-4/14	4/15-5/10	5/11-6/6	6/7-7/8 9/21-9/24	7/9-9/20 9/25-11/9
1960	4-10/5-3	5/4-5/28	5/29-6/21	6/22-7/15	7/16-8/9	8/10-9/2
1961	2-3/6-5	6/6-7/7	7/8-8/3	8/4-8/29	8/30-9/23	9/24-10/17
1962	3/11-4/3	4/4-4/28	4/29-5/22	5/23-6/17	6/18-7/12	7/13-8/8
1963	4/24-5/18	5/19-6/12	6/13-7/7	7/8-7/31	8/1-8/25	8/26-9/18
1964	2/11-3/7	3/8-4/4	4/5-5/9 6/18-8/5	5/10-6/17 8/6-9/8	9/9-10/5	10/6-10/31
1965	3/26-4/18	4/19-5/12	5/13-6/6	6/7-6/30	7/1-7/25	7/26-8/19
1966	5/6-6/31	6/1-6/26	6/27-7/21	7/22-8/15	8/16-9/8	9/9-10/2
1967	2/24-3/20	3/21-4/14	4/15-5/10	5/11-6/6	6/7-7/8 9/10-10/1	7/9-9/9 10/2-11/9
1968	4/9-5/3	5/4-5/27	5/28-6/20	6/21-7/15	7/16-8/8	8/9-9/2
1969	2/3-6/6	6/7-7/6	7/7-8/3	8/4-8/28	8/29-9/22	9/23-10/17
1970	3/11-4/3	4/4-4/27	4/28-5/22	5/23-6/16	6/17-7/12	7/13-8/8
1971	4/24-5/18	5/19-6/12	6/13-7/6	7/7-7/31	8/1-8/24	8/25-9/17
1972	2/11-3/7	3/8-4/3	4/4-5/10 6/12-8/6	5/11-6/11 8/7-9/8	9/9-10/5	10/6-10/30
1973	3/25-4/18	4/18-5/12	5/13-6/5	6/6-6/29	7/1-7/25	7/26-8/19
1974						
	5/5-5/31	6/1-6/25	6/26-7/21	7/22-8/14	8/15-9/8	9/9-10/2
1975	2/24-3/20	3/21-4/13	4/14-5/9	5/10-6/6	6/7-7/9 9/3-10/4	7/10-9/2 10/5-11/9

VENUS SIGN 1910–1975

Libra	Scorpio	Sagittarius	Capricorn	Aquarius	Pisces
8/9-9/6	9/7-10/22	10/23-10/27	1/1-1/22	1/23-2/15	2/16-3/11
	10/28-12/31				
9/19-10/13	1/1-1/6	1/7-2/5	2/6-3/4	3/5-3/30	3/31-4/24
	10/14-11/5	11/6-11/30	12/1-12/24	12/25-12/31	
11/1-11/25	11/26-12/19	12/20-12/31		1/1-1/17	1/18-2/11
8/20-9/14	9/15-10/9	1/1-1/12	1/13-2/5	2/6-3/1	3/2-3/25
		10/10-11/5	11/6-12/16	12/7-12/31	
10/4-10/27	10/28-11/20	11/21-12/14	12/15-12/31	1/1-4/6	4/7-5/5
11/10-12/7	12/8-12/31		1/1-1/7	1/8-1/31	2/1-2/24
9/3-9/26	1/1-1/2	1/3-1/27	1/28-2/20	2/21-3/15	3/16-4/9
	9/27-10/21	10/22-11/15	11/16-12/10	12/11-12/31	
10/18-11/11	11/12-12/4	12/5-12/28	12/29-12/31	1/1-1/5	1/6-2/2
8/9-9/6	9/7-12/31		1/1-1/21	1/22-2/14	2/15-3/10
9/19-10/12	1/1-1/6	1/7-2/5	2/6-3/4	3/5-3/29	3/30-4/23
	10/13-11/5	11/6-11/29	11/30-12/23	12/24-12/31	
11/1-11/24	11/25-12/19	12/20-12/31		1/1-1/16	1/17-2/10
8/20-9/13	9/14-10/9	1/1-1/12	1/13-2/5	2/6-3/1	3/2-3/25
		10/10-11/5	11/6-12/7	12/8-12/31	
10/3-10/26	10/27-11/19	11/20-12/13	2/7-2/25	1/1-2/6	4/7-5/5
			12/14-12/31	2/26-4/6	
11/10-12/7	12/8-12/23		1/1-1/6	1/7-1/30	1/31-2/23
9/3-9/26	1/1	1/2-1/26	1/27-2/20	2/21-3/15	3/16-4/8
	9/27-10/21	10/22-11/14	11/15-12/9	12/10-12/31	
10/18-11/10	11/11-12/4	12/5-12/28	12/29-12/31	1/1-1/4	1/5-2/2
8/9-9/7	9/8-12/31		1/1-1/21	1/22-2/14	2/15-3/10
9/18-10/11	1/1-1/7	1/8-2/5	2/6-3/4	3/5-3/29	3/30-4/23
	10/12-11/5	11/6-11/29	11/30-12/23	12/24-12/31	
	11/25-12/18	12/19-12/31		1/1-1/16	1/17-2/10
10/31-11/24					
8/20-9/13		1/1-1/12	1/13-2/4	2/5-2/28	3/1-3/24
		10/9-11/5	11/6-12/7	12/8-12/31	
			1/30-2/28	1/1-1/29	
10/3-10/26	10/27-11/19	11/20-12/13	12/14-12/31	3/1-4/6	4/7-5/4
			1/1-1/6	1/7-1/30	1/31-2/23
11/10-12/7	12/8-12/31				

MARS SIGN 1910–1975

	Jan.	Feb.	Mar.	Apr.	May	June	July	Aug.	Sept.	Oct.	Nov.	Dec.
1910	AR	TA	GE	GE	CA	CA	LE	VI	VI	LI	SC	SC
1911	SA	CP	AQ	AQ	PI	AR	TA	TA	GE	GE	GE	TA
1912	TA	GE	GE	CA	CA	LE	LE	VI	LI	LI	SC	SA
1913	CP	CP	AQ	PI	AR	AR	TA	GE	CA	CA	CA	CA
1914	CA	CA	CA	CA	LE	LE	VI	LI	LI	SC	SA	SA
1915	CP	AQ	PI	PI	AR	TA	GE	GE	CA	LE	LE	LE
1916	LE	LE	LE	LE	LE	VI	VI	LI	SC	SC	SA	CP
1917	AQ	AQ	PI	AR	TA	GE	GE	CA	LE	LE	SA	VI
1918	LI	LI	VI	VI	VI	LI	LI	SC	SC	SA	VI	CP
1919	AQ	PI	AR	TA	GE	CA	CA	LE	VI	VI	CP	LI
1920	LI	SC	SC	SC	LI	LI	SC	SC	SA	SA	VI	AQ
1921	PI	AR	AR	TA	GE	GE	CA	LE	LE	VI	LI	LI
1922	SC	SC	SA	SA	SA	SA	CA	SA	SC	SC	AQ	AQ
1923	PI	AR	TA	TA	GE	CA	CA	LE	VI	VI	LI	SC
1924	SC	SA	CP	CP	AQ	CA	PI	PI	AQ	AQ	PI	PI
1925	AR	TA	TA	GE	CA	AQ	LE	VI	VI	LI	SC	SC
1926	SA	CP	CP	AQ	PI	AR	AR	VI	VI	TA	TA	TA
1927	TA	TA	GE	GE	CA	LE	LE	VI	LI	LI	SC	SA
1928	SA	SA	AQ	PI	PI	AR	TA	GE	GE	CA	CA	CA

MARS SIGN 1910-1975

	Jan.	Feb.	Mar.	Apr.	May	June	July	Aug.	Sept.	Oct.	Nov.	Dec.
1929	GE	GE	CA	CA	LE	LE	VI	VI	LI	SC	SC	SA
1930	CP	AQ	AQ	PI	AR	TA	GE	GE	CA	CA	LE	LE
1931	LE	LE	CA	LE	LE	VI	VI	LI	LI	SC	SA	CP
1932	CP	AQ	PI	AR	TA	TA	GE	CA	CA	LE	VI	VI
1933	VI	VI	VI	VI	VI	VI	GE	LI	SC	SA	SA	CP
1934	AQ	PI	AR	AR	TA	GE	LI	CA	SC	LE	VI	LI
1935	LI	LI	LI	LI	LI	LI	LI	SC	LE	SA	CP	AQ
1936	PI	PI	AR	TA	GE	GE	CA	LE	LE	VI	LI	LI
1937	SC	SC	SA	SA	SC	SC	SC	SA	SA	CP	AQ	AQ
1938	PI	AR	TA	TA	GE	CA	CA	LE	VI	VI	LI	SC
1939	SC	SA	SA	CP	CP	AQ	AQ	CP	CP	VI	AQ	PI
1940	AR	AR	TA	GE	GE	CA	LE	LE	VI	AQ	LI	SC
1941	SA	SA	CP	AQ	AQ	PI	AR	AR	AR	VI	AR	AR
1942	TA	TA	GE	GE	CA	LE	LE	VI	VI	LI	SC	SC
1943	SA	CP	AQ	AQ	CA	AR	TA	TA	GE	GE	GE	GE
1944	GE	GE	GE	GE	CA	LE	VI	VI	LI	SC	SC	SA
1945	CP	AQ	AQ	PI	AR	TA	TA	GE	CA	CA	LE	LE
1946	CA	CA	CA	CA	LE	LE	VI	LI	LI	SC	SA	SA
1947	CP	AQ	PI	AR	AR	TA	GE	CA	CA	LE	LE	VI

77

MARS SIGN 1910–1975

	Jan.	Feb.	Mar.	Apr.	May	June	July	Aug.	Sept.	Oct.	Nov.	Dec.
1948	VI	LE	LE	LE	LE	VI	VI	LI	SC	SC	SA	CP
1949	AQ	PI	PI	AR	TA	GE	GE	CA	LE	LE	VI	VI
1950	LI	LI	LI	VI	VI	LI	LI	SC	SC.	SA	CP	CP
1951	AQ	PI	AR	TA	TA	GE	CA	CA	LE	VI	VI	LI
1952	LI	SC	SC	SC	SC	SC	SC	SC	SA	CP	CP	AQ
1953	AR	AR	AR	TA	GE	GE	CA	SA	VI	LI	LI	LI
1954	SC	SA	SA	CP	CP	CP	SA	SA	SA	CP	AQ	PI
1955	PI	AR	TA	TA	GE	CA	SA	LE	VI	LI	LI	SC
1956	SA	SA	SA	GE	AQ	PI	PI	PI	PI	PI	SC	AR
1957	AR	TA	TA	GE	CA	CA	LE	VI	VI	LI	SC	SC
1958	SA	CP	CP	AQ	PI	AR	AR	TA	TA	GE	TA	TA
1959	TA	GE	GE	CA	CA	LE	LE	VI	LI	LI	SC	SA
1960	CP	CP	AQ	PI	AR	AR	TA	GE	GE	CA	CA	CA
1961	CA	CA	CA	CA	CA	TA	VI	VI	LI	SC	SA	SA
1962	CP	AQ	PI	PI	AR	LE	GE	GE	CA	LE	TA	LE
1963	LE	LE	LE	LE	AR	TA	VI	GE	SC	LE	SC	CP
1964	AQ	AQ	PI	AR	AR	TA	GE	LI	LE	SC	SA	VI
1965	VI	VI	VI	VI	VI	VI	LI	LI	LE	SA	VI	CP
1966	AQ	PI	AR	AR	TA	GE	CA	CA	LE	VI	VI	LI

78

MARS SIGN 1910–1975

	Jan.	Feb.	Mar.	Apr.	May	June	July	Aug.	Sept.	Oct.	Nov.	Dec.
1967	LI	SC	SC	LI	LI	LI	LI	SC	SA	SA	CP	AQ
1968	PI	PI	AR	TA	GE	GE	CA	LE	LE	VI	LI	LI
1969	SC	SC	SA	SA	SA	SA	SA	SA	SA	CP	AQ	PI
1970	PI	AR	TA	TA	GE	CA	CA	LE	VI	VI	LI	SC
1971	SC	SA	CP	CP	AQ	AQ	AQ	AQ	AQ	AQ	PI	PI
1972	AR	TA	TA	GE	CA	CA	LE	LE	VI	LI	SC	SC
1973	SA	CP	CP	AQ	PI	PI	AR	TA	TA	TA	AR	AR
1974	TA	TA	GE	GE	CA	LE	LE	VI	LI	LI	SC	SA
1975	SA	CP	AQ	PI	PI	AR	TA	GE	GE	GE	CA	GE

AR—Aries
TA—Taurus
GE—Gemini
CA—Cancer
LE—Leo
VI—Virgo
LI—Libra
SC—Scorpio
SA—Sagittarius
CP—Capricorn
AQ—Aquarius
PI—Pisces

9

The Planets As "Stars"

The Astrological Cast of Characters in Order of Their Appearance

As you learned in the chapter "Defining Terms," the planets are the *sine qua non* of astrology—the factor without which there would be no such study. It is the placement of the planets in the signs of the zodiac that give those signs meaning in human terms, and the placement of the planets in an individual horoscope that "spell out" that individual's character/personality. As for forecasting, it is the movement (transits) of the planets throughout our lifetime that activate one part of our chart or another and bring out certain life conditions.

Those planets are moving bodies and not "stars" in the astrological sense, though they are sometimes referred to with that word. In Shakespeare's play, *Julius Caesar*, Cassius, one of the conspirators, states, "The fault, dear Brutus, is not in our stars but in ourselves that we are underlings." Shakespeare (Cassius) actually knew what he was talking about because astrology was part and parcel of daily life in Elizabethan times when the play was written, as well as in Caesar's ancient Rome. However, Shakespeare seems to have preferred "stars" as a more poetic word than "planets." He also was right about another thing: The "stars" (planets) don't push people around unless you let them. The key is to understand the role each planet plays in your basic astrological makeup through your natal chart and to get to know yourself via this ancient and pragmatic science. Then you will better understand how the transits of the different planets are most likely to affect you.

Though the planets are not stars by astronomical definition (except for the sun), they do play the starring roles in the great cosmic drama that is acted out every day of our lives, and has been since the beginning of life on earth. There are other heavenly bodies—like the asteroids—that play supporting roles, but most astrologers take the Big Ten into consideration when they do a chart or a personal forecast: the sun, the moon, Mercury, Venus, Mars, Jupiter, Saturn, Uranus, Neptune, and Pluto. (Some of these planets, like the Moon, Venus, and Mars, are touched on in other parts of this book, and you may want to read those sections to get a better understanding of their characteristics.)

Each planet rules one or more signs of the zodiac—i.e., is very closely associated with that sign or signs. The one that rules your sun sign is your own personal planet, so to speak, and its description will fill in more of the background of your sign.

The following is a rundown of the planetary cast of characters, presented in their order of appearance, their actual position in our solar system As you know, the sun is the center of our solar system, and the orbits of the planets form rings around it. Looking at the planets this way underscores the fact that the *closer* planets influence us much more strongly as individuals. Planets farther out in the solar system are not only farther away, they also move much more slowly. While a transit of the moon lasts two days, for instance, a transit of Uranus (which takes eighty-four years to circle the zodiac) may influence your life for many months. However, even with these distant planets, their position in a specific *house* of your own horoscope will greatly influence your astrological makeup.

The Sun

Vital Statistics: 864,000 miles in diameter; average distance from earth, 93 million miles; gaseous nature. Appears to circle the zodiac in 365 days.

Rules: The sign of Leo
Fourth period of life: ages 23 to 41
Role: The true "star" ... the male lead ... the doer ... the activator.

Facts and Foibles: The position of the sun in anyone's horoscope is the central fact about that person, astrologically speaking. Your sun sign is your core—your individuality. It is your ego in the best sense of the word, the part of you that moves you in a certain life direction. No matter what your sun sign is, true self-development means developing the highest potential of that sign. People really grow into their sun signs as they mature, and the sun symbolically governs that stage of life (23 to 41) at which we are (or should be) mature individuals who are concerned with creating something in our own right. The sun is considered a masculine planet, because it is the fiery, animating force of life. We are meant to *express* our sun sign; those who do not can literally have a lifeless quality about them.

Those born under the sign of Leo have been said to be favored because of their rulership by the most important "planet" of them all. In ancient times, the sun was often the chief deity and was worshipped for its extraordinary power. It was recognized that without the sun, life on earth could not exist, and the dimming of its light via an eclipse was a terrifying experience for early civilizations that recognized their dependence upon its warmth and vitalizing nature. Whether or not Leo is a special sign is debatable, but there is no doubt that there is a tendency in some Leo sun sign people to become overly self-centered. Perhaps even unconsciously, they sense that it is a heady destiny to be ruled by the sun, but they are unable to handle its tremendous energies properly.

The Moon

Vital Statistics: 238,857 miles from the earth; 2,160 miles in diameter (one-fourth earth's size). Revolves around the earth (circles the zodiac) in about 27 ½ days
Rules: The sign of cancer
The first four years of human life

Role: The leading lady ... the "feeler" ... the mother ... the reactor.

Facts and Foibles: The moon is not exactly a planet, either; it is a satellite of our own planet, earth. However, it is the largest satellite with respect to its parent planet anywhere in the solar system that we know of. It has a tremendous gravitational pull, which is demonstrated on earth by the changing of the tides and other natural phenomena.

The moon has no light of its own, and we can see it shining only because it reflects the sun. Therefore, the moon is considered a *receptive* or "feminine" planet, rather than an active one like the sun. The moon in mythology has always been a woman—often the "Great Mother" to ancient peoples who saw the sun as the "Great Father." Accordingly, the moon rules the first four years of human life, when we are totally dependent on our mothers, and the motherly sign of Cancer, which is closely associated with nurturing and growth. In an individual horoscope, the position of the moon indicates our ability to feel and to respond emotionally. It is our impressionability and sensitivity, i.e., our subjective rather than our objective sign. The moon reacts to experience and remembers it. All our memories are stored in our subconscious, which is the part of the human psyche the moon signifies. In a sense, as the moon rules the night, it rules our dark or hidden side. As it takes some time for us to develop or grow into our sun sign, the moon sign manifests itself much more strongly in young children than the sun sign does. The moon represents the instinctual nature connected with infantile responses; our moon sign acts from habit, often without thinking.

Mercury

Vital Statistics: 36 million miles away from the sun; 2,900 miles in diameter; orbits sun at 108,000 miles per hour; goes through zodiac in 88 days.

Rules: The signs of Gemini and Virgo
Age of curiosity: 4 through 14

Role: The young male lead ... the observer ... the messenger ... the communicator.

Facts and Foibles: Mercury is the hottest, quickest, and smallest of the planets, and is closest to the sun. It is so closely associated with the sun in an astronomical sense, that Mercury is very often in the same sign as the sun in a natal chart. In any horoscope, it is never more than two signs away from your sun sign.

In ancient times Mercury was regarded as the sun's messenger, and the gods with whom it was associated always had some kind of communicating function. In Egypt, Mercury was Thoth—scribe to the gods, keeper of the divine books. The Greeks called him Hermes, the messenger; the Romans renamed him Mercury, but assigned similar functions. Hermes/Mercury always had a golden tongue, and was regarded as the great persuader. Quickness and deftness also associate Mercury with all kinds of human skills requiring manual and mental dexterity.

Mercury has a double role to play as ruler of the signs of Gemini and Virgo. In a sense, Mercury is two-faced; the communicative side in Gemini, his precise specialist side in Virgo. No matter what your sun sign is, in your horoscope Mercury symbolizes your style of thinking and communicating—not so much how intelligent you are as how you tend to put things together mentally.

Mercury is a very human planet, and has a very human foible; occasionally he gets things all mixed up and causes a lot of trouble. About three times a year, for about three weeks at a time, Mercury seems to be going *backwards*. (That appearance is caused by the varying rates of speed of various planets—like two trains traveling in the same direction that can seem as if they are traveling in two different directions.) During these periods Mercury is said to be *retrograde*, it is known to cause problems in all kinds of human interactions. People get the wrong message, or don't get it at all. People who are supposed to meet on a street corner never find each other. Trains and planes are missed, luggage is lost, orders simply never get transmitted or seem to vanish in thin air. There has been quite a bit of research on Mercury retrograde, and it all proves out. Even if people don't know *why* retrograde Mercury

makes things go wrong, they sure know it does. In 1986 Mercury will be retrograde during these periods:
   March 7 through March 30.
   July 9 through August 3.
   November 2 through November 22.

Venus

Vital Statistics: 67.2 million miles from the sun; 26 million to 160 million miles from earth; approximately the same size and volume as earth. Goes through all twelve signs of the zodiac in about 225 days.
Rules: The signs of Taurus and Libra
   Period of developing sexuality: ages 14 to 21
Role: The young, nubile female lead . . . the love interest . . . the artist.
Facts and Foibles: Like Mercury, Venus follows the sun very closely, so in anyone's horoscope it is never very far away from your sun sign. Symbolically, Venus represents your capacity to love and relate, and the capacity to appreciate beauty. In ancient myth, Venus was seen as the daughter of the moon, a feminine planet associated with many of the earthly things traditionally associated with women: the providing of food and shelter, the beautifying of the home, the harmonizing of opposites and settler of strife. Venus is a peaceful planet in every sense of the word. Aphrodite to the Greeks, Venus to the Romans, this goddess/planet was seen as the bounteous giver of life's gifts and pleasures—the personification of beauty. She is supposed to inspire us with the desire for both material and spiritual growth.

Like Mercury, Venus has two faces, but, strangely, one rules a feminine sign, Taurus, and one rules a masculine sign, Libra. In Taurus, Venus shows her earthier side, more concerned with creature comforts, sex, and material prosperity. In Libra, a more refined Venus shines forth as the graceful "hostess," the one who beautifies things and relates to others.

Though most Libra males are quite virile, their rulership by the planet Venus often manifests itself in extremely good looks and a great appreciation of beauty. The virile male hairdresser or interior decorator is the personification of this side of Venus. Because Venus seeks peace rather than war, harmony rather than discord, she rules lawyers, mediators, and arbitrators.

Since Venus rules one feminine earth sign and one masculine air sign, she is sometimes seen as a symbol for the fact that all things in the universe can be made to work in harmony—even the incompatible elements of air (Libra) and earth (Taurus) and the often antagonistic principles of male and female—in real life as in astrology. Divorce courts come under the rulership of Venus.

Mars

Vital Statistics: 14 million miles from the sun; 35 million miles from earth; 10 percent of earth's size; circles the zodiac in about 687 days.
Rules: The sign of Aries
Ages 42 to 56
Role: The virile male antagonist . . . the lover . . . the warrior.
Facts and foibles: Mars is a rather small planet and has sometimes been called "Earth's little brother." However, since ancient times Mars has been attributed with great powers—possibly because of its fiery red color. Even the earliest peoples associated Mars with strife and sex and a warriorlike attitude. In fact, Mars has had a rather bad reputation in astrology and was sometimes known as the "lesser malefic." But some groups assigned Mars another role and gave him a different dimension. The Egyptians called Mars Artes, and connected him with personal creative expression; to the Hebrews he played a similar role. When you think about it, sex, strife, and creative expression are only a few steps away from each other. Certainly, the act of procreation is a creative one, as it gives new life. War and strife are divisive, but often a new order comes out of them as well.

Mars is pure masculine energy—sometimes a bit rough, but always determined. In a personal horoscope, the sign position of Mars tells how you tend to assert yourself, how aggressive you are likely to be when going after what you want, even how much you will want it. Mars is our desire nature. (See the chapter on Venus and Mars to find out more about Mars in your own horoscope.) As the god of war, Mars is associated with courage and bravery, traits that are available to the Aries sun sign person if he/she cares to develop them. Mars is moral courage too, and the Mars-ruled Aries sun sign person at his/her best will never desert a cause or a person—no matter how rough the going gets.

About once every two years Mars returns to the same place it occupied on the day of your birth; to astrologers this is known as the "Mars return." It is a period of time during which one can make great strides, because Mars is stimulating that area of the natal chart connected with taking on the world. People often feel a great surge of energy during their Mars return, but if that energy is not directed in a productive channel, it can cause a lot of problems in relationships. You are far better taking out your Mars return aggressiveness on another job or another creative project rather than another person.

Jupiter

Vital Statistics: Largest planet in the solar system, 318 times larger than earth; 365 million to 600 million miles from earth; gaseous nature; circles the zodiac in about 12 years.
Rules: The sign of Sagittarius
     Ages 57 to 68
Role: The hero ... the "father confessor" ... the one who saves the day.
Facts and Foibles: From earliest times, Jupiter was assigned a role in the "cosmic drama" almost as important as that of the sun. Huge and luminous, Jupiter was easily visible to the naked eye eons before the age of the telescope. The sun may have been god in the all-encompassing sense, but Jupiter was *the* god who could make things happen, even interfere in human affairs if he was needed. And he has always been a "good guy." The Hindus, whose roots lie in antiquity, call him Vishnu, the preserver. To the Greeks, he was Zeus, the god

who reigned supreme on Mount Olympus; he became Jupiter under the Romans. The important thing about this masculine god-planet is that it has always been very godly but very human at the same time. Zeus frequently came down from Mount Olympus to bestow his favors on people—particularly women who caught his fancy (causing his wife Hera to become jealous). Jupiter-Zeus is the god who keeps one foot in heaven and one foot firmly planted on the earth. Since the planet itself is large and impressive-looking, it has always been associated with benevolence and expansiveness. Our English word "jovial" has its roots in the name Jove, by which name Jupiter was sometimes called.

Joviality is one of the characteristics that is available to people born under the sign of Sagittarius, which Jupiter rules. Some Sagittarians are jovial, they spend all their money and all their energy on making life one long party.

But Jupiter has a serious side, too. Jupiter is associated with the divine law, and the ability to make that law known to men on earth. The higher Sagittarian, ruled by Jupiter, has a sense of this mission, and often takes the real-life role of priest-missionary or teacher of higher studies. While Venus and Libra, the sign Venus rules, are associated with the *practice* of law, Jupiter and Sagittarius are connected with the *making* and *interpretation* of laws.

Saturn

Vital Statistics: 75,000 miles in diameter, 95 times as big as earth; 886 million miles from the sun; takes 29 years to circle the zodiac.
Rules: The sign of Capricorn
   Ages 68 on
Role: The "older man" ... the taskmaster ... the disciplining father.
Facts and Foibles: Like Jupiter, Saturn is so large it can be seen with the naked eye from earth and was watched carefully by early peoples. It was quickly observed that certain transits of Saturn brought trials and troubles on earth and so the planet earned itself the name of the

"greater malefic" by the time astrologers had begun to record their findings. Is Saturn really a "bad guy" as so many astrology books will tell you? There is no question that Saturn represents the principle of limitation; when you go too far out on a limb or get over expansive, Saturn is always there to teach you that there are rules and restrictions. However, as Saturn also represents the principle of contraction, this planet can and does bring periods of time in which we can consolidate our forces and make a secure place for ourselves in this world.

Saturn is also sometimes called the "lord of Karma." Translated into human terms, that means that Saturn represents our inevitable responsibilities, our "fated" duties in this world. Once again, there is a positive side. When Saturn is strongly placed in an individual's chart, that individual is exceptionally able to handle responsibility and achieve worldly success. As ruler of the sign of Capricorn, Saturn brings to that sign an extraordinary talent for working long and hard as well as reaping the material rewards that come with dedication to a task.

Kronos (or Chronos) was the ancient Greek god who is generally regarded as the prototype for Saturn's particular personality or role, and his story sheds a lot of light on the perceptions of this planet. Kronos was born to the very highest ancient god, Ouranos, and to the original earth mother, Ge. Kronos got a little carried away with this position and overthrew his father (castrating him) to take over the throne. When Kronos was told one of his own children would do the same to him, he swallowed them all—except Zeus, who was miraculously saved and became the "avenger." Later on, Zeus banished Kronos into exile. We know Kronos as Father Time—that shadowy old man who reminds us that it's later than we think. Kronos/Saturn also cautions against runaway ambitions, which is often punished by a downfall like his.

One of the most fascinating aspects of Saturn is that it is an uncannily accurate cosmic clock. Taking about 29 years to make a full circle of the zodiac, Saturn returns to the same place it occupied in your horoscope at your birth when you are about 29 years old. The "Saturn return" is regarded by astrologers as the true end of childhood (astrology is kind to us weak mortals by giving us more time to "grow up" than conventional earthly wisdom does). When Saturn begins to creep up on us in our late twenties, we generally begin to feel that it's time to settle down and do something big in the way of taking on earthly responsibility. Many people go through a "life crisis" at this time, because they feel the push that Saturn is giving them, but have trouble knowing what to do about it. Many, many people resolve the dilemma by getting married, buying a home, having a child, or getting divorced. The point is that it is time to *do something decisive* and to take responsibility for our own lives and actions. There are an incredible number of "Saturn return babies" because having a child is probably the most joyful as well as the biggest responsibility a person can assume.

On its second return—at about the human age of 58—people are generally ready to start relaxing their responsibilities and enjoying the fruits of their labors. It is a wise precaution to make ready for the second Saturn return, because just as Saturn tells us we have to *work*, he also tells us when it is time to *stop* working. But remain a productive human being, with real interests and the wherewithal to pursue them.

Uranus

Vital Statistics: 1.7 billion miles from earth; 29,300 miles in diameter, 15 times larger than earth; takes 84 years to circle the zodiac; has an erratic orbit.
Rules: The sign of Aquarius
Teenagers
Role: The rebel ... the home-wrecker ... the visionary.
Facts and Foibles: Uranus is the first of the "modern" planets, i.e., those unknown to the ancients, and only discovered via the telescope. Uranus, the first planet to be discovered in this manner, was thus a shock to both astronomers and astrologers. Both groups believed the orbit of Saturn defined the limits of our solar system,

and both had to revise their thinking at this discovery. Astrologers took things in their stride by calling Uranus a "planet of the higher octave" and interpreting it as a breakthrough from the realm of purely earthly influences (with Saturn as the dividing line) to the "cosmic" or "higher" order of things. They decided that Uranus—an unconventional planet in many respects—must be the ruler of the quirky sign of Aquarius (which had been formerly ruled by Saturn). In a way it is uncanny that the sudden discovery of Uranus in 1781 heralded all the breakthrough discoveries of the 19th and 20th centuries. In a sense, Uranus ushered in the modern world; it also rules our current Age of Aquarius. As that age (approximately 2000 years long) will continue to shock us with discovery after discovery, it hopefully will also bring us the sense of brotherhood of humanity that is the hallmark of the sign of Aquarius.

As Uranus takes 84 years to circle the zodiac, it stays in each sign about seven years. (It is currently about two-thirds of the way through the sign of Sagittarius.) Whatever Uranus touches as it transits a person's natal chart gets a real jolt. Sometimes very suddenly. Uranus hates the status quo and almost always shakes it up. That means that a lot of changes take place when Uranus comes along, but for most people those changes are eventually positive ones. Uranus gets you out of whatever rut you happen to be in and does it quite forcefully. However, those who resist the changes Uranus "suggests" can cause themselves a lot of trouble. If you aren't willing to bend, Uranus can really "break you up."

Uranus is appropriately associated with the teen years, during which young people are often in a state of rebellion. However, here too, it is a *necessary* fact of life that people must eventually rebel against the strictures of childhood in order to become separate individual human beings. Uranus is associated not only with teenagers, but also with many of the things that represent their rebellion, like rock music, blaring radios, and all that goes with them. In essence, Uranus is the symbol of the electronic modern world.

Neptune

Vital Statistics: 2.6 billion miles from earth; 2.7 billion miles from the sun; takes about 165 years to circle the zodiac.

Rules: The sign of Pisces
No specific age.

Role: The fascinating stranger ... the poet ... the one who confuses the issue... the dreamer of great dreams.

Facts and Foibles: As it is difficult to get a handle on people heavily influenced by Neptune (like Pisceans), it took astronomers a while to figure out what Neptune really was. At first they observed nothing but some rather weird abberations in the orbit of Uranus as they began to plot that planet's orbit. In the early 1840s, some of them proved mathematically that there *must* be another planet out there, although it couldn't be seen. Finally, using all the data at hand, a German astronomer spotted Neptune in 1846.

There is a rather "sneaky" character to Neptune, but what this nebulous planet really symbolizes is the love that passes all understanding, the all-encompassing universal love that is virtually impossible for mortals to feel and give. Venus represents two-way love, the sharing kind. Neptune's love goes only in one direction. Neptune gives in a sense of self-sacrifice, and takes nothing in return.

There is evidence that even though no one really *saw* Neptune until 1846, the ancients knew all about its principles, and embodied them in the mythical figure of Poseidon (later called Neptune), the lord of the seas, master of the deep. When you think that more than three-quarters of the earth's surface is covered by water, you realize that Neptune was pretty important in the overall scheme of things. In fact, according to the Greeks, when the universe was created, it was divided among Zeus-Jupiter, who took the heavens, Hades-Pluto who took the underworld, and Poseidon-Neptune who took the oceans.

Just as water is difficult to contain, it is difficult for many people to get in touch with Neptune's higher qualities in their own charts. Water is soul and spirit, metaphysically speaking, so Neptune should make us aspire to much higher things. Not only universal love, but poetry, music and art in its purest forms. However, what Neptune touches in most people's natal charts often turns into an area of confusion rather than creativity. Neptune rules liquid in all its forms and, unfortunately, some people react to Neptune's confusing vibes by turning to alcohol or drugs. For many drug and alcohol abusers, however, the real goal of their vice is to attain a kind of "cosmic consciousness" which is the real realm of Neptune.

Since Neptune takes 165 years to circle the zodiac, it stays in one sign for 13 years or more. Therefore, it is the zodiacal *sign* Neptune makes to the "personal planets" in your chart that really count. People positively influenced by Neptune make the true artists and poets of this world—as well as the visionaries who interpret its meaning in more philosophical and metaphysical terms.

Pluto

Vital Statistics: 3,666 billion miles from the sun; takes about 242 years to circle the zodiac.
Rules: The sign of Scorpio
Prenatal
Role: The "heavy" . . . the transformer . . . the tragic hero.
Facts and Foibles: As you will note, Pluto is a little light on vital statistics. That's because this immensely distant planet, only discovered in 1930, has yet to reveal some of its secrets to astronomers. Like Neptune, it was discovered only because of the erratic nature of the orbit of Uranus. But, even when Pluto was conclusively sighted in 1930, its small size relative to its extremely strong gravitational pull didn't make sense to astronomers. Either Pluto is much larger than we now think or it is so dense that it exerts a force much greater than its size should account for.

Either way, there's no doubt that Pluto represents *power*. In fact, many astrologers connect the discovery of Pluto with the discovery by man of the extraordinary power in matter itself—the power of the atom. As with Neptune, Pluto's "realm" had been staked out in myth and astrology long before its actual discovery. Pluto is Hades, lord of the underworld—the place of darkness that all men fear. However, since most older religions regard life and death as a cycle, Pluto represents rebirth as well. We die only to be reborn. One of the symbols for Pluto is the Phoenix that rises triumphantly from its own ashes. Pluto—and the sign of Scorpio that it rules—hold onto their secrets, but have an incredible power to endure and triumph over life's circumstances. The extremes of life and death that Pluto/Scorpio is associated with connect neatly with the extremism of this astrological sign. "Plutonic" Scorpios often regard the world as totally black and white, with very few grays in between. They can also be the "best" of people, like reformers and religious leaders, or the "worst" of people, like criminals and those who manipulate others for their own purposes.

10

Astrotrivia

How Do You Rate in the Best Game in Town?

The ancient art of astrology is loaded with bits and pieces of miscellaneous information—all of it fascinating, and some of it more useful than you may think. For instance, did you know that every zodiac sign has a special day of the week and certain colors assigned to it? And, how good are you at guessing sun signs of celebrities—those larger-than-life models of sun signs in the flesh? The Astrotrivia that follows is partly in quiz form, partly in short-take astrological facts. In the first part, you can test your own astrological perceptivity; in the second, you can add a lot to your fund of astrological information—and maybe even learn a few things, you can use in your daily life.

Astrotrivia Part I
Sun Signs of the Rich and Famous

Try to answer the following questions yourself; if you're stumped you'll find the answers on page 103–104.

1. What famous stripper and the famous actress who played her mother in a Broadway show have the sign of Capricorn in common?

2. What two show biz buddies—who run in the same pack—are both Sagittarians?

3. What do these people have in common: Joseph Stalin, Richard Nixon, Herman Goering, Al Capone, and Mao Tse Tung?

4. What two handsome male movie stars, both known for their progressive ideas, have the same sun sign? And, what is it?

5. What highly Scorpionic actor had an on-again, off-again lifetime romance with a glamourous Pisces actress?

6. What two female tennis pros are both athletic Sagittarians?

7. What U.S. president had a "show-me-I'm-from-Missouri" personality, and what was his sun sign?

8. What two famous "lonely hearts" columnists get their soft Cancerian shoulders cried on all the time?

9. What two "greats" of American popular music were both thoroughly American, and both born on the Fourth of July?

10. Under what sign were these warrior peacemakers all born: Dwight D. Eisenhower, David Ben Gurion, Jimmy Carter, Mohandus Ghandi, and Eleanor Roosevelt?

11. What anti-American villainess of World War II was born on the Fourth of July?

12. What sun sign do these people have in common: Oscar Wilde, Truman Capote, and Gore Vidal?

13. What two famous rock stars—one early, one late—were born not only under the same sign, but on the same day?

14. Which of the following is/was not a Scorpio?
    Charles Manson   Robert Kennedy
    Bo Derek   Pablo Picasso
    Katherine Hepburn   Indira Ghandi
    Princess Grace   Johnny Carson
    Henry Kissinger   Billy Graham

15. All of the following were born under the two most musical signs of the zodiac. What are they?

Judy Collins	Michael Jackson
Barbra Steisand	George Gershwin
Stevie Wonder	Luciano Pavarotti
Fred Astaire	Paul Simon
Irving Berlin	Julie Andrews
Bing Crosby	Anthony Newly
Beverly Sills	John Lennon
Bobby Darin	Guiseppe Verdi

16. All the following ladies of the stage and screen are masters of their craft. Which craftsman-like sun sign were they all born under?

Lauren Bacall	Celeste Holm
Anne Bancroft	Greer Garson
Ingrid Bergman	Twiggy
Greta Garbo	Jo Ann Worley
Sophia Loren	Claudette Colbert
Lilly Tomlin	Raquel Welch

17. What sun sign do the following famous rebels and rule-breakers have in common: Marlon Brando, Warren Beatty, Eddie Murphy, Charlie Chaplin, Hugh Hefner?

18. What sun sign do these medical and research geniuses have in common: Madame Curie, Jonas Salk, Christian Bernard?

19. What present-day famous Leo "princess" lived in Camelot with her Gemini "prince"?

20. What two great ballet stars were both born in the same country, and share the graceful sun sign, Pisces?

Answers on p. 103–104

Astrotrivia Part II
More Celebrity Sun Sign Lore

Just a handful of the many, many stage/screen-struck Leos:

Robert DeNiro	Julia Child
Mike Jagger	Arlene Dahl
Lucille Ball	Alfred Hitchcock
Dustin Hoffman	Mae West
Cecil B. Demille	George Bernard Shaw
John Derek	Dino D. Laurentis
Mike Douglas	Robert Mitchum
Robert Redford	Peter O'Toole
Jason Robards Jr.	Roman Polanski
Esther Williams	Jill St. John
Stanley Kubrick	Robert Taylor
Shelly Winters	Keenan Wynn

And here are some Leos who make/made the international scene their stage:

Fidel Castro	Henry Ford
Jackie Onassis	Alex Haley
Coco Chanel	Lawrence of Arabia
Benito Mussolini	Mata Hari
Rasputin	Napoleon
Neil Armstrong	Andy Warhol
Mike Conners	

Librans are often lovely, like Catherine Deneuve and Brigitte Bardot. Barbara Walters is the ultimate "cool" Libra.

Cancer is the second fame sign, because Cancer rules the public. Cancers who have made it somehow or other are:

Bill Cosby	Ringo Starr
Jimmy Cagney	John Glenn
Ernest Hemingway	Arthur Ashe
Gerald Ford	The Mayo brothers (of the Mayo clinic)

Some outspoken, inventive Aquarians whose opinions have not always been popular, but were always ahead of their time:

Norman Mailer Ralph Nader
Charles Darwin Thomas Edison
Jules Verne Betty Friedan
Ayn Rand Vanessa Redgrave
Galileo Franklin D. Roosevelt

Astrotrivia Part III
Fascinating Facts About the Signs

Here are the colors that, by tradition, match each of the signs of the zodiac:

1. Aries: bright red, scarlet, magenta

2. Taurus: pastels in most shades, especially pink and turquoise

3. Gemini: beiges and light gray

4. Cancer: shimmery and irridescent shades of gray and silver; anything luminous

5. Leo: bright golds and yellows

6. Virgo: dark navy, brown, gray

7. Libra: cloudy pales, especially blue-green

8. Scorpio: murky colors, especially blood red and black

9. Sagittarius: rich blues, purples, greens

10. Capricorn: black, "no-color" colors

11. Aquarius: checks, stripes, patterns, electric blue

12. Pisces: deep lilac, mauve, sea green

Each Sign/Planet owns a day of the week:

Sunday = Sun/Leo

Monday = Moon/Cancer

Tuesday = Mars/Aries, Mars/Scorpio

Wednesday = Mercury/Gemini, Mercury/Virgo

Thursday = Jupiter/Sagittarius, Neptune/Pisces

Friday = Venus/Taurus, Venus/Libra

Saturday = Saturn/Capricorn, Saturn/Aquarius

(Since there are only seven days and twelve signs, some of the signs double up. Also, since the ancients only knew seven planets, there are only enough days to match seven of the ten planets we now recognize.)

Astrotrivia Part IV
Where Do You Belong?

Each sign is said to have certain places where it belongs. Long ago, the world was divided up according to astrological tradition, so there are certain countries, cities, and areas that have the vibrations of certain signs. Tradition divides up other kinds of spaces, too, as you will see.

- *Aries places:* In the world: Birmingham, Oldman, Leicester, and Blackburn, *England* ... Florence, Naples, Verona and Padua *Italy* ... Marseilles and Burgundy *France* ... *Denmark, Germany, Palestine, Syria, Japan.*

    Anywhere: sheepfolds, forges, tool houses, fireplaces, on sandy soil, kilns, ceilings, fire houses, emergency rooms.
- *Taurus places:* In the world: Dublin, *Ireland* ... Mantua, Parma, Palermo, *Italy* ... St. Louis, *U.S.A.* ... *The Greek Islands, Asia Minor,* the *Caucasus.*

    Anywhere: banks, dairies, pastures, shady places, corn fields, middle rooms of houses, altars, maypoles.
- *Gemini places:* In the world: San Francisco, *U.S.A.* ... London and Plymouth, *England* ... Bruges, *Belgium* ... Versailles and Louvaine, *France* ... Nurenburg, *Germany* ... *Lower Egypt, Armenia, Wales.*

    Anywhere: buildings with pillars, bookcases, hills and mountains, upper back rooms, graineries.
- *Cancer places:* In the world; St. Andrews, *Scotland* ... Amsterdam, *Holland* ... New York City, *U.S.A.* ... Stockholm, *Sweden* ... Genoa, Venice, Milan, *Italy* ... *Paraguay, North and West Africa.*

Anywhere: lakes and brooks, salt marshes, pubs, kitchens, cellars, corner houses facing north.

- *Sagittarius places:* In the world: Avignon, *France* ... Stuttgart, Cologne, *Germany* ... Nottingham, Sheffield, Bradford, *England* ... Provence, *France* ... *Hungary, Arabia, Tuscany.*

   Anywhere: highest place around, topmost room in house, stables for racing horses, obelisks, places near fire, where incense is burned.

- *Capricorn places:* In the world: Brussels, *Belgium* ... Port Said, *Egypt* ... *India, Afghanistan, Mexico, Lithuania, Orkney Islands, Macedonia.*

   Anywhere: vaults, convents, thick forests, gates and hinges, old trees, jails, cattle barns, door knockers, game preserves.

- *Aquarius places:* In the world: Brighton and Trent, *England* ... Salszburg, *Austria* ... Hamburg, *Germany* ... the Piedmont, *Italy* ... *Prussia, Red Russia, Westphalia.*

   Anywhere: buses, bridges, ladders, garages, airplanes, power transmitters, fountains, springs and streams, sleds, ice caps.

- *Pisces places:* In the world; Alexandria, *Egypt* ... Seville, *Spain* ... Southport, Lancaster, Bournemouth, Tiverton, *England* ... *Portugal, Calabria, Normandy, Sahara.*

   Anywhere: fish ponds, oceans, oil fields, submarines, séances, flooded areas, bars, aquariums, boat yards, swimming pools, hospitals.

- *Leo Places:* In the world: Rome, Ravenna, *Italy* ... Bath, Bristol, Portsmouth, Blackpool, *England* ... Philadelphia, Chicago, *U.S.A.* ... *Bohemia, Sicily, the Alps, Damascus.*

   Anywhere: wild animal preserves, deserts and forests, castles, furnaces, gold mines, porches, forts.

- *Virgo places:* In the world: Paris, Lyons, Toulouse, *France* ... Boston, Los Angeles, *U.S.A.* ... Heidelberg, *Germany* ... *Turkey, West Indies, Brazil, Silesia, Switzerland.*

   Anywhere: pantries, restaurants, refrigerators, medicine cabinets, desks, malt houses.

- *Libra places:* In the world: Dover, Liverpool, Newcastle, *England* ... Messina, *Italy* ... Halifax, *Nova Scotia* ... *China, Norway, The Transvaal, the Barbary coast.*
  Anywhere: windmills, wood sheds, harbors, tops of mountains, garrets and lofts, guest rooms, tops of dressers, domed buildings.
- *Scorpio places:* In the world: Copenhagen, *Denmark* ... Leeds, Nottingham, *England* ... Johannesburg, *South Africa* ... Burma, *India* ... *Tibet, North China, Argentina.*
  Anywhere: junk yards, meat markets, laboratories, low gardens and streams, vineyards, deepest part of ocean.

Astrotrivia Part V
Which Animal Best Suits You?

Each sign is said to have an affinity with certain kinds of pets. Here's the rundown.

Aries: No animal that needs a lot of taking care of; but if Aries has one pet, he/she will usually have two, so the animals can take care of each other.

Taurus: Almost any kind of soft, warm creature. Taurus is a great nature lover, so even a skunk would be welcome.

Gemini: Anything with fascinating habits, like bees or ants, or anything that talks, like a parrot or a minah bird.

Cancer: Anything in need of a mother is welcome in Cancer's house, no matter how sloppy or in need of care.

Leo: Cats, of course, preferably with good breeding. Peacocks or anything with bright colors or plumage are fine too.

Virgo: Cats are preferable, because they are clean animals, but any animal in distress brings out Virgo's warmth.

Libra: This sign would just as soon do without, but if a pet is preferred, it's the perfectly groomed poodle or other refined breed of dog or cat.

Scorpio: This sign goes for rather dangerous pets, such as snakes, or anything with a sting. Basically, animals are creatures to be observed, not coddled.

Sagittarius: Horses—at home or at the race track. Any very large dog in the city, almost anything of immense size in the country.

Capricorn: Capricorns *need* pets to help pull them out of their frequent depressions. The friendliest kind of animals are the best bet, like sheepdogs.

Aquarius: This sign needs a very smart animal, so is picky about the breed of dog or cat. Actually, birds are preferable to this cool sign.

Pisces: Many people born under this sign will take in any stray that strays into their path, no matter how scraggly or ugly. They often put animals before humans in their scheme of things.

Astrotrivia Part I answers

1. Gypsy Rose Lee and Ethel Merman (who played Gypsy's mother in *Gypsy).*
2. Frank Sinatra and Sammie Davis, Jr.
3. They were all born under the calculating sign of Capricorn.
4. Paul Newman and Alan Alda were both born under the sign of Aquarius.
5. Richard Burton was the Scorpio; Liz Taylor the Pisces.
6. Billie Jean King and Chris Evert.
7. Harry S. Truman, a Taurus.
8. Abigail Van Buren ("Dear Abby") and Ann Landers.

9. George M. Cohan ("Yankee Doodle Dandy") and Louis "Satchmo" Armstrong.
10. Libra.
11. Tokyo Rose.
12. Libra.
13. Elvis Presley and David Bowie (January 5—Capricorn).
14. Henry Kissinger. He's a wily Gemini, but he could easily fool you, because his moon sign is Scorpio.
15. The column on the left are Taureans; those on the right are Librans.
16. Virgo.
17. Aries.
18. Scorpio.
19. Jackie Kennedy Onassis is a Leo; John F. Kennedy was a Gemini.
20. Rudolph Nureyev and Vaslav Nijinsky.

11

Sun Sign Changes. 1920–1975

If you were born "on the cusp" (very near the end or the beginning of a sign) you can find out what your sign really is by using the chart that follows. Many people do not realize that the sun does not "change signs" on the same day every year—or, for that matter, at the same time. For this reason the chart of sun sign changes is calculated to the minute.

How to Use the Chart

Locate your year of birth, then the month in which you were born. Let's say you were born in April of 1942. In the box for that month and year you will see

20–Tau
12:30 P.M.

That means if you are born *after* 12:30 p.m. on April 20 in 1942, you are a Taurus. If you were born before that date and time, your sun sign is the preceding one, Aries.

In this chart (as well as in the rising-sign chart) the signs are abbreviated as follows:

Ar = Aries
Tau = Taurus
Gem = Gemini
Can = Cancer
Leo = Leo
Vir = Virgo
Lib = Libra
Sc = Scorpio

Sag = Sagittarius
Cap = Capricorn
Aq = Aquarius
Pis = Pisces

NOTE: All times given in the sun sign changes chart are Eastern Standard. You must correct for daylight savings time (subtract one hour) and for time zone. For Central Standard Time subtract one hour; for Mountain Standard Time subtract two hours; for Pacific Standard Time subtract three hours.

	1920	1921	1922	1923	1924	1925	1926	1927	1928	1929
Jan	21–Aq 4:05 am	20–Aq 8:55 am	20–Aq 2:48 pm	20–Aq 8:35 pm	21–Aq 2:29 am	20–Aq 8:20 am	20–Aq 2:13 pm	20–Aq 8:12 pm	21–Aq 1:57 am	20–Aq 7:42 am
Feb	19–Pis 5:29 pm	18–Pis 11:21 pm	19–Pis 5:16 am	19–Pis 11:00 am	19–Pis 4:51 pm	18–Pis 11:43 pm	18–Pis 4:35 am	19–Pis 10:35 am	19–Pis 4:20 pm	18–Pis 10:07 pm
Mar	20–Ar 5:00 pm	20–Ar 10:51 pm	21–Ar 4:49 am	21–Ar 10:29 am	20–Ar 4:20 pm	20–Ar 11:13 pm	21–Ar 4:01 am	21–Ar 11:59 am	20–Ar 3:44 pm	20–Ar 9:35 pm
Apr	20–Tau 4:39 am	20–Tau 10:32 am	20–Tau 4:29 am	20–Tau 10:06 pm	20–Tau 3:59 am	20–Tau 10:51 pm	20–Tau 3:36 pm	20–Tau 9:32 pm	20–Tau 3:17 am	20–Tau 9:11 am
May	21–Gem 4:22 am	21–Gem 10:17 am	21–Gem 9:11 pm	22–Gem 9:45 pm	21–Gem 3:41 am	21–Gem 10:33 pm	21–Gem 3:15 pm	21–Gem 9:08 pm	21–Gem 2:53 am	21–Gem 8:48 am
June	21–Can 12:40pm	21–Can 6:36 pm	22–Can 12:27 pm	22–Can 6:03 am	21–Can 12:noon	21–Can 5:50 pm	21–Can 5:21 pm	22–Can 11:30 pm	21–Can 11:07 am	21–Gem 5:01 pm
July	22–Leo 11:40 pm	23–Leo 5:31 am	23–Leo 11:20 am	23–Leo 5:01 pm	22–Leo 11:58 pm	23–Leo 4:45 am	23–Leo 10:25 am	23–Leo 4:17 am	22–Leo 11:02 pm	23–Leo 3:54 am
Aug	23–Vir 6:22 am	23–Vir 12:15 pm	23–Vir 6:04 pm	23–Vir 11:52 pm	23–Vir 5:48 am	23–Vir 11:33 am	23–Vir 5:14 pm	23–Vir 11:06 pm	23–Vir 4:53 am	23–Vir 10:41 am
Sept	23–Lib 3:25 am	23–Lib 11:20 am	23–Lib 5:10 am	23–Lib 9:04 pm	23–Lib 2:58 am	23–Lib 8:43 am	23–Lib 2:25 pm	23–Lib 8:17 pm	23–Lib 2:36 am	23–Lib 7:52 am
Oct	23–Sc 12:31 pm	23–Sc 6:03 pm	23–Sc 11:53 pm	24–Sc 5:51 am	23–Sc 11:44 am	23–Sc 5:31 pm	23–Sc 11:18 pm	24–Sc 5:07 am	23–Sc 10:55 am	23–Sc 4:41 pm
Nov	22–Sag 9:15 pm	22–Sag 3:21 pm	22–Sag 8:55 pm	23–Sag 2:54 am	22–Sag 8:46 am	22–Sag 2:36 pm	22–Sag 8:28 pm	23–Sag 2:14 am	22–Sag 8:00 am	22–Sag 1:48 pm
Dec	21–Cap 10:17 pm	22–Cap 4:08 am	22–Cap 9:57 pm	22–Cap 3:53 pm	21–Cap 10:45 pm	22–Cap 3:37 am	22–Cap 9:34 am	22–cap 3:18 pm	21–Cap 9:04 pm	22–Cap 2:53 am

	1930	1931	1932	1933	1934	1935	1936	1937	1938	1939
Jan	20–Aq 1:33 pm	21–Aq 7:18 pm	20–Aq 1:07 am	20–Aq 6:53 am	20–Aq 10:37 am	20–Aq 6:29 pm	21–Aq 12:12am	20–Aq 6:01 am	20–Aq 11:59 am	20–Aq 5:51 pm
Feb	19–Pis 4:00 am	19–Pis 9:06 am	19–Pis 3:29 pm	19–Pis 9:16 pm	19–Pis 3:02 am	19–Pis 8:52 am	19–Pis 2:33 pm	18–Pis 3:21 pm	19–Pis 2:20 am	19–Pis 8:10 am
Mar	21–Ar 3:30 am	21–Ar 9:40 am	20–Ar 2:54 pm	21–Ar 8:43 pm	21–Ar 2:28 am	21–Ar 8:19 am	20–Ar 1:58 pm	20–Ar 7:45 pm	21–Ar 1:43 am	21–Ar 7:29 am
Apr	20–Tau 3:06 pm	20–Tau 8:40 pm	20–Tau 2:28 am	20–Tau 8:19 am	20–Tau 2:00 pm	20–Tau 7:50 pm	20–Tau 1:31 am	20–Tau 7:20 pm	20–Tau 1:15 pm	20–Tau 6:55 pm
May	21–Gem 2:42 pm	21–Gem 8:15 pm	21–Gem 2:07 am	21–Gem 7:57 am	21–Gem 1:35 pm	21–Gem 7:25 pm	21–Gem 1:08 am	21–Gem 6:57 am	21–Gem 12:51 pm	21–Gem 6:27 pm
June	21–Can 11:53 pm	23–Can 4:28 am	21–Can 10:23 am	21–Can 4:12 pm	21–Can 9:48 pm	22–Can 3:32 am	21–Can 9:22 am	21–Can 3:12 pm	21–Can 9:04 pm	22–Can 2:40 am
July	23–Leo 10:42 am	23–Leo 3:21 pm	22–Leo 9:18 pm	23–Leo 3:06 am	23–Leo 8:42 am	23–Leo 2:33 pm	22–Leo 8:18 pm	23–Leo 2:07 am	23–Leo 7:57 am	23–Leo 1:37 pm
Aug	23–Vir 4:27 pm	23–Vir	23–Vir 4:06 am	23–Vir 9:53 am	23–Vir 3:32 pm	23–Vir 9:24 pm	23–Vir 3:11 am	23–Vir 8:58 am	23–Vir 2:46 pm	23–Vir 8:31 pm
Sept	23–Lib 1:35 pm	23–Lib 10:10 pm	23–Lib 1:16 am	23–Lib 7:01 am	23–Lib 10:45 am	23–Lib 6:38 pm	23–Lib 12:26 pm	23–Lib 6:13 pm	23–Lib 12:noon	23–Lib 5:50 pm
Oct	23–Sc 11:25 pm	24–Sc 4:15 am	23–Sc 10:04 am	23–Sc 3:48 pm	23–Sc 9:35 pm	24–Sc 3:29 am	23–Sc 10:18 am	23–Sc 3:06 pm	23–Sc 8:54 pm	24–Sc 2:46 am
Nov	22–Sag 7:34 pm	23–Sag 1:25 am	22–Sag 7:10 am	22–Sag 10:53 am	22–Sag 6:44 pm	23–Sag 12:35 am	22–Sag 6:25 pm	22–Sag 12:17 pm	22–Sag 6:06 pm	22–Sag 11:59 pm
Dec	22–Cap 8:40 am	22–Cap 2:30 pm	21–Cap 8:14 pm	22–Cap 1:58 am	22–Cap 5:49 pm	22–Cap 1:37 pm	21–Cap 7:27 pm	22–Cap 1:22 am	22–Cap 7:13 am	22–Cap 1:05 pm

	1940	1941	1942	1943	1944	1945	1946	1947	1948
Jan	20–Aq 11:44 pm	20–Aq 5:34 am	20–Aq 11:16 am	20–Aq 5:20 pm	20–Aq 11:09 pm	20–Aq 4:55 am	20–Aq 10:44 am	20–Aq 4:23 pm	20–Aq 10:18 pm
Feb	19–Pis 2:04 pm	18–Pis 7:59 pm	19–Pis 1:39 am	19–Pis 7:41 am	19–Pis 1:28 pm	18–Pis 7:15 pm	19–Pis 1:10 am	19–Pis 6:53 am	19–Pis 12:37 pm
Mar	20–Ar 1:24 pm	20–Ar 7:21 pm	21–Ar 1:03 am	21–Ar 7:03 am	21–Ar 12:49 pm	20–Ar 6:38 pm	21–Ar 12:34 am	21–Ar 6:13 am	20–Ar 11:57 am
Apr	20–Tau 12:51 am	20–Tau 6:51 am	20–Tau 12:30 pm	20–Tau 6:32 pm	20–Tau 12:18 am	20–Tau 6:08 am	20–Tau 12:03 pm	20–Tau 5:40 pm	19–Tau 11:25 pm
May	21–Gem 12:23 am	21–Gem 6:23 am	21–Gem 12:01 pm	21–Gem 6:03 pm	20–Gem 11:51 pm	22–Gem 5:41 am	21–Gem 11:34 am	21–Gem 5:04 pm	20–Gem 10:58 pm
June	21–Can 8:37 am	21–Can 2:33 am	21–Can 8:08 pm	22–Can 2:13 am	21–Can 9:03 am	21–Can 1:52 pm	21–Can 7:45 pm	22–Can 1:19 am	21–Can 7:11 am
July	22–Leo 7:34 pm	23–Leo 1:26 am	23–Leo 6:59 am	23–Leo 1:05 pm	22–Leo 6:55 pm	23–Leo 12:48 am	23–Leo 6:37 am	23–Leo 12:12 pm	22–Leo 6:06 pm
Aug	23–Vir 2:21 am	23–Vir 8:30 am	23–Vir 1:50 pm	23–Vir 7:55 pm	23–Vir 1:47 am	23–Vir 7:36 am	23–Vir 1:23 pm	23–Vir 7:09 pm	23–Vir 1:03 am
Sept	22–Lib 11:46 pm	23–Lib 5:33 am	23–Lib 11:10 am	23–Lib 5:12 pm	22–Lib 11:02 pm	23–Lib 4:50 am	23–Lib 10:41 am	23–Lib 4:29 pm	22–Lib 10:22 pm
Oct	23–Sc 8:39 am	23–Sc 2:22 pm	22–Sc 8:01 pm	24–Sc 2:09 am	23–Sc 7:57 am	20–Sc 1:45 pm	23–Sc 7:37 pm	24–Sc 1:27 am	23–Sc 7:19 am
Nov	22–Sag 5:49 am	22–Sag 11:38 am	22–Sag 5:23 pm	22–Sag 11:22 pm	22–Sag 5:09 am	22–Sag 10:56 am	22–Sag 4:47 pm	22–Sag 10:38 pm	22–Sag 4:29 am
Dec	21–Cap 6:55 pm	22–Cap 12:44 am	22–Cap 6:31 am	22–Cap 12:30 pm	21–Cap 6:15 pm	22–Cap 12:04 am	22–Cap 5:54 am	22–Cap 11:44 am	21–Cap 5:23 pm

	1949	1950	1951	1952	1953	1954	1955	1956	1957
Jan	20–Aq 4:11 am	20–Aq 10:00 am	20–Aq 3:53 pm	20–Aq 9:38 pm	20–Aq 3:22 am	20–Aq 9:14 am	20–Aq 3:03 pm	20–Aq 8:49 pm	20–Aq 2:43 am
Feb	18–Pis 6:27 pm	19–Pis 12:16 am	19–Pis 6:10 am	19–Pis 11:57 am	18–Pis 5:41 pm	19–Pis 11:33 pm	19–Pis 5:19 am	19–Pis 11:05 am	18–Pis 5:01 pm
Mar	20–Ar 5:49 pm	20–Ar 11:30 pm	21–Ar 5:26 am	20–Ar 11:14 am	20–Ar 5:01 pm	20–Ar 10:54 pm	21–Ar 4:36 am	20–Ar 10:21 am	20–Ar 4:17 pm
Apr	20–Tau 5:18 am	20–Tau 11:00 am	20–Tau 4:49 pm	20–Tau 10:37 pm	19–Tau 4:26 am	20–Tau 10:20 am	20–Tau 3:58 pm	19–Tau 9:44 pm	20–Tau 3:45 am
May	21–Gem 5:18 am	21–Gem 11:00 am	21–Gem 4:49 pm	20–Gem 10:37 pm	21–Gem 4:26 am	21–Gem 10:20 am	21–Gem 3:58 pm	20–Gem 9:44 pm	21–Gem 3:45 am
June	21–Can 4:51 am	21–Can 10:27 am	21–Gem 4:15 pm	20–Gem 10:04 pm	21–Gem 3:53 am	21–Gem 9:48 am	21–Can 3:25 am	21–Can 9:13 pm	21–Can 3:09 am
July	22–Leo 1:03 pm	22–Leo 6:37 pm	22–Can 12:25 am	21–Can 6:13 am	21–Can noon	21–Can 5:55 pm	21–Can 11:32 pm	21–Can 5:24 am	21–Can 11:21 am
Aug	23–Vir 1:58 pm	23–Leo 5:30 am	23–Leo 11:29 am	22–Leo 5:05 pm	22–Leo 10:53 pm	23–Leo 4:45 am	23–Leo 10:25 am	22–Leo 4:20 pm	22–Leo 10:13 pm
Sept	23–Lib 6:49 pm	23–Vir 12:24 pm	23–Vir 6:22 pm	23–Vir 12:03 am	23–Vir 5:46 am	23–Vir 11:37 am	23–Vir 5:19 pm	22–Vir 11:15 pm	23–Vir 5:07 pm
Oct	23–Sc 4:05 pm	23–Lib 9:44 pm	23–Lib 3:38 am	22–Lib 9:24 am	23–Lib 3:07 am	23–Lib 8:56 am	23–Lib 2:42 am	22–Lib 8:30 am	23–Lib 2:27 am
Nov	22–Sag 1:04 pm	22–Sag 6:48 pm	23–Sc 12:37 am	23–Sc 6:22 am	23–Sc 12:07 pm	23–Sc 5:58 am	22–Sc 11:44 am	23–Sc 5:35 pm	23–Sc 11:33 am
	22–Sag 10:17 am	22–Sag 4:03 pm	22–Sag 9:52 pm	22–Sag 3:36 am	22–Sag 9:23 am	22–Sag 3:14 pm	22–Sag 9:02 pm	22–Sag 2:51 am	22–Sag 8:45 am
Dec	21–Cap 11:24 am	22–Cap 5:14 am	22–Cap 11:01 am	21–Cap 4:44 pm	21–Cap 10:22 pm	22–Cap 4:25 am	22–Cap 10:12 am	21–Cap 4:00 pm	21–Cap 9:49 pm

	1958	1959	1960	1961	1962	1963	1964	1965	1966
Jan	20–Aq 2:20 pm	20–Aq 2:20 pm	20–Aq 8:11 pm	20–Aq 2:02 am	20–Aq 7:49 pm	20–Aq 1:55 pm	19–Aq 7:43 pm	20–Aq 1:30 am	20–Aq 8:21 am
Feb	18–Pis	19–Pis	19–Pis 10:26 am	18–Pis 6:27 pm	18–Pis 10:16 am	19–Pis 4:09 am	19–Pis 10:25 am	18–Pis 3:49 pm	18–Pis 9:39 pm
Mar	20–Ar 10:49 pm	21–Ar 4:38 pm	20–Ar	20–Ar 5:27 am	20–Ar 9:30 am	21–Ar 3:20 am	20–Ar 9:43 am	20–Ar 3:05 pm	20–Ar 8:53 pm
Apr	20–Tau 10:06 pm	20–Tau 3:55 am	20–Tau 9:43 am	20–Tau 2:33 pm	20–Tau 8:51 pm	20–Tau 2:37 pm	19–Tau 9:00 pm	20–Tau 2:27 am	20–Tau 8:12 am
May	21–Gem 9:28 am	21–Gem 3:17 pm	20–Gem 10:06 pm	21–Gem 2:33 am	21–Gem 8:17 am	21–Gem 1:59 pm	20–Gem 8:33 pm	21–Gem 1:27 am	21–Gem 7:33 am
June	21–Can 8:52 am	21–Can 2:38 pm	21–Can 8:33 pm	21–Can 1:51 am	21–Can 8:17 am	21–Can 1:59 pm	21–Can 4:43 am	21–Can 1:27 am	21–Can
July	4:57 pm	22–Leo 10:50 pm	22–Leo 4:43 am	22–Leo 10:12 am	22–Leo 4:24 pm	23–Leo 11:04 pm	22–Leo 4:43 am	22–Leo 9:56 am	23–Leo 3:33 pm
Aug	23–Leo 3:51 am	23–Leo 9:45 am	22–Vir 5:38 pm	22–Leo 9:12 pm	23–Leo 3:19 am	23–Leo 9:00 am	22–Leo 3:38 pm	22–Leo 8:49 pm	23–Leo 2:24 am
Sept	23–Vir 10:47 am	23–Vir 4:44 pm	22–Vir 10:35 pm	23–Vir 3:46 am	23–Vir 10:13 am	23–Vir 3:58 pm	22–Vir 10:35 pm	23–Vir 3:43 am	23–Vir 9:18 am
Oct	23–Lib 5:10 am	23–Lib 2:09 pm	23–Lib 8:00 pm	23–Lib 1:26 am	23–Lib 7:35 am	23–Lib 1:24 pm	23–Lib 8:00 pm	23–Lib 1:06 am	23–Lib 6:43 am
Nov	23–Sc 5:12 am	23–Sc 11:12 pm	23–Sc 5:03 am	23–Sc 10:46 am	23–Sc 4:41 pm	23–Sc 11:30 pm	23–Sc 5:03 am	23–Sc 10:11 am	23–Sc 3:52 pm
	22–Sag 2:30 am	22–Sag 8:23 am	22–Sag 2:19 pm	22–Sag 8:10 am	22–Sag 2:02 pm	22–Sag 7:50 pm	22–Sag 2:19 am	22–Sag 7:30 am	22–Sag 1:15 pm
Dec	22–Cap 3:40 am	22–Cap 9:35 am	21–Cap 5:27 pm	21–Cap 9:25 pm	22–Cap 3:15 am	22–Cap 9:02 am	21–Cap 3:27 pm	21–Cap 8:41 pm	22–Cap 2:29 pm

	1967	1968	1969	1970	1971	1972	1973	1974	1975
Jan	20–Aq 1:05 pm	20–Aq 6:54 pm	20–Aq 12:30 am	20–Aq 6:25 am	20–Aq 12:14 pm	20–Aq 6:00 pm	19–Aq 11:49 pm	20–Aq 5:47 am	20–Aq 11:37 am
Feb	19–Pis 3:25 am	19–Pis 9:11 am	18–Pis 2:47 pm	18–Pis 8:43 pm	19–Pis 2:28 am	19–Pis 8:12am	18–Pis 2:02 pm	18–Pis 8:00 pm	19–Pis 1:51 am
Mar	21–Ar 2:37 am	20–Ar 8:22 am	20–Ar 2:08 pm	20–Ar 7:59 pm	21–Ar 1:28 am	20–Ar 7:22 am	20–Ar 1:13 pm	20–Ar 7:08 pm	21–Ar 12:58 am
Apr	20–Tau 1:56 pm	19–Tau 7:42 pm	20–Tau 1:18 am	20–Tau 5:16 am	20–Tau 12:54 pm	19–Tau 6:38 pm	20–Tau 12:31 am	20–Tau 5:19 am	20–Tau 12:08 pm
May	21–Gem 1:19 pm	20–Gem 7:07 pm	21–Gem 12:41 am	21–Gem 6:32 am	21–Gem 12:16 pm	20–Gem 6:00 pm	20–Gem 11:54 pm	21–Gem 5:37 am	21–Gem 1:25 pm
June	21–Can 4:23 pm	21–Can 1:13 am	21–Can 6:55 am	21–Can 2:43 pm	21–Can 8:21 pm	21–Can 2:07 am	21–Can 8:01 am	21–Can 1:38 pm	21–Can 7:27 pm
July	23–Leo 8:16 pm	22–Leo 2:13 pm	22–Leo 8:05 pm	23–Leo 1:38 am	23–Leo 7:15 am	22–Leo 1:03 pm	22–Leo 6:56 pm	23–Leo 12:30 am	23–Leo 7:23 am
Aug	23–Vir 3:13 pm	22–Vir 9:52 pm	23–Vir 2:35 am	23–Vir 6:35 am	23–Vir 2:16 pm	22–Vir 8:04 pm	23–Vir 1:55 am	23–Vir 7:29 am	23–Vir 1:24 pm
Sept	23–Lib 12:38 pm	22–Lib 6:26 pm	23–Lib 12:07 am	23–Lib 5:59 am	23–Lib 11:47 am	22–Lib 5:34 pm	22–Lib 11:22 pm	23–Lib 4:59 am	23–Lib 10:56 am
Oct	23–Sc 9:44 pm	23–Sc 1:30 am	23–Sc 9:03 am	23–Sc 3:05 pm	22–Sc 8:53 pm	23–Sc 2:42 am	23–Sc 8:31 am	23–Sc 2:12 pm	23–Sc 8:07 pm
Nov	22–Sag 7:05 pm	22–Sag 12:59 am	22–Sag 6:23 am	22–Sag 12:25 pm	22–Sag 6:15 pm	22–Sag 12:04 am	22–Sag 5:55 am	22–Sag 11:39 am	22–Sag 5:32 pm
Dec	22–Cap 8:17 am	21–Cap 2:00 pm	21–Cap 7:44 pm	22–Cap 1:36 am	22–Cap 5:26 am	21–Cap 1:14 pm	21–Cap 7:09 pm	22–Cap 12:57 am	22–Cap 7:47 am

12

Virgo: The Big Picture

Because the twelve signs of the zodiac represent twelve ways of being in the world, you will know more about yourself and why you tend toward certain types of behavior and attitudes by knowing more about Virgo. If you read about the elements and qualities in "Defining Terms," for instance, you'll find out that you are one of the practical, resourceful *earth signs*, and, as one of the *mutable signs*, you should be able to display multiple talents. You can "meet yourself" in the Virgo prototype described in "Twelve Places at the Table," and your clever planetary ruler, Mercury, provides some excellent clues about the Virgo style.

However, even with these broad brush strokes, your Virgo portrait is still an abstract; to see yourself in totality, you need more of the background filled in. That means going back to some very important basics: your sixthplace position in the zodiac, your picture symbol, the virgin, and the shorthand figure, or glyph, that astrologers use to indicate Virgo when they draw up a horoscope. In Virgo, as in every astrological sign, these three factors link together, forming a strong chain of meaning that holds together everything that is Virgo.

When the sun reaches zero degrees Virgo, on or about August 23, the second cycle of the zodiac and summer, the second earthly season, begins to draw to a close. Virgo is the third of the summer signs and has waited patiently for the hot sun of Leo to bring all the fruits of the earth to full ripeness. Virgo is the sign of the harvest, that busy but joyful time when people have traditionally gathered and carefully put away the food that will sustain them throughout the long fall and winter. In a sense, Virgo is the back to work sign, coming after the traditional month of rest and recreation from late July through late August. The typical person born under the sign of Virgo senses the fact that he/she is put on this earth to work and to serve both the earth and other people. For some, this leads to self-sacrifice, as well as the self-pity that often accompanies it. However, people born under the sign of Virgo should also possess an awareness that life is good, and full of good things, because as the Virgo cycle begins, there is evidence of life's bounty everywhere. One of the challenges for the person born under this sign is to combine dedication to work with the joy of fulfillment that can come from a job well done. For perfectionist Virgo, it is often a big challenge.

Virgo's Position in the zodiac has another meaning as well for this sign's temperament. The gathering of the harvest must be done at precisely the right time if the best and fullest crop is to be gotten; Virgo's legendary efficiency is very much a function of the right timing. The good Virgo knows exactly the right amount of time and effort to put out at exactly the right time in order to maximize the end product. Unfortunately, too many Virgos become overanxious and bogged down in detail to make the most of this excellent gift.

The legendary symbol of the virgin for Virgo is very often misunderstood. It is a symbol of purity, not of prudery; in fact, sexual activity is usually very important to a person born under the sign of Virgo. For those who "evolve," it is one of the areas of life where Virgos can combine efficiency of technique with great pleasure. The Virgo virgin is the original feminine principle, the great mother fertilized by the force of creation, capable of bringing forth the best the earth has to give. In Roman mythology, she was worshipped as Ceres, goddess of the harvest, and her festival was marked by a procession of women in white wearing crowns of ripe corn. Earlier, the Greeks worshipped the virgin as Demeter, goddess of agriculture. If the virgin is "pure," her purity is a purity of purpose and dedication to the important role of fertility in creation.

One little recognized symbol of the virgin is the Great Sphinx of Egypt. Its lion's body symbolizes the animal passions of the sign of Leo, which immediately precedes Virgo. However, the head is that of a maiden. The full meaning is that the sign of Virgo represents mind over matter. Like Virgo, the Sphinx sits patiently—perhaps through eternity—waiting for the exact moment when its "secret" should be revealed. The ultimate Virgo, symbolically speaking, is the Virgin Mary whose earthly purity made her worthy of bearing God's child. The gods of antiquity, like Zeus and Jupiter, were also worshipped by virgin priestesses who became "impregnated" with the essence of divinity and brought forth divine knowledge. In effect, the sign of Virgo represents the "holy" state of femaleness, which is very close to God.

The glyph or shorthand symbol astrologers use to indicate Virgo (see illustration) is sometimes interpreted as the coils of female energy, or, literally, the female sexual parts. The symbol is self-enclosed, once more reflecting the self-containment of this zodiac sign. Others see in Virgo's glyph the coils of the human intestines, and the sign of Virgo is said to rule or be connected with the human digestive system. On a mundane level, many Virgo people are overly concerned about the purity of their food and the state of their body's nourishment. Health food stores are very "Virgo." On a more symbolic level, it is in the intestines that food is absorbed and made useful for the body. Usefulness is one of the main life goals for many a Virgo.

13

Virgo: Objectives and Obstacles

A Game Plan for Being the Most Successful Virgo Under the Sun

Every astrological sign is a set of possibilities; being born under a particular sign does not guarantee you *are* or *will be* all those things that sign is capable of being. Nor would you want to. There are positive characteristics to be cultivated, as well as negative ones you can avoid or overcome. Living "à la carte"—selecting what you want from all the options available—is open to you, within the overall context of your sign.

You can, of course, order the "prix fixe" dinner by living your life as it comes without attempting to direct it. The choice is yours, which is one good reason it is incorrect to regard your astrological destiny as preordained. You are responsible for how you embody your sign, and what results from that embodiment.

Astrologically speaking, your life as a sign is a journey with a starting point, the raw, or "primitive" end of the side, and a destination, the evolved or "ideal" realization of that sign. Once again, you don't have to take the full trip; there are plenty of exits if you choose to use them, and few people are ever totally "finished." But if you at least know where you are going and what potential booby traps lie along the way, you will be way ahead of the game.

Regard the following as a map and use it in charting your course. The most successful way to be the best of your astrological sign is to work with it, in full knowledge of its upside-down side. The happiest people of any astrological sign are those who aim high and are not afraid to stretch their understanding of themselves in order to reach their goal.

Where Virgo Starts

Because becoming an evolved Virgo is one of the most difficult trips in the zodiac, you may find many born under this sign falling prey to the worst of themselves. Astrology books abound with descriptions of the "Classic" Virgo—the critical, carping, dissatisfied, unhappy, sharp-tongued person who is never satisfied with anything or anyone. At its best, Virgo is the sign of the great analyzer who can dissect almost anything and give a carefully detailed picture of how it is put together. Turned inside out, this facility makes Virgo the ultimate critic—the one who sees only the flaws and the weak spots. In many cases, Virgo plays this role of critic out of envy of people who seem to express themselves much more easily than Virgo can. And the reason Virgo has such difficulty expressing him-/herself is that he/she censors every word before it is uttered and every thought before it becomes action. The terrible trap of the unevolved Virgo is the frustrated desire for *self*-perfection. Since nobody is perfect, this kind of Virgo inevitably ends up an unhappy, and often bitter, person. Some suffer so much that others find them unpleasant company, and Virgo faces yet another problem—loneliness. Here are some of the buzz words by which you can recognize the primitive or unevolved Virgo type:

Worried	Complaining
Fussy	Pessimistic
Narrow-minded	Martyrish
Obsessive	Servile
Unable to admit guilt	Irritable

Where Virgo Can Go

For those with the stamina to make the full trip, the prize at the end of the rainbow for the evolved Virgo is a wonderful one indeed. His/her body and mind work together very efficiently. He/she works with a purpose, and enjoys to the fullest the rewards that work can bring. Rather than being servile, this kind of Virgo has carved out a very personal niche in this world, and is happy to occupy it—and value it.

One of the reasons becoming a high Virgo rather than a low Virgo is difficult is that Leo, the sign before Virgo, is a very hard act to follow. Symbolically (and actually, as far as temperament goes), Leo represents the ultimate in self-expression. Leo's role in the world is to become a personality, and there are very few hindrances laid upon the sign to prevent him/her from doing so. Virgo's got a much tougher path fo follow, because practical Virgo must find a way to express him-/herself via service in this world. Philosophically speaking, it does not matter whether or not Leo's self-expression really makes a contribution; for Virgo, that is a must. In a sense, Virgo must make a big leap to a whole new level in the human experience.

The evolved Virgo has the clearest of minds and the sharpest of visions; it is virtually impossible to fool this kind of person with anything shoddy or imperfect. Instead of being sarcastic, the evolved Virgo is witty in the best sense of the word, combining intelligence with a well-balanced, humorous attitude toward the ways of the world. Because they have learned to give the pure love Virgo is capable of, they receive it as well and are generally quite fulfilled people.

Here are some buzz words by which you can recognize the evolved Virgo:

Analytical
Superb
Thorough

Honest
Systematic
Humorous

- Self-disciplined
- Productive
- Caring
- Logical

How Virgo Can Get There

Though it may seem like a paradox, the best route to happiness and success for Virgo is through his/her perfectionism. The trick is to use it rather than become a slave to it. An internal drive for the best is a formidable weapon in this all-too-often sloppy world. What Virgo must do is turn those incredibly clear eyes outward rather than inward and concentrate on the job at hand, whatever it may be. The thing that will eventually bring self-confidence to this often uncertain sign is seeing the results of his/her competence. In order to see those results, Virgo has got to force a wider vision upon him-/herself, and not get lost in the forest because all Virgo can see is the trees.

Most Virgos have a specialty, even if it is buried deep within them. For success, Virgo has got to discover that specialty, then sharpen it as only Virgo can do. Instead of being narrow-minded, the Virgo bent on success should choose the path or calling that best suits his/her abilities. Then practice that calling better than anyone else. For many, it will be a service career that beckons, because to serve others with joy is one of Virgo's natural birthrights. However, Virgo can "serve" in many different capacities; it is important that people born under this sign do not impose limitations on themselves. The world does enough of that for them.

Potential Pitfalls

If a particular Virgo is lucky, he/she was raised by parents who understood their child's desperate need for signals that he or she was "okay." The worst demon Virgo has to wrestle with in this life is a lack of self-esteem. If one is born with an innate need for perfection, it follows logically that the need is rarely, if ever, met. The Virgo person who gets down on him-/herself is one of the most pitiful people in the zodiac. Unlike some other signs who may seem attractive in their need for love, the unhappy Virgo sends out some very negative vibes. Worse still, the Virgo who feels that he/she doesn't deserve happiness simply will not find it. In fact, this kind of Virgo is often the one who ends up in a desperately unhappy marriage or work environment, but sticks it out because he/she believes it is his/her lot in life.

It's not easy for some to build self-esteem, and for Virgo it may be even harder. However, if Virgo finds that special talent and perfects it, he/she at least has a chance of feeling successful. It doesn't really matter what that talent is—it could be anything from competence in the kitchen to a skill with a musical instrument. The point is that if Virgo does something he/she *likes* to do and does it well, then Virgo can start building up self-esteem. The bricks of confidence may not be very large, but if Virgo keeps piling them up he/she can build a very powerful wall against those self-negative feelings.

14

Pairing Off with Virgo

Your Compatibility with Other Signs of the Zodiac

Since there are only twelve signs of the zodiac, it would be unusual to go through life without having to interact with each of them at one time or another. Obviously, your astrological makeup is more complex than your Virgo sun sign, but there are some basic truths about how you tend to react when face to face with someone of another sun sign. If you have read about "The Geometry of Relationships," you already know that being an earth sign means Virgo relates more easily to certain elements than to others. Now, getting more specific, you will see what the odds are on your match-ups with each of the other signs, including your own.

When people talk about "relationships," they are usually referring to the romantic kind, and there is no doubt that since time immemorial love has been observed to have a great deal to do with keeping the earth revolving in its orbit. However, we also have a lot of other personal interactions, from important ones, like boss-employee and parent-child to more casual ones, like waitress-patron, cabdriver-rider, and buddy-buddy. The general rules that follow apply in all cases; just change the language a little and do a bit of interpretation. You will find that there is more truth than poetry in the matter of astrological compatibility.

Virgo with Aries You two are unlikely to make it

living under the same roof. Your need for things to be neat and orderly would be constantly frustrated by Aries' slapdash living style and constant movement and activity. However, as friends you would be very good for each other. You're both very smart, and you could help Aries focus his/her talents in the right direction. Aries could show you a lot about how fun life can really be. With luck, there is the possibility that you will click.

Virgo with Taurus You will probably be very attracted to sweet Taurus, and—if you play your cards right—Taurus will feel the same. Playing your cards right means overlooking some of Taurus's rather loose and imprecise ways; he/she means so well, that it would be a shame to criticize. Of the two, you will be the far more adaptable, so you might as well make up your mind at the start that you're going to do a lot of compromising to make things work. If you do, things will work quite beautifully.

Virgo with Gemini It is likely that you two will make each other nervous, at least at the start. Gemini is a little too ephemeral for you to pin down; Gemini finds you a bit too reserved. However, on closer inspection, you may both decide this is a good thing. Gemini really needs your practicality, and you will find Gemini's lively mind a delight. Together, you could make a relationship, but not one without problems. Believe it or not, you will have to grow up almost as much as Gemini.

Virgo with Cancer Though earth signs like you and water signs like Cancer technically mix well, in this particular case the outlook is a little dim. In fact, that's what life could be like if you two both decided to get moody and irritable at the same time. Another problem: you could make Cancer feel rather inadequate, and Cancer won't like that. In a way, it's too bad the prognosis is not good here, because you would ultimately benefit from Cancer's brand of all-enveloping love. Try this one in business instead.

Virgo with Leo Leo is probably the sign that will make you feel most Virgolike. It isn't Leo's fault, and you should not make him/her think so. If you decide you are going to benefit from Leo's outgoing, expressive nature, you will eventually realize that you can't live life through someone else. With you, Leo will be gracious—but a little confused. He/she simply doesn't understand how such an intelligent person as you has such problems coping with the world. He/she is liable to never discover just how loving you can be.

Virgo with Virgo You two could make a love relationship an awful lot of work, with very little play to compensate. In effect, you could simply analyze each other to death—at least the death of any positive feeling that exists. On the other hand, you both have similar goals, so if you apply your combined intelligence to working out an intelligent arrangement, you could make each other very happy. In business there isn't enough fire here to accomplish anything really creative. You need a more inspiring opposite number.

Virgo with Libra This is a surprisingly good combination—surprising because earth signs like you and air signs like Libra are sometimes at odds. Where you and Libra come together is in the refinement of your tastes and ideas. You are amazingly alike in your interests and pleasures. The love between you will be of a rather idealistic nature, but that's just fine by the two of you. In other kinds of pair-offs, like parent-child and boss-employee, things are a little more difficult.

Virgo with Scorpio You two are just about made for each other—at least in the emotional and physical senses. You are all too happy to put Scorpio in control of things, because you derive such satisfaction from Scorpio's all-consuming love and passion. Scorpio sees in you a person as determined as he/she is to master some aspect of life. All will go well if you don't disappoint Scorpio by giving in to your feelings of inadequacy. A relationship with Scorpio can be an excellent way for you to develop your powers.

Virgo with Sagittarius   Like you, Sagittarius is a "mutable" or adaptable sign, and in spite of some surface flakiness, most Sagittarians have a built-in organizational system. Your appeal for one another, however, will be more mutual esteem than hot-blooded passion. Sagittarius thinks in much broader terms than you do, and constantly has his/her eyes on the stars. You are a bit too realistic to truly fire up Sagittarius feelings. As a work combination, you two are virtually unbeatable.

Virgo with Capricorn   You simply adore Capricorn's strong ways and decisiveness; Capricorn respects and admires your dedication to work. You could build a wonderful and stable life together. However, you are both going to have to learn to admit your faults and to gain some humility. Together you may feel way above it all and lose touch with the simpler things in life. If you have children, you must take care to give them a sense that life is more than material things.

Virgo with Aquarius   In some ways, you are both "strange birds," and could easily flock together. Each would be tolerant of the other's eccentricities, and your clear, logical minds would click well together. However, Aquarius' brand of love is a little chilly, and it could make you rather anxious if he/she doesn't appear to be paying attention. The other danger is that you will criticize each other too much; it may be meant in a constructive way, but the results could be disastrous.

Virgo with Pisces   While you are a saver, Pisces is a spender, in every sense of the word. Pisces' emotional excuses are very likely to raise your contempt after the fascination has worn off. You will eventually drive Pisces away with your demands that he/she shape up. On one level, however, this combination has a lot of merit. With your practical intelligence, you could make the most of some of Pisces' creative but impractical schemes. Keep this one of a light nature, however, or Pisces could drown you out.

15

The Virgo Sex Role Dilemma

One of the most important ways in which the twelve signs of the zodiac are divided is into "masculine" signs and "feminine" signs, and there are six of each. The reason is simple: As one sign follows the other in the zodiac, they alternate energies, much like the Yin/Yang principle of eastern philosophy. The universe is made up of opposites that complement each other; light and dark, hot and cold, black and white, hard and soft. One is not better than the other; rather, each is essential to the existence of its opposite. In other words, you can't have one without the other.

The six fire and air signs are "masculine," since fire and air are connected with *active, assertive, outgoing* energy.

Aries	Gemini
Leo	Libra
Sagittarius	Aquarius

The six water and earth signs are "feminine," because water and earth represent *reactive, inner-directed, receptive* energy.

Taurus	Cancer
Virgo	Scorpio
Capricorn	Pisces

To put it simply, *the masculine fire and air signs are positive, while the earth and water signs are negative.* To remain neutral and avoid placing a higher value on one or the other kind of energy (or sign) it is useful to think of a battery with positive and negative poles. Without both, it simply doesn't work.

Though the masculine-feminine division of the signs has nothing whatever to do with human physical sexuality or sexual preference, it has very important implications for human behavior. Bluntly put, women born into male signs can be more "masculine"/achieving/competitive than men born into female signs. On the other hand, men born in female signs can be more "feminine"/nurturing/cooperative than women born into male signs. Both men and women born into signs that match their own sex may overemphasize the behavior and attitudes connected with that gender. The "ideal" person, psychologically and metaphysically speaking, has a healthy mix of both masculine and feminine attitudes. Without at least some of both, we cannot be whole people, able to encompass and understand the total range of human emotions, desires, drives, and goals. Since none of us is perfect, just about everyone could stand a bit more "gender blending." Your astrological sign offers some excellent clues about how you can accomplish that.

As a "feminine" sign, Virgo embodies the principles of receptiveness and reaction; being *acted upon* rather than taking action. For Virgos of both sexes, passivity can be a serious problem. For men born under the sign, it is—curiously enough—less of a problem. Virgo men may serve others, but their physical masculinity keeps them from appearing to be "wimps," at least in a majority of cases. And, to their credit, they are closer to their feelings than many males born under masculine signs. Virgo women, on the other hand, are all too easily cast in the role of servile females whose role in life is to support and be at the beck and call of someone else—very often a male.

Therefore, the Virgo sex role dilemma is clear: For success, Virgo men should cultivate their outward masculinity without losing any of the supportive inner femaleness that comes naturally to them. Virgo women, on the other hand, must drag themselves up and out of their female personalities and make the tremendous effort of asserting themselves in the world. Being a Virgo makes the number two role even easier for her to fall into than it is for other women. Keep these facts in mind as you read the following Virgo portraits, and you—man or woman—will better understand the "why" of your Virgo behavior.

16

The Virgo Female

Passionate Pilgrim

Just as white gloves and a perfect hairdo do not a lady make, the Virgo woman's composed but often tense outward appearance conceals anything but a sexually repressed woman. Her sexual standards are high, however, and she is rarely promiscuous; what the Virgo woman is passionate about is going to any lengths to achieve union with that "perfect" man. Virgos care a lot about what others think, and their behavior is generally quite socially acceptable. However, the Virgo woman who has made up her mind that a particular male is the one for her will brave the worst kind of publicity to be with him.

The other side of the "passionate Pilgrim" is the Virgo woman's unfortunate tendency to let the world happen to her rather than the other way round. She can be extraordinarily passive. In the myth, beautiful Psyche loses her lover, Eros, when a mean trick is played on her by her jealous sisters. Psyche then must go through all kinds of trials in order to be reunited with Eros. As determined as she is, her methods of coping with these trials is typically female; Psyche worries a lot, but doesn't make any real effort. Help comes to her, appropriately enough, from the small, weak creatures of the earth, and she eventually gets her man. The Virgo woman is not necessarily a clinging vine, but she all too often resembles Psyche in her unwillingness to take the bull by the horns and change her situation. Let alone take the world by storm.

As a child, the Virgo girl is generally docile and quiet and much tidier than a lot of other children. Some Virgo youngsters have a real problem about getting dirty; the wise mother, as much as she likes the trait, should not let it go too far, because a lot of Virgo obsessiveness begins in childhood. Bright and quick as well, the Virgo girl can appear to be the perfect child. Unfortunately, what that means is that the slightest deviation from perfect behavior, which her parents come to expect, brings criticism which is the last thing in the world the Virgo girl's easily bruised ego needs. Sometimes Virgo children appear cold to their parents, because they are not overly demonstrative, or receptive to hugs and kisses. Once again, it is a trap of sorts, because this child needs as much, if not more, physical demonstrations of love from her parents as any other child. Many Virgo girls become teachers' pets and thereby get removed from the circle of the other kids—often setting up a pattern for a lifetime.

As a young woman, the Virgo female often starts out by dipping a tentative toe into life rather than plunging into it wholeheartedly. At this point, she has already typically fallen victim to the Virgo's lack of confidence. Whatever level of education she reaches, it is unlike the Virgo female to aggressively pursue the best job available. What she usually does is take the position where she feels most comfortable—and that is often where she is virtually invisible. However, since competence is built in to the Virgo personality, she will do well. If she learns to trust herself, she may even do *very* well; but it will be extremely difficult for her ever to like being the boss. In fact, the Virgo female can be very unhappy if she doesn't *have* a real boss to back up and serve.

In her emotional and sexual life the Virgo female faces a problem. Many Virgo women have a lot of trouble coming to terms with their sexuality; the roots of the difficulty may lie in her childhood, where she somehow got the idea that bodily functions are "not nice." Or, with her tendency to follow the rules, the Virgo woman may not allow herself to enjoy sex outside of a permanent and socially acceptable relationship. Because of this, many Virgo women marry very early. Even the more open-minded Virgo woman is confused about how to handle her emotional and physical needs. The real problem is that Virgo females often do not have a very positive image of womanhood; many have a love/hate relationship with their mothers, who really were not very good models. And the emphasis is on the hate side.

As a mate, the Virgo woman can really come into her own—if she marries the right man. That would be someone wise enough to realize that he has his Virgo woman's total love and fidelity and that he need not exploit her. It is uncanny how many Virgo women end up under the thumb of a demanding and sometimes brutal male. The other common pattern for the Virgo wife is to take out her own bad feelings about herself on her husband. The comic-book stereotype of the nagging wife is unfortunately often an accurate picture of the Virgo female who is unhappy with herself—and hence her marriage. Can the Virgo woman achieve happiness in a relationship? Yes, but only after she has learned to love, or at least to accept, the person she herself is. And that is usually the hardest thing the Virgo woman ever has to do in her life.

As a mother, the Virgo woman must be very careful not to repeat the "sins" of her own upbringing with her children. And she must understand that even the best of children are never perfect. The biggest mistake she may make is to care about the physical needs of her children so totally that she neglects them in the emotional area. If a Virgo mother's children are warm, dry, and fed, she can easily think that all is right with the world. She may also tend to over-teach and try to make her kids the best in the class. Motherhood can be a blessing for the Virgo woman, however, because through it she may finally begin to feel a sense of accomplishment as well as a real connection with other warm, loving creatures like herself.

17

The Virgo Male

He's a "Puzzlement"

Virgo men probably have more trouble with women than men born under any other sign in the zodiac. The "typical" Virgo male has been brought up in an atmosphere where "mommy" ruled the roost—and, even through silence, communicated to her children that "daddy" really wasn't worth much. To put it bluntly, many Virgo men are afraid of women, because—subconsciously at least—they believe that women have really got more power. Even if they are only moderately neurotic on this subject, they still have a lot of trouble developing free and easy communication with members of the opposite sex. The Virgo man's woman trouble spills over into his professional life, where he may run himself ragged trying to be perfect in order to avoid the trap of humiliation he saw his father face. The real trouble is that the Virgo male does not understand the feminine principle; this is true even of those who were not raised in the "classic" Virgo atmosphere. The solution for the male Virgo is to come to terms with his *own* femaleness in order to appreciate it in the opposite sex. If he is not to go through life overreacting to women—as well as to the female principle in everything—he's got to learn to value his own maternal tendencies. Evolved Virgo men excel at jobs that require building things in the material universe—either physically or intellectually—and of making those things the best they can be.

As a child, the Virgo male was most likely a very good little boy. His parents were probably delighted at his ability to amuse himself and require so little traditional discipline. A lot of Virgo boys show an interest in things like cooking, dressmaking, and other traditionally female pursuits. The wise parent does not discourage these creative outlets, but lets them run their course, allowing the child to grow. Woodworking and other hobbies that require manual dexterity and patience are also often chosen by the Virgo boy. He is very prone to minor deceptions like pretending to be sick, usually to get his mother's attention. If she is not alert, the mother of the Virgo boy will play right into his hands by coddling him—and maybe setting up a lifetime pattern of hypochondria. What the Virgo boy is trying to ward off by his little game is the criticism he sees his mother leveling at his father. After all, if you're sick, people *have* to be nice to you!

As a young man, the Virgo male often works and worries himself right into an excellent job. Virgos are highly competent people, and—no matter how hard he tries to hide it—the Virgo male can be the shining light in any organization. There are, of course, many Virgo men who end up in positions of great power, but success rarely makes them as happy and satisfied as it does more self-seeking signs like Leo. More power means more responsibility and more work. Scratch many a workaholic, and you will find a typical Virgo male. In his emotional life the Virgo man is equally tentative about his position. It is typical of the men of this sign to marry late—usually after a long search for the woman who will understand him. Like their female counterparts, Virgo men are usually quite healthy in their desire for sexual experience. If the Virgo man is a "virgin," it is in his purity of desire for a match that combines intellectual companionship as well as physical compatibility. His standards are extremely high, and he tests every potential partner he meets. The woman who enters into a romantic relationship with a Virgo male can expect a very high-level courtship—i.e., one in which books, films, the theater, and everything else of an intellectual nature are given more than equal time with the physical side of the union. Many women find Virgo men absolutely fascinating at first, because their taste is so good, their minds are so active, and they are so respectful of women. Total disillusionment can set in when the woman involved with the Virgo male discovers that he really has a problem communicating anything about his feelings—and that often what he communicates to her is nothing but a put-down in the end.

As a mate and the vast majority do eventually marry, the Virgo man can be the most devoted partner, particularly in the sense of sexual fidelity. He will also rarely forget an anniversary or other special occasion, although his celebration of it may not be the most sentimental occasion. The Virgo male will also prove to be exceptionally stable in hard times; the problem is that he may project his own unusual willingness to sacrifice upon his wife, and expect the same attitude from her. If he has chosen the most likely partner for a Virgo male—a rather docile, hard-working type—all will go well. However, if the Virgo man's constructive criticism gets out of hand, his marriage may fall apart. Even the most submissive of females is capable of reacting loudly to the kind of constant nitpicking the Virgo male is prone to. Once his wife shows this kind of threatening behavior, the Virgo man is no longer comfortable. It all sounds too familiar, and the scenario begins to look like the one he was exposed to in his childhood. He may then step up the frequency and sharpness of his criticism, and from that point on the marriage may go straight downhill. And, as traumatic as the upheaval is for the Virgo male, he may even be the one to make the break. More often, however, it is the woman who walks away, leaving the hapless Virgo man wondering what he did wrong.

Obviously, a lot of Virgo men remain married to the

same woman for many years, and not all of them conform to this textbook case. But you can be sure of one of two things: A steadily married Virgo male has either lucked out and found the "perfect mate," or he is simply suffering in silence.

As a father, the Virgo male can be the most diligent father, carrying out his paternal responsibilities to a tee. Even though fatherhood is generally not a role he aspires to, when he does have children he is more than willing to share the load of caring for them with his wife. In some ways, he would rather do that than go out and compete in the business world. His children may get their own fill of his put-downs, but Virgo's natural warmth will usually come through to them, and they will realize that, no matter what he says or does, he really believes it is for their good and that his fatherly love is real.

18

Virgo Help Wanted

Selecting a Career and Your On-the-Job Style

A vitally important aspect of a successful Virgo game plan is making sure you land in the right job or career—i.e., the one that best suits your native talents and tendencies. It is more than a truism that people perform better doing what comes naturally. There are some natural careers for Virgo, and they all have several common denominators: mastery of technical details and a desire to serve through useful activity. It is not possible to list *all* the specific jobs a Virgo should do well at, but there are some "Virgo images" that provide useful guidelines. Though you may not literally end up *doing* any of these things, try to conjure up an idea of what it takes to do the following jobs, and you will have a better handle on what kind of inner resources Virgo people have available to them for career success.

Nutritionist	Technical editor/writer
Piano teacher/tuner	Nurse/physical therapist
Pharmacist/chemist	Computer scientist
Film/book critic	Telephone operator/worker
Mathematician/accountant	Fashion designer/pattern maker
Tool and die worker	Veterinary surgeon

Equally important to finding the best job slot for you

is understanding how your Virgo sun sign affects your modus operandi on the job and your potential for moving up. Every sun sign has certain success skills that can smooth and widen the career path, as well as blind spots that can cause roadblocks. The more you know about both, the better off you will be.

Some of the very things that plague the Virgo sun sign person in their personal lives can be to their benefit in the business world. One is your incredible ability to see that teeny speck of dust or that minor technical error. Virgo, of all the signs, is the master of detail. If you cultivate it, your patience is greater than that of any other sign, particularly when it comes to wrestling with a problem and finding out exactly where the glitch is. The computer science field is probably populated with Virgos, although no one has done a real study.

Hand-in-hand with your good mind for detail goes your extreme desire for perfection. No matter what a particular Virgo decides to do in his/her life, this tendency is an asset. Famous Virgos in show business, like Anne Bancroft and Peter Sellers, perfected their craft to such a point that they reached "master craftsman" status. Virgo singer Maurice Chevalier appeared cool and debonair, but every little movement and syllable was worked on intensely. Virgos who go into a field like fashion are able to turn out tailoring that far exceeds the norm; like everything a Virgo does, the Virgo designer's clothes *work*.

Despite all Virgo's resources, however, it is a sign that often finds it rough going in the world of competition. In point of fact, Virgo hates to compete and usually gravitates toward number two spots where they can prop up someone else. The efficient administrative secretary without whom a great titan of industry could not exist is one of the all-too-true Virgo stereotypes. The problem for the particularly competent Virgo who shuns the spotlight is that eventually he will outshine his superior. Then, Virgo's boss is likely to react badly, or the underling Virgo him-/herself will begin to resent the situation. It is so easy for the Virgo sun sign person to be unhappy that he/she should try to avoid this hidden success syndrome at all costs. The best thing to do is recognize your own strengths and abilities, and point them out *before* superiors just simply notice them. Go for the top rather than the second rung on the ladder, because you have every bit of talent necessary to do so. Another of the labels that is often slapped on Virgo is "the martyr." Keep this in mind, and the next time you feel yourself going in that direction, correct your course.

19

How "Pure" a Virgo Are You?

Your Moon Sign ... Your Rising Sign

No one is a "pure Virgo"—or pure anything, for that matter—when it comes to astrological signs. As you will learn when you read "Defining Terms," there are many other factors in a horoscope that add up to the total person that is "you." Yes, there are twelve basic personality types, according to the zodiac, but within those broad groups there are almost infinite variations.

Though you are a Virgo at the core, and can count on the portrait of your sun sign to define you in essence, the two other horoscope factors that count most are in your personality profile: your moon sign and your rising sign. Many people know their moon sign; anyone can quickly determine it via an ephemeris. If you know your birthtime at least within one hour, you can use the table in this book to find out what your rising sign is.

The Moon—Your "Dark Side"

Almost more than your sun sign, your moon sign indicates what makes you run. Most of the time, you do not know it yourself, because the moon is your subconscious, your "dark side" not because it is bad, but because it is hidden. When the meaning of your moon sign is added to your Virgo sun sign, it is a fuller picture and a better indicator of your probable personality. Here's how a Virgo sun sign mixes with each of the moon signs.

Virgo sun sign/Aries moon sign   You are a particularly quick-thinking, quick-on-the-trigger Virgo. The good news is that you are excellent at repartee and often take the lead in a discussion. The bad news is that you sometimes get a little too smug for your own good, and are a bit too hard to get along with. Soften up.

Virgo sun sign/Taurus moon sign   If it's possible to be too practical, you fit the bill. Extremely cautious, you are the kind of Virgo who can go through life missing out on a lot of opportunities. However, people like you, and you would make an excellent boss.

Virgo sun sign/Gemini moon sign   You are a particularly friendly Virgo, which helps you a lot. However, with both your sun and moon in "mutable" or flexible signs, you tend to lack decisiveness. While you can do two things at once, it is often difficult for you to decide which of them deserves your closest attention.

Virgo sun sign/Cancer moon sign   Your mind is so subtle it could play tricks on you; that means you may believe people are against you when there is no truth in that whatsoever. Despite your tendency to paranoia, however, you can be very persuasive when you want to. This gives you a golden tongue which should be put to good use.

Virgo sun sign/Leo moon sign   You are one of the warmer Virgos under the sun—and a bit more self-expressive than the average as well. It is even possible for you to be a little too proud of your accomplishments and brag a bit. Undoubtedly you love all things fine and elegant—and expensive.

Virgo sun sign/Virgo moon sign   You are most likely to be the classic Virgo type who carps and is too meticulous—even obsessive—about small things. While your success potential is great, you could spend a lot of your time down in the dumps. Don't work so hard, and loosen up with a dollar—and spend it on yourself.

Virgo sun sign/Libra moon sign Your judgment, perception, and reason are excellent, and you've even got a good imagination. However, it is possible for you to be overly impatient—with both yourself and with others. The arts undoubtedly attract you, and you should have some ability in that direction. Interior decoration is a field you have a flair for.

Virgo sun sign/Scorpio moon sign It is all too easy for you to be selfish and unforgiving. Your willingness to work hard and your persistence are so great that you may expect too much of others. In fact, people may feel they have to be extra cautious around you. For the greatest happiness, you should cultivate the warmth that Virgo is capable of.

Virgo sun sign/Sagittarius moon sign Though you are inclined to make hasty judgments, you are a much more broadminded Virgo than others. Your desire to teach is strong, and you should do well in any profession related to instructing others. Your biggest problem is lack of persistence, but you can lick it.

Virgo sun sign/Capricorn moon sign You are very shrewd—almost calculating. Your desire for success and everything that goes with it is very strong. But your mind tends to be so serious that you could appear to walk around with the proverbial "black cloud" over your head. Cultivate your wit and warmth.

Virgo sun sign/Aquarius moon sign You could be positively ingenious; in fact, this is a combination that makes for the "mad but brilliant" scientist. Your problem is that once you make up your mind no one can make you see that it's possible you are wrong. Don't be so opinionated, because people really like you—and you wouldn't want to change that.

Virgo sun sign/Pisces moon sign You are a great giver, but a great taker as well. In fact, you are the kind of Virgo who might prefer that others serve *you*.

You've got all the technical ability of the typical Virgo, but sometimes you don't know how to apply it. Cultivate your fine sense of detail.

Your Rising Sign—Know Your "Cover"
The third of the big three astrological factors is your rising sign, which you can think of as an *overlay* to your sun sign. Although it does not carry the psychological weight your moon sign does, your rising sign is also unconscious because it is a mode of external behavior that comes so naturally to you that you may not be aware of it. In a sense, your rising sign is your "cover." It can never totally obscure the real you of your sun sign, but it can temporarily mask that sign, especially when people first meet you. Here's what happens to Virgo when you lay a rising sign over typical Virgo behavior:

Virgo with Aries rising Whatever your sex, you could get the reputation for being a shrew. Tone it down a little when you tell people what they're doing wrong—as you often do.

Virgo with Taurus rising The sweet Taurus facade is a nice one for Virgo. You come across as much easier to please than you really are, and people accept you readily.

Virgo with Gemini rising You are too interested in other people for your own good, and may come off as a busybody. In some cases, you seem hostile. Back off a little.

Virgo with Cancer rising It would be all too easy for you to get the label of crab; everything, but everything bothers you. Try to do more of your suffering in silence.

Virgo with Leo rising This is an excellent rising sign for Virgo, because it gives you the appearance of warmth and amiability. However, you do tend to preach to others too often.

Virgo with Virgo rising What you see is what you get with this combination. Try to cultivate some of the softer Virgo characteristics, like wanting to help other people.

Virgo with Libra rising Regardless of sex, you are the "hostess with the mostest." Your precise performance could make you an excellent diplomat.

Virgo with Scorpio rising There could be a genuine sting in the way you appear to others—even if you don't mean it. When you're feeling mean, keep your mouth shut.

Virgo with Sagittarius rising You are a serious type who loves to have fun—a rather good combination. Your casual exterior can cover up a lot of irritation too.

Virgo with Capricorn rising Though you are probably very impressive physically, you could come off as a boor. Brush up that sparkling Virgo wit.

Virgo with Aquarius rising You are not one to give a quick and easy answer, so you may appear a little cold in casual company. However, people value your opinion when you give it.

Virgo with Pisces rising People get a shock when they get to know you, because you are far from the pushover you first appear to be. However, your soft covering is a great asset, in most cases.

20

Find Your Rising Sign

It is easier than many people think to find out your rising sign. One reason is that it is based on "universal" or "sidereal" time—the measure used in space travel. To ascertain your rising sign, look through the following chart and locate the birthdate nearest your birth date; look across and locate the time nearest your birth time. Remember that if daylight saving time was in effect at your birth, you must subtract one hour from the time stated on your birth certificate. In the section for your date and time, you will find an abbreviation for the sign that was rising when you were born. For instance, if your birthdate is June 12 at 9:30 a.m., your rising sign is Leo; if you were born on the same date at 9:30 p.m., your rising sign is Capricorn.

You will notice that the *year* you were born does not affect your rising sign. However, the geographical latitude does. These tables are calculated for the middle latitudes of the United States. If you were born far to the south, it is wise to look at the sign that *follows* your rising sign as well. If you were born far to the north, check out the *previous* sign.

Rising Signs—A.M. Births

	1 AM	2 AM	3 AM	4 AM	5 AM	6 AM	7 AM	8 AM	9 AM	10 AM	11 AM	12 NOON
Jan 1	Lib	Sc	Sc	Sc	Sag	Sag	Cap	Cap	Aq	Aq	Pis	Ar
Jan 9	Lib	Sc	Sc	Sag	Sag	Sag	Cap	Cap	Aq	Pis	Ar	Tau
Jan 17	Sc	Sc	Sc	Sag	Sag	Cap	Cap	Aq	Aq	Pis	Ar	Tau
Jan 25	Sc	Sc	Sag	Sag	Sag	Cap	Cap	Aq	Pis	Ar	Tau	Tau
Feb 2	Sc	Sc	Sag	Sag	Cap	Cap	Aq	Pis	Pis	Ar	Tau	Gem
Feb 10	Sc	Sag	Sag	Sag	Cap	Cap	Aq	Pis	Ar	Tau	Tau	Gem
Feb 18	Sc	Sag	Sag	Cap	Cap	Aq	Pis	Pis	Ar	Tau	Gem	Gem
Feb 26	Sag	Sag	Sag	Cap	Aq	Aq	Pis	Ar	Tau	Tau	Gem	Gem
Mar 6	Sag	Sag	Cap	Cap	Aq	Pis	Pis	Ar	Tau	Gem	Gem	Cap
Mar 14	Sag	Cap	Cap	Aq	Aq	Pis	Ar	Tau	Tau	Gem	Gem	Can
Mar 22	Sag	Cap	Cap	Aq	Pis	Ar	Ar	Tau	Gem	Gem	Can	Can
Mar 30	Cap	Cap	Aq	Pis	Pis	Ar	Tau	Tau	Gem	Can	Can	Can
Apr 7	Cap	Cap	Aq	Pis	Ar	Ar	Tau	Gem	Gem	Can	Can	Leo
Apr 14	Cap	Aq	Aq	Pis	Ar	Tau	Tau	Gem	Gem	Can	Can	Leo
Apr 22	Cap	Aq	Pis	Ar	Ar	Tau	Gem	Gem	Can	Can	Leo	Leo
Apr 30	Aq	Aq	Pis	Ar	Tau	Tau	Gem	Can	Can	Can	Leo	Leo
May 8	Aq	Pis	Ar	Ar	Tau	Gem	Gem	Can	Can	Leo	Leo	Leo
May 16	Aq	Pis	Ar	Tau	Gem	Gem	Can	Can	Can	Leo	Leo	Vir
May 24	Pis	Ar	Ar	Tau	Gem	Gem	Can	Can	Leo	Leo	Leo	Vir
June 1	Pis	Ar	Tau	Gem	Gem	Can	Can	Can	Leo	Leo	Vir	Vir
June 9	Ar	Ar	Tau	Gem	Gem	Can	Can	Leo	Leo	Leo	Vir	Vir
June 17	Ar	Tau	Gem	Gem	Can	Can	Can	Leo	Leo	Vir	Vir	Vir
June 25	Tau	Tau	Gem	Gem	Can	Can	Leo	Leo	Leo	Vir	Vir	Lib
July 3	Tau	Gem	Gem	Can	Can	Can	Leo	Leo	Vir	Vir	Vir	Lib
July 11	Tau	Gem	Gem	Can	Leo	Leo	Leo	Vir	Vir	Vir	Lib	Lib
July 18	Gem	Gem	Can	Can	Leo	Leo	Vir	Vir	Vir	Lib	Lib	Lib
July 26	Gem	Gem	Can	Can	Leo	Leo	Vir	Vir	Vir	Lib	Lib	Lib
Aug 3	Gem	Can	Can	Can	Leo	Leo	Vir	Vir	Vir	Lib	Lib	Sc
Aug 11	Gem	Can	Can	Leo	Leo	Leo	Vir	Vir	Lib	Lib	Lib	Sc
Aug 18	Can	Can	Can	Leo	Leo	Vir	Vir	Vir	Lib	Lib	Sc	Sc
Aug 27	Can	Can	Leo	Leo	Leo	Vir	Vir	Lib	Lib	Lib	Sc	Sc
Sept 4	Can	Can	Leo	Leo	Leo	Vir	Vir	Vir	Lib	Lib	Sc	Sc
Sept 12	Can	Leo	Leo	Leo	Vir	Vir	Lib	Lib	Lib	Sc	Sc	Sag
Sept 30	Leo	Leo	Leo	Vir	Vir	Vir	Lib	Lib	Sc	Sc	Sc	Sag
Sept 28	Leo	Leo	Leo	Vir	Vir	Lib	Lib	Lib	Sc	Sc	Sag	Sag
Oct 6	Leo	Leo	Vir	Vir	Vir	Lib	Lib	Sc	Sc	Sc	Sag	Sag
Oct 14	Leo	Vir	Vir	Vir	Lib	Lib	Lib	Sc	Sc	Sag	Sag	Cap
Oct 22	Leo	Vir	Vir	Lib	Lib	Lib	Sc	Sc	Sc	Sag	Sag	Cap
Oct 30	Vir	Vir	Vir	Lib	Lib	Sc	Sc	Sc	Sag	Sag	Cap	Cap
Nov 7	Vir	Vir	Lib	Lib	Lib	Sc	Sc	Sc	Sag	Sag	Cap	Cap
Nov 15	Vir	Vir	Lib	Lib	Sc	Sc	Sc	Sag	Sag	Cap	Cap	Aq
Nov 23	Vir	Lib	Lib	Lib	Sc	Sc	Sag	Sag	Sag	Cap	Cap	Aq
Dec 1	Vir	Lib	Lib	Lib	Sc	Sc	Sag	Sag	Cap	Cap	Aq	Aq
Dec 9	Lib	Lib	Lib	Sc	Sc	Sc	Sag	Sag	Cap	Cap	Aq	Pis
Dec 18	Lib	Lib	Sc	Sc	Sc	Sag	Sag	Cap	Cap	Aq	Aq	Pis
Dec 28	Lib	Lib	Sc	Sc	Sag	Sag	Sag	Cap	Aq	Aq	Pis	Ar

Rising Signs—P.M. Births

	1 PM	2 PM	3 PM	4 PM	5 PM	6 PM	7 PM	8 PM	9 PM	10 PM	11 PM	12 MIDNIGHT
Jan 1	Tau	Gem	Gem	Can	Can	Can	Leo	Leo	Vir	Vir	Vir	Lib
Jan 9	Tau	Gem	Gem	Can	Can	Leo	Leo	Leo	Vir	Vir	Vir	Lib
Jan 17	Gem	Gem	Can	Can	Can	Leo	Leo	Vir	Vir	Vir	Lib	Lib
Jan 25	Gem	Gem	Can	Can	Leo	Leo	Leo	Vir	Vir	Lib	Lib	Lib
Feb 2	Gem	Can	Can	Can	Leo	Leo	Vir	Vir	Vir	Lib	Lib	Sc
Feb 10	Gem	Can	Can	Leo	Leo	Leo	Vir	Vir	Lib	Lib	Lib	Sc
Feb 18	Can	Can	Can	Leo	Leo	Vir	Vir	Vir	Lib	Lib	Sc	Sc
Feb 26	Can	Can	Leo	Leo	Leo	Vir	Vir	Lib	Lib	Lib	Sc	Sc
Mar 6	Can	Can	Leo	Leo	Leo	Vir	Vir	Lib	Lib	Sc	Sc	Sc
Mar 14	Can	Leo	Leo	Vir	Vir	Vir	Lib	Lib	Lib	Sc	Sc	Sag
Mar 22	Leo	Leo	Leo	Vir	Vir	Lib	Lib	Lib	Sc	Sc	Sc	Sag
Mar 30	Leo	Leo	Vir	Vir	Vir	Lib	Lib	Sc	Sc	Sc	Sag	Sag
Apr 7	Leo	Leo	Vir	Vir	Lib	Lib	Lib	Sc	Sc	Sc	Sag	Sag
Apr 14	Leo	Vir	Vir	Vir	Lib	Lib	Sc	Sc	Sc	Sag	Sag	Sag
Apr 22	Leo	Vir	Vir	Lib	Lib	Lib	Sc	Sc	Sc	Sag	Sag	Cap
Apr 30	Vir	Vir	Vir	Lib	Lib	Sc	Sc	Sc	Sag	Sag	Cap	Cap
May 8	Vir	Vir	Lib	Lib	Lib	Sc	Sc	Sag	Sag	Sag	Cap	Cap
May 16	Vir	Vir	Lib	Lib	Sc	Sc	Sc	Sag	Sag	Cap	Cap	Aq
May 24	Vir	Lib	Lib	Lib	Sc	Sc	Sag	Sag	Sag	Cap	Cap	Aq
June 1	Vir	Lib	Lib	Sc	Sc	Sc	Sag	Sag	Cap	Cap	Aq	Aq
June 9	Lib	Lib	Lib	Sc	Sc	Sag	Sag	Sag	Cap	Cap	Aq	Pis
June 17	Lib	Lib	Sc	Sc	Sc	Sag	Sag	Cap	Cap	Aq	Aq	Pis
June 25	Lib	Lib	Sc	Sc	Sag	Sag	Sag	Cap	Cap	Aq	Pis	Ar
July 3	Lib	Sc	Sc	Sc	Sag	Sag	Cap	Cap	Aq	Aq	Pis	Ar
July 11	Lib	Sc	Sc	Sag	Sag	Sag	Cap	Cap	Aq	Pis	Ar	Tau
July 18	Sc	Sc	Sc	Sag	Sag	Cap	Cap	Aq	Aq	Pis	Ar	Tau
July 26	Sc	Sc	Sag	Sag	Sag	Cap	Aq	Aq	Pis	Ar	Tau	Tau
Aug 3	Sc	Sc	Sag	Sag	Cap	Cap	Aq	Aq	Pis	Ar	Tau	Gem
Aug 11	Sc	Sag	Sag	Sag	Cap	Cap	Aq	Pis	Ar	Tau	Tau	Gem
Aug 18	Sc	Sag	Sag	Cap	Cap	Aq	Pis	Pis	Ar	Tau	Gem	Gem
Aug 27	Sag	Sag	Sag	Cap	Cap	Aq	Pis	Ar	Tau	Tau	Gem	Gem
Sept 4	Sag	Sag	Cap	Cap	Aq	Pis	Ar	Tau	Gem	Gem	Can
Sept 12	Sag	Sag	Cap	Aq	Aq	Pis	Ar	Tau	Tau	Gem	Gem	Can
Sept 20	Sag	Cap	Cap	Aq	Pis	Pis	Ar	Tau	Gem	Gem	Can	Can
Sept 28	Cap	Cap	Aq	Aq	Pis	Ar	Tau	Tau	Gem	Gem	Can	Can
Oct 6	Cap	Cap	Aq	Pis	Ar	Ar	Tau	Gem	Gem	Can	Can	Leo
Oct 14	Cap	Aq	Aq	Pis	Ar	Tau	Tau	Gem	Gem	Can	Can	Leo
Oct 22	Cap	Aq	Pis	Ar	Tau	Tau	Gem	Gem	Can	Can	Leo	Leo
Oct 30	Aq	Aq	Pis	Ar	Tau	Tau	Gem	Can	Can	Can	Leo	Leo
Nov 7	Aq	Aq	Pis	Ar	Tau	Tau	Gem	Can	Can	Can	Leo	Leo
Nov 15	Aq	Pis	Ar	Tau	Gem	Gem	Can	Can	Can	Leo	Leo	Vir
Nov 23	Pis	Ar	Ar	Tau	Gem	Gem	Can	Can	Leo	Leo	Leo	Vir
Dec 1	Pis	Ar	Tau	Tau	Gem	Gem	Can	Can	Leo	Leo	Vir	Vir
Dec 9	Ar	Tau	Tau	Gem	Gem	Can	Can	Leo	Leo	Leo	Vir	Vir
Dec 18	Ar	Tau	Gem	Gem	Can	Can	Can	Leo	Leo	Vir	Vir	Vir
Dec 28	Tau	Tau	Gem	Gem	Can	Can	Leo	Leo	Vir	Vir	Vir	Lib

21

Virgo Astro-Outlook for 1986

Expect the world to open up to you in a lot of ways this year, Virgo. One reason will be that you are a lot more outgoing and enthusiastic about life in general. As you broaden your horizons and become involved with people outside your usual circle, you will find yourself a lot more popular. Among the unexpected, rather wonderful things that will happen because of your wider outlook is a chance to travel farther and wider than you ever have.

As a Virgo, you generally do things to improve yourself that are essentially practical. Now you are ready to get involved with something new that has little to do with your everyday world. Your explorations should bring you in touch with some adventurous people who are ready to take the world by storm. You will do well to get involved.

As far as relationships go, you are more likely to seek out intellectual companionship and social compatibility than serious commitment. It could mean that you are going to have to be realistic about what you can expect from someone you get involved with; he/she may be determined to keep things platonic, no matter what your wishes.

In your home and family life, you may find yourself with new responsibilities due to some unexpected changes. If you maintain your sense of humor, and resist your tendency to criticize, you will come smiling through. For more concrete details about what the course of your life is likely to be in 1986, consult the day-by-day forecasts on the following pages.

22

Fifteen Months of Day-by-Day Predictions

OCTOBER 1985

Tuesday, October 1 (Moon in Taurus) You will need to maintain a sense of self-discipline today, especially if you want to carry out your goals. These goals include the desire to increase your knowledge of the world through study and travel, so involve yourself with cultural exhibits or learning institutions. If you remain perceptive and aware of every detail, you will be well rewarded in the long run.

Wednesday, October 2 (Moon in Taurus) A major change is well in view now, as you find yourself moving toward new possibilities and a broadening of ideas. Your desire for change could cause you to travel to new places, where you may find someone who really "speaks your language." Don't let any small differences of opinion stand in the way of an incredible friendship. Look to 5 as today's lucky number.

Thursday, October 3 (Moon Taurus to Gemini 8:26 a.m.) You will be in a good mood today, especially if you receive word from a loved one who is far away. Your high spirits will make you the center of attention, so don't try to suppress your fun-loving, merry attitude—it will make others admire you. If any disagreements come up, don't lie back and expect things to work out—make the first move yourself.

Friday, October 4 (Moon in Gemini) Someone may

make lots of big promises today, but don't rely too heavily on their word. Be cautious and aware that things might fall through, and be ready to make a rebound in case they do. This person is not trying to be dishonest, but you may be putting words in their mouth and then believing them to be true. Make sure everything is perfectly spelled out for you—don't take chances.

Saturday, October 5 (Moon Gemini to Cancer 8:42 p.m.) Today you will concern yourself with matters of finance and business opportunities. There may be some "power plays" at work, so try to avoid any unnecessary competition or hidden traps. However, don't stay on the sidelines—get right into the action by being bold and expressing ideas. Don't hesitate to make negotiations, just remember to maintain a serious attitude.

Sunday, October 6 (Moon in Cancer) A humanitarian urge will cause you to join a group or organization and fight for what you believe in. Don't try to bury your concern for others because you think it will be harmful to your own success. Follow through with your instincts and true feelings. Thinking on a more worldwide level will enable you to gain admiration and support from many different people.

Monday, October 7 (Moon in Cancer) Today is fast-moving and full of accomplishments for you. However you cannot take a passive approach—you must be ready to take action, to work hard, and to cooperate with other people. A daring attitude will help you overcome any fears or apprehensions—then you will feel ready to have all eyes on you, and will enjoy your time under the spotlight!

Tuesday, October 8 (Moon Cancer to Leo 6:38 a.m.) Yesterday commanded an outgoing and daring attitude, but today you will feel like being more secluded and more in tune with yourself. Don't be overly ambitious or expect too much from yourself—it's alright to take a break and take time to sort out your thoughts. Your instincts and intuitions are right on target, so don't ignore or push aside any ideas.

Wednesday, October 9 (Moon in Leo) You may be feeling quite shy today, even though something inside tells you to get out and meet people. You could either drown in a little self-pity or try to overcome it by thinking positively and counting your blessings. If you decide to get moving, it could be a very active day. Body language and subtle "signs" will seem to stand out more than usual, so observe people closely in order to learn more about them.

Thursday, October 10 (Moon Leo to Virgo 1:24 p.m.) You have been doing a lot of hard work behind the scenes, and may be feeling a little discouraged because you think no one is noticing your efforts. Well don't worry, in time you will receive the praise and the gratitude you deserve. Just make sure you keep to your tasks and prove that you have staying power. An Aquarius may cross your path today.

Friday, October 11 (Moon in Virgo) Everything should go your way today, because the moon is in Virgo and your motivation is extremely high. Let yourself loose in order to travel, meet people, and bring about greater variety in your life. Focus some attention on self-expression, as you will have a lot to say, and someone who cares will gladly listen. Try your luck with number 5.

Saturday, October 12 (Moon Virgo to Libra 2:38 p.m.) You could find yourself with a "sweet tooth" today or an uncontrollable urge to indulge in a major feast. Watch your weight—overeating could be quite harmful physically *and* mentally. Keep in mind any promises you made to yourself. If any family trouble arises, try to serve as the peacemaker and take a leadership position in order to guide others to a state of harmony.

Sunday, October 13 (Moon in Libra) Your mind could easily drift from matters of business and finance, and thoughts on this subject could become rather fuzzy. Therefore try to clear your head a little and be extra careful about decisions concerning money—some opportunities are around the corner. Wishful thinking will be strong, so you must think realistically as well.

Monday, October 14 (Moon Libra to Scorpio 2:50 p.m.) You will feel ambitious today, and very self-confident in your abilities. You are doing a good job and those in charge recognize your hard work—so it's a perfect opportunity to ask for a raise or some other kind of advancement. Others will be impressed by your drive and your willingness to take on extra duties. A Capricorn may play an important role.

Tuesday, October 15 (Moon in Scorpio) Try to recognize your full potential. If you are pessimistic and fail to put all your energy into your work, it will be harmful to both you and your co-workers. Strive to communicate openly with those who can help you; don't keep any secrets or ideas to yourself. Be prepared to let go of the past in order to take on new projects—especially any doubts which have been holding you back.

Wednesday, October 16 (Moon Scorpio to Sagittarius 2:25 p.m.) It's time to make a new start, to let go of problems from the past, and to reach new levels of closeness and caring. You should strive to put relationships with close relatives on a new basis as well. You will be feeling independent and innovative, ready for change and variety—perhaps a new romantic adventure! Keep an eye out for a Leo.

Thursday, October 17 (Moon in Sagittarius) Today you will feel like staying inside and being alone to think and contemplate your situation. This will be your center of attention as material concerns make way for new spiritual values. Strive to get to know yourself and to improve family situations as well. Old memories may resurface, stirring feelings of nostalgia and sentiment.

Friday, October 18 (Moon Sagittarius to Capricorn 3:37 p.m.) Concern for family affairs will continue to be strong, and you will be ready to stay at home and smooth out any rough spots in your domestic life. However, your urge to travel will be strong as well, so plan your day in order to include both. Your popularity is high, and people will be attracted to your good mood. Take time to indulge in conversation with a philosophical Sagittarius.

Saturday, October 19 (Moon in Capricorn) You will have to pay special attention to details, especially if someone else is relying on you. Watch out for little kinks in the system and try to get rid of them in order to carry through. If you devote yourself to duty, you could be rewarded with a romantic outing or an evening of entertainment with someone special. This special person could be an Aquarius or a Leo.

Sunday, October 20 (Moon Capricorn to Aquarius 8:04 p.m.) After all your hard work, you are entitled to some fun and recreation—don't let anything keep you from enjoying yourself today! You will feel restless and itching for new adventures and excitement. Put your energy to good use by trying to fulfill your social desires. Your verbal ability is also high; so don't hesitate to speak your mind freely.

Monday, October 21 (Moon in Aquarius) Be willing to give advice and support to a friend who needs your help, especially if he/she shares your concerns about work and employment. You may feel obliged to comfort them as well—perhaps a gift of wine, art or music will do the trick. Rearrange your schedule so that you have time to socialize and talk to people. Try your luck with number 6.

Tuesday, October 22 (Moon in Aquarius) Your level of imagination is very high today, so use it to come up with creative new ideas—this could play a big role in terms of your career. You may find yourself solely in charge of a current project, and you will be able to take command with optimism. Just be careful not to conjure up problems that don't really exist—you are extra sensitive today.

Wednesday, October 23 (Moon Aquarius to Pisces 3:35 a.m.) A relationship could reach better and friendlier terms today, but you must be willing to work for it. Don't expect things to work themselves out on their own, you must make a strong effort. Be honest to yourself and to others, be careful not to make promises you can't keep. If any decisions are riding on you, make sure you consult people who have more experience. Their advice is worth a lot.

Thursday, October 24 (Moon in Pisces) Your positive side and your negative side are fighting an inner battle today. Your negative feelings are strong even though you know a positive attitude will gain wider appeal. Stir up any love and hope that have been buried inside and let them come out—don't be scared away by the possibility of crushed dreams. Try to associate with those who have the same hopeful visions.

Friday, October 25 (Moon Pisces to Aries 2:09 p.m.) You won't feel like listening to other people's ideas or suggestions, instead you will feel a desire to be independent. This may cause more problems at work, so be careful, and go slow. Once a mellow atmosphere has been established, you can put your own bright ideas to work. New opportunities may include a possible financial increase, so keep your eyes and ears open.

Saturday, October 26 (Moon in Aries) You will think a lot about your loved ones today, and how you could help to improve any existing situations concerning security and comfort. Budget-making and savings are also on your mind, as you will feel like saving up assets for a rainy day. However, don't be *too* miserly—investigate a bargain; it may well be worth the money.

Sunday, October 27 (Moon in Aries) An ability to ask the right questions will be extremely helpful today, especially if you are striving to solve a mystery. Insightful answers will clear up any confusions and lift any foggy thoughts. You will feel like engaging in social activity, but they may be more expensive than you originally expected. Don't spend lots of money without careful consideration.

Monday, October 28 (Full Moon 1:59 p.m. Moon Aries to Taurus 2:11 a.m.) You may feel like wandering off track today, and some rigid self-discipline will be needed to keep you from straying from your responsibilities. You will also feel the urge to expand your intellectual capacity through studying and higher education; so prepare yourself for a few "lessons." Don't try to pin your duties on someone else—the only way to get things accomplished is to do it yourself.

Tuesday, October 29 (Moon in Taurus) Your spirits will be brightened today by a well-needed change of scenery. This new atmosphere could bring about new feelings of spunk and ambition—so get out and go places! Someone from a different background may help you see "the other side of the coin," so get ready for an alteration of views and a new realization.

Wednesday, October 30 (Moon Taurus to Gemini 2:35 p.m.) A situation may occur today that calls for a tactful handling of feelings—don't be hesitant or evasive, it will just make things more difficult. Be careful not to take too much on your shoulders, don't try to be a hero or a big shot, as it could disrupt your family balance. Talk things out and reach a fair agreement. A Taurus or a Libra may play an important role.

Thursday, October 31 (Moon in Gemini) Yesterday you were concerned with family matters, but today your attention will turn to career and work possibilities. Be realistic about demands made on your time—don't take on more than you can handle just because you want praise and recognition. It would do you good to put aside selfish desires and focus on desires that include helping other people. Have a happy Halloween!

NOVEMBER 1985

Friday, November 1 (Moon in Gemini) Communication is very important today, whether it is verbal or written. Try to express yourself openly to those who can help you make vital changes, and who will offer valuable advice. You may find yourself involved in a short journey which brings you closer to a loved one; and a romantic situation may occur. A Gemini may step into the picture, and luck lies with number 5.

Saturday, November 2 (Moon Gemini to Cancer 3:12 a.m.) You are the one who must organize a social happening today, perhaps involving the family. Your energy level is high, so you may find yourself running around, trying to beautify your surroundings, and trying to find entertainment. You will be drawn to gourmet foods and good music. You also may find yourself face to face with someone who you have not been on good terms with, so try to cool things off. Forgive and forget!

Sunday, November 3 (Moon in Cancer) Be careful—your wishes and dreams are a bit unrealistic today. You must be honest with yourself in order to avoid a crushing disappointment. You may have a tendency to search the crowd for someone to idealize and strive to be like; make sure you know that person well and have good reason for your admiration. Don't fool yourself. Use your current feelings of sympathy to comfort a pal.

Monday, November 4 (Moon Cancer to Leo 3:12 a.m.) Maintain a serious attitude today, and show that you mean business. Carry through with your promises and do your job well in order to gain the prestige and admiration you so strongly desire. This applies to a love relationship as well—prove to your partner that you really care, that you are ready to make commitments. Try your luck with number 8 today.

Tuesday, November 5 (Moon in Leo) Today you will have a desire to put aside selfish goals and focus on helping those less fortunate. Others may not recognize your efforts at first, but it won't matter, because it will bring you inner satisfaction and help you to feel good about yourself. You will also feel quite creative, so let your artistic talents come out! An Aries may be involved in today's events.

Wednesday, November 6 (Moon Leo to Virgo 9:14 p.m.) Don't blindly follow others today; instead create your own, unique path and leave room for others behind you. You will feel like being a leader and letting some original, daring ideas clear your way. Some of these ideas may be old, hidden thoughts that have now resurfaced—use them well! You may find that a Leo is perfectly willing to support you.

Thursday, November 7 (Moon in Virgo) The moon moves into Virgo today! Expect some sort of psychic revelation—you will be feeling unusually perceptive and intuitive, and perhaps even blessed with certain powers of ESP! However be careful not to force issues, even though you are feeling "in command" of a personal situation. Don't become too involved with yourself and your own thoughts—family members need attention and consideration.

Friday, November 8 (Moon in Virgo) Congratulations! Your social world is expanding, you are ready for new activities, new journeys, perhaps a whole new image for yourself. You're in prime condition for a personal makeover, which may help to jolt you out of any rut you may have fallen into. However, be cautious—

don't take on *too* much, or you will feel too weighed down to carry on.

Saturday, November 9 (Moon Virgo to Libra 1:14 a.m.) Focus your attention on matters of money today. Try to balance your checkbook, review your savings account, and get all details straightened out. You must remain disciplined and stick to your daily routine in order to ensure a stable, comfortable situation. It will pay off in the long run, with more money and greater security.

Sunday, November 10 (Moon in Libra) Financial concerns continue to linger in your thoughts, as you strive to promote exciting developments. Great changes could occur, but you must be willing to make an extra effort. If things don't turn out exactly the way you wanted, don't hesitate to discuss and negotiate methods that will enable greater satisfaction. Try your luck with number 5 today.

Monday, November 11 (Moon Libra to Scorpio 1:53 a.m.) A family member will need extra warmth and support today, so be fully willing to express your love. It may be a good idea to add a special little touch—perhaps a gift of flowers, music, or another token of love. Your mood will be incredibly gracious, so use it to its full advantage. In return, your friends will feel honored, and will let you know it.

Tuesday, November 12 (Moon in Scorpio) Today you will feel like avoiding crowded, noisy places, social events, or superficial small talk. Your mood will be evasive and secretive, as well as unusually sensitive to the words of others—a good day to stay inside and avoid conflict. However don't let this distaste for other's opinions keep you completely isolated—a good talk with someone who cares may be just what you need.

Wednesday, November 13 (Moon Scorpio to Sagittarius 1:12 a.m.) A quality repair job in your home will help you feel more secure and more content with your living conditions. Repairs may also need to be made in a relationship—try to put down some roots, establish a greater permanency and a more solid position for yourself. Someone at the "top of the social ladder" will help you promote your interests, so be grateful.

Thursday, November 14 (Moon in Sagittarius) The completion of a current project looms into view, and will inspire you to get moving and keep busy. The possibility of a successful venture will cause you to think about the future, to start planning and generating new ideas. Try to look at the whole picture in order to understand how everything works and links together. Watch out for an Aries or a Libra today.

Friday, November 15 (Moon Sagittarius to Capricorn 1:10 a.m.) Today you will possess an unusually large amount of personal magnetism, which will cause admirers to flock around you. You will be feeling particularly flirtatious, but watch out! An innocent flirtation just may lead to something quite intense. You will be drawn to the magic of the theater, and may even feel like being a bit theatrical yourself—so put on a show, your friends will love it!

Saturday, November 16 (Moon in Capricorn) The romance of yesterday continues through this Saturday, bringing some tender and sentimental moments. Someone wants to depend on you, and is expecting quite a lot—so show you really care by catering to their whims and fancies. It is alright to expect a lot in return, as your desires to please are mutual. The lucky number of today is 2.

Sunday, November 17 (Moon Capricorn to Aquarius 3:54 a.m.) Don't hesitate to push business concerns aside for a little while, and to participate in a little social diversion. Say "yes!" to party or travel invitations. You will feel extra ready to join in some fun and adventure. Aside from all this lighthearted activity, you will also feel like seeking philosophical answers to some problems—so ask friends to lend ideas if you think it will help.

Monday, November 18 (Moon in Aquarius) You have been "playing" a lot lately, so now it's time to settle down and get back to serious hard work. A more disciplined routine is in store for you. Don't allow other people to take on your duties—do it yourself! This will provide you with self-confidence and well-needed motivation. Health matters are also important, so take good care of your body so that your mind will feel healthy as well.

Tuesday, November 19 (Moon Aquarius to Pisces 10:04 a.m.) Don't stick too hard to old-fashioned methods, even if you feel comfortable and secure with them. It's time to move on now, and to show that you are flexible, versatile, and willing to take on new methods. This daring attitude will be greatly welcomed by fellow employees, so don't be scared off by the threat of disapproval. Let your true emotions lead the way.

Wednesday, November 20 (Moon in Pisces) A dominating person whom you must deal with today may scare you into being soft-spoken and evasive of the issue at hand. You must try to muster up some tact, and get right into the heart of the matter as avoidance will only prolong the problem. Don't jump right into a decision, wait patiently until all the facts are uncovered. Saving time is not as important as making the right decision.

Thursday, November 21 (Moon Pisces to Aries 8:00 p.m.) Your romantic dreams may run a little wild today, creating a situation in your head that does not really exist. Be honest with yourself about someone whom you are very interested in—he/she may not be as perfect as you thought. Go slow in this relationship; don't rush things or make any hasty judgments. In any event, spiritual values will dominate your need for pleasure.

Friday, November 22 (Moon in Aries) Use any power you may possess in order to deal with a financial matter—a "pulling of strings" will be quite beneficial. Dig right into the problem, and go right to the top instead of dealing with underlings. Above all, don't worry too much—you may not know it, but a powerful ally is on your side. Speak up with ease and confidence, your voice will be heard and appreciated.

Saturday, November 23 (Moon in Aries) You have been serving as a crutch for someone who is afraid to walk on his/her own two feet. This person needs you to let go, even if it seems cruel at the time. You must help to encourage him/her towards independence; be friendly, but firm. Step back a few paces in order to view this relationship from a new perspective. This will make you feel as if you really helped someone—you did.

Sunday, November 24 (Moon Aries to Taurus 8:37 a.m.) Today a great transformation will take place inside of you. This change could bring a new feel for self-expression and some clever new ideas. You will feel like showing off, like dashing under the spotlight, like letting everyone see the new you! And it will work— your new image won't go unnoticed. Watch out for a passionate Leo.

Monday, November 25 (Moon in Taurus) You will feel very dreamy today, and your head will be filled with fantasies of faraway places. However these will only be fantasies, as you will actually prefer the warmth and security of your own home. Your imagination will be very strong, so try to use it not only to dream, but to think up some creative new methods. Number 2 is today's lucky number.

Tuesday, November 26 (Moon in Taurus) Yesterday you felt quite lazy and passive, but today will bring you to the other extreme as you find yourself feeling restless and ready to move. In fact, you will feel *too* restless, both mentally and physically, to deal with routine matters, so now is a perfect time to put travel plans in motion. Study and learn in order to satisfy your curiosity, and engage in a fiery discussion if that will help vent some energy.

Wednesday, November 27 (Moon Taurus to Gemini 9:02 p.m.) Today you will feel like pursuing some personal goals, and you may realize that career matters are standing in your way. You must make a decision as to which is more important at this point. However, you are building for the future now, so remember to be diligent, see projects through, and read between the lines. Steer away from a person who may distract you from your concentration.

Thursday, November 28 (Moon in Gemini) Some restrictions that have been holding you back may lift today, making you feel free and ready to move on. Keep active and strive to make new contacts in order to advance your professional life—you have no excuse not to go for your dreams! You may be tempted by a possible romantic affair, but think carefully about the consequences before jumping in.

Friday, November 29 (Moon Gemini to Cancer 8:59 a.m.) If you are involved in any disagreements that come up at home or at work, try to smooth things out by serving as "peacemaker"—someone's got to do it, so it might as well be you. Try not to lean too heavily on one side, be realistic yet diplomatic to everyone involved. Whatever you do will most likely be noticed by a lot of people, so make sure you do it right.

Saturday, November 30 (Moon in Cancer) You will feel like establishing a warm, loving friendship today. However, try not to be too sensitive, as your head is in the clouds and you are unusually susceptible to disappointment. Try to learn the true story before you suffer hurt feelings—a little reality now will help you avoid a lot of pain later. If you feel like "spilling your guts," an equally sensitive Pisces will be glad to listen.

DECEMBER 1985

Sunday, December 1 (Moon Cancer to Leo 8:04 p.m.)
Today you're in the mood for luxurious entertainment and lavish feasts, but be careful not to overdo it. An equal amount of time should be devoted to business matters. Your artistic talents will be quite strong, so use them in order to start a creative project. You will also be in the mood for romance, so keep your eye on a sentimental, distinctive person whom you admire.

Monday, December 2 (Moon in Leo) You will feel extra sensitive to vibrations today, and unusually susceptible to extreme emotions. Try to stay away from crowds or social events, you will feel much more comfortable at home. Find a warm, cozy atmosphere in which you can contemplate spiritual values, search for inspirations, and strive to find deeper meanings. A Pisces may cross your path.

Tuesday, December 3 (Moon in Leo) Don't hesitate to ask for favors today, but make sure you do so in private. You just may get what you are looking for, as long as you are careful not to make a public issue of your requests. The person who is granting your favor would prefer it to be a secret. If you show your reliability, it just may lead to a boost in status or a financial gain. Today's lucky number is 8.

Wednesday, December 4 (Moon Leo to Virgo 4:38 a.m.) The moon is in your own house, Virgo, today, so you will be feeling expecially motivated and energetic. You may even receive some unexpected publicity which will make you feel good about yourself. Strive to let go of old chains which have been restricting your movement. Now is the time to explore your full potential, and to move on to new accomplishments.

Thursday, December 5 (Moon in Virgo) Your face will definitely stand out in the crowd today, as you are blessed with personal magnetism. Renewed vitality and optimism are in abundance, and your improved spirits will cause your looks to improve as well. A Leo could be among the people who notice you today, and your lucky number is 1.

Friday, December 6 (Moon Virgo to Libra 9:44 a.m.) You may be treated to an incredible meal today, but keep your eyes on the scale and keep the consequences in mind. A family member or friend may be acting lost and alone, so this is where you should step in to provide extra comfort. You are feeling emotional, so put your sensitivity to good use. You may find luck with number 2.

Saturday, December 7 (Moon in Libra) Your financial picture will be a little foggy today, and you may end up spending a lot more than you originally planned. This is because you are in an extravagant mood, and at the same time unusually gullible, so you are the perfect victim for a fast-talking salesperson—watch out! Have fun today, but make sure you don't burn yourself out with a lot of frantic running around. Take it easy!

Sunday, December 8 (Moon Libra to Scorpio 1:05 p.m.) Yesterday's careless spending will cause you to take a more conservative course, which is your best bet. Count every penny, balance your checkbook, and decide just how much you should allow yourself to spend for the rest of the season. This is a day where you must put practical money details before luxurious desires. Today's lucky number is 4.

Monday, December 9 (Moon in Scorpio) Expect a well-needed change of scenery today, or new variety of some sort. An alteration of daily matters will help you overcome feelings of boredom and futile routine. Communication is very important, especially if you come in contact with an active, mentally quick individual who seems romantically interested. Just make sure you get the story behind the story.

Tuesday, December 10 (Moon Scorpio to Sagittarius 1:11 p.m.) If you have been feeling sad or guilty about losing contact with a friend, don't hesitate any longer. The holiday season provides a great opportunity for you to send a card, letter, or gift; do it, it will make you feel better. You may receive some news about relatives or neighbors, and may find yourself involved in some gossip. Don't believe everything you hear!

Wednesday, December 11 (Moon in Sagittarius) Try to clear up any confusions that exist within the family today, especially ones pertaining to basic values. You may find yourself in the middle of a nasty conflict, so do all you can to make the situation better for everyone involved. You will have to try to remove yourself from the action in order to see the situation clearly from an outsider's perspective.

Thursday, December 12 (Moon Sagittarius to Capricorn 1:03 p.m.) A current relationship could reach new levels of intensity, stirring some discussion about putting down roots. Try to follow your true emotions, they will lead you to the right path and the right decision. Any plans for the future will receive praise and approval from the family, so don't hesitate to be honest and straightforward.

Friday, December 13 (Moon in Capricorn) You may feel self-indulgent today, but you will find that the day will be more enjoyable if you think of other people first. Try to let your concern for others overpower your selfish motives, and try to get across your feelings of hope and optimism. If you express them strongly enough, you may inspire others to be equally hopeful. Working for a cause would add to your feelings of self-satisfaction.

Saturday, December 14 (Moon Capricorn to Aquarius 1:34 p.m.) This day has the potential to be incredibly romantic—don't let an independent attitude spoil your chances. Feel free to be dependent on someone, it could actually improve your relationship. Make the first move if your partner seems slow, and try to entertain him/her with your wit and imagination. You're a winner today, so let it show.

Sunday, December 15 (Moon in Aquarius) Your intuition will be quite remarkable today, as you find that you are almost able to read minds! This unique talent will be very handy. Try to be where you will prove most helpful, and spread some love and affection where it is needed. If you have been putting off any chores, it's time to get moving now! Don't save things for the last minute.

Monday, December 16 (Moon Aquarius to Pisces 6:21 p.m.) Today you will experience a strong sense of adventure, but you'll find that you must focus your attention on work. Instead of trying to kill your adventurous spirit, try to combine them with your work obligations in order to create a bolder approach to your job. You will be blessed with charm and a particularly abundant sense of humor, so use them to their fullest extent.

Tuesday, December 17 (Moon in Pisces) Don't be overly ambitious to take a leadership position today; go along with associates and allow another to take the lead while you focus on practical details. Instead of trying to come up with flashy new plans, it would be a better idea to stick to routine and disciplined activities until you feel more comfortable. Today's lucky number is 4.

Wednesday, December 18 (Moon in Pisces) You won't feel like being alone today, you would much rather spend time communicating and talking to other people. This fear of loneliness will cause you to listen eagerly to a romantic proposal, which will spark new interests and opportunities. Your artistic talents will be strong, so try to get involved in a project that calls for creativity.

Thursday, December 19 (Moon Pisces to Aries, 2:55 a.m.) Your tastes are becoming incredibly luxurious, so be extra careful how much you spend today. Some simple items may cost a lot more than you expected, and the price of entertaining also seems to be going up. However don't let this stop you from organizing a holiday party—it will provide the perfect atmosphere for you to rediscover old sentimental ties.

Friday, December 20 (Moon in Aries) Money worries continue to dominate your mind, as you find cash rapidly disappearing. It is imperative that you keep track of your expenditures and remain realistic about the cost of future plans. Careful planning now will save you a lot of hardship later. An air of mystery and aloofness is surrounding you today, so you may stir up a lot of curious minds.

Saturday, December 21 (Moon Aries to Taurus 3:09 p.m.) This is a day of power struggles at work, but you won't have to compete for attention. You will get all the praise you deserve through hard work, diligence, and ability—not through sneaky schemes or maneuvers. Someone in an authority position will recognize this, admire you, and will show it with warm affection—perhaps even financial recognition.

Sunday, December 22 (Moon in Taurus) Travel and greater communication will inspire you today, and cause you to feel especially ambitious and ready to move on to new ways of life. You may reach a higher level of understanding if you take the time to think and contemplate new situations. Strive to see the whole, full picture instead of wallowing in petty details. Today's lucky number is 9.

Monday, December 23 (Moon in Taurus) You're a leader today! Your style is distinctive, causing you to stand out in a glamorous way. Other people will be attracted to you like magnets, and you will feel ready to run off on exciting new adventures. Your leadership attitude will be obvious, so don't expect others to make the first move. Follow your bold, aggressive instincts.

Tuesday, December 24 (Moon Taurus to Gemini 3:46 a.m.) Your family is extremely important in helping you to realize your dreams and ambitions. They will gladly urge you on and give you all the strength and support you need to carry through. Their caring attitudes will cause you to feel very emotional, and your gratitude will be stirred even more by a thoughtful gift from a relative. Show your warmth and appreciation.

Wednesday, December 25 (Moon in Gemini) Merry Christmas! Today will be socially active and intellectually stimulating at the same time. Your sense of humor will keep everyone laughing, and your charm will keep everyone interested. However, beware of *too* much activity. Try to deal with one event at a time—too many irons in the fire will prove to be quite dangerous! The lucky number of today is 3.

Thursday, December 26 (Moon Gemini to Cancer 3:41 p.m.) It's time to get back to practical concerns and clear up any details surrounding a project. There may be an obstacle in your way, so this is a perfect opportunity to prove yourself to others by successfully overcoming that obstacle. You can do so by cutting through a little red tape. If the job is well done, you'll glow with pleasure and pride.

Friday, December 27 (Full Moon 2:46 a.m. Moon in Cancer) Your social life improves today with the lifting of old restrictions. You will feel free to pursue personal desires, or to plan a journey that you have been putting off. You may experience a friendly exchange of ideas with an intelligent person, and he/she will help you expand your own intellectual capacity. Be receptive to exciting changes!

Saturday, December 28 (Moon in Cancer) You will be right in the middle of a family gathering today, and you may find yourself the main "organizer." Don't shun your obligations if other people are relying on you, you may even have to smooth out some ruffled feathers if that becomes necessary. Take some extra time off to visit a loved one whom you haven't seen in a while. A Libra or a Taurus may play an important role.

Sunday, December 29 (Moon Cancer to Leo 1:57 a.m.) You will come upon a fork in the road today—one path leads to new heights of inspiration, the other leads to new depths of despair. The road you find yourself on all depends on your attitude, so maintain a positive one. Wherever you end up, be careful, because you are extra sensitive today and your reactions will be extreme. Solitude will be helpful in order to think things through.

Monday, December 30 (Moon in Leo) If you hear about new career opportunities, don't go flapping your tongue all over town—remain quiet until you obtain all the information and all the facts. Someone could be watching you and secretly discussing your abilities, so be wary of any observant eyes. You have a chance to gain more recognition if you do your job right. Today's lucky number is 8.

Tuesday, December 31 (Moon Leo to Virgo 10:00 a.m.) The arrival of the new year brings the dawning of a new day for you—but don't think only of yourself, share some of life's privileges with those less fortunate. Try not to have a defeatist attitude for the future, as it will do nothing but stunt your mental growth. Don't be influenced by those who are pessimistic about the upcoming year—celebrate with people who will share your optimism and good cheer. Have fun!

JANUARY 1986

Wednesday, January 1 (Moon in Virgo) What a way to start out the year! With the moon in your own sign, you should be off and running—and have a head start. All your best qualities are highlighted today, and you are able to be much more optimistic than usual. Your sparkling Virgo wit will be required today—as you entertain others. All in all, your sense of balance is excellent now.

Thursday, January 2 *(Moon Virgo to Libra 3:45 p.m.)* This is "good news" day. For some, the subject is money—and it could be a surprise. Good reports come in from other people too, and you may have the occasion to congratulate someone in your own family. Things are even running smoothly on the homefront after a successful adjustment. The lucky number is 6.

Friday, January 3 *(Moon in Libra)* You may have to set someone straight today, and you should not hesitate to define your terms the way you want them defined. Someone gives you an excellent suggestion, and you should recognize it as such—and respond. Try to start clearing the decks for a much more active time to come. That may mean getting rid of some things you definitely do not need.

Saturday, January 4 *(Moon Libra to Scorpio 7:44 p.m.)* Many Virgos are involved in a relationship which is beginning to intensify; you will learn a lot about love now. Others are getting more responsibility, along with a chance to increase their income. Trust your judgment today. And a Capricorn who comes along. The lucky number is 8.

Sunday, January 5 *(Moon in Scorpio)* Many of you will be relieved by some good news about someone's progress today. Others will be talking about an upcoming trip or visit to someone they haven't seen in a while. All in all, you should be happy and optimistic. An Aries or a Libra could help you maintain that mood.

Monday, January 6 *(Moon Scorpio to Sagittarius 9:47 p.m.)* Try to assert your own individuality now, even though you may feel a bit restricted. It is important to know that you are not without allies, and that you can "score points." A Leo may help you get to the heart of an important matter.

Tuesday, January 7 (Moon in Sagittarius) Don't try to be your own appraiser; you need someone more expert to tell you the true value of something. Be absolutely positive about what you have and what you need; it's time to begin a "new deal" where your security is concerned, both emotional and financial. The lucky number is 2.

Wednesday, January 8 (Moon Sagittarius to Capricorn 10:42 p.m.) Ask as many questions as you feel like asking now, because you deserve the answers. Many Virgos will find that their contributions are appreciated, and that they can safely be a bit more experimental. Some should start thinking about getting more space, in every sense of the word.

Thursday, January 9 (Moon in Capricorn) If you feel that someone is not telling you the truth today, you are probably right. Just realize that this person is trying to be diplomatic, even if he/she isn't being completely honest. Children may figure big in the day's activities and require some attention. Some can expect to be contacted by an old flame. Be confident about your physical attractiveness.

Friday, January 10 (Moon in Capricorn) Some will be experiencing the excitement of discovery now. Others will be delighted to realize that what seemed to be a casual romance is turning into a strong, meaningful relationship. Any of you should be able to really show your own style now. Take some tips from a Gemini or a Sagittarian.

Saturday, January 11 (Moon Capricorn to Aquarius 12:01 a.m.) Accept a token of someone's affection, because it is meant sincerely. You may not feel the same way, however. People around you should be rather cooperative today, and you may even find someone telling you how to do something a better way. You can always learn.

Sunday, January 12 (Moon in Aquarius) Once again, you should be feeling in harmony with those around you—and realizing that they share your purposes and goals. It should give you the confidence to make a definite decision. Some may have to be decisive of getting rid of junk that's been accumulating and is no longer needed. Be ruthless about it! The lucky number is 7.

Monday, January 13 (Moon Aquarius to Pisces 3:39 a.m.) You should realize that you are in a strong position now—possibly even a winner. Some Virgos will have to pay more attention to the rules and regulations than they have in the recent past. In some cases, the law is involved. Take some time out today to pay attention to your most important partnership—possibly your marriage. It may need some help.

Tuesday, January 14 (Moon in Pisces) You should feel a strong sense of accomplishment about finishing something now. It should be a great load off your mind. For some, it is definitely time to start doing some self-promotion. It does not come naturally to you, but you have every opportunity to do it now. Let a Libra help you.

Wednesday, January 15 (Moon Pisces to Aries 11:03 a.m.) Watch it! Someone may attempt to trip you up. Don't let that happen, and show this person just how on your toes you are. It will be a rude awakening. Some will find out that what appeared to be a setback is actually a good thing—for ultimate success. The lucky number today is 1.

Thursday, January 16 (Moon in Aries) It would be easy for you to overindulge today—particularly in rich food. Try to be smart about it, because you recently made some resolutions about your health. In all ways, stick to familiar ground today. Someone you have been in doubt about shows that he/she does have your best interest at heart.

Friday, January 17 (Moon Aries to Taurus 10:14 p.m.) Someone may be brutally frank with you today—possibly about your appearance. Try not to overreact, because this person is sincere in wanting to help you. Before the end of the day, many Virgos will receive an exciting invitation—possibly involving future travel. Try not to get down on yourself today. The lucky number is 3.

Saturday, January 18 (Moon in Taurus) Some kind of a restriction comes to an end. Many of you will feel moved to show your appreciation in some tangible way. You are right to be generous with this person. For some, education is a prime interest now. For others, romance is very much on their minds.

Sunday, January 19 (Moon in Taurus) It is important to make your views known now; if you get the facts on the record, you will be protecting yourself for the future. Some Virgos should be aware that somebody is taking "poetic license" with the truth; try to sort out fact from fiction. A Gemini could be very important.

Monday, January 20 (Moon Taurus to Gemini 11:12 a.m.) Someone may be very free with his/her advice today, and it could get on your nerves. Be polite, but do not waste your time. Some Virgos will find a way to elevate their prestige; others will become concerned about the status of a relationship. Is it going to last much longer? Go slow, and be very specific.

Tuesday, January 21 (Moon in Gemini) Something unexpected may happen today that threatens to throw you off-balance. Don't panic, things will not only calm down, they will ultimately go in your favor. There's a lot going on behind the scenes, and you have someone important backing you up all the way. The lucky number today is 7.

Wednesday, January 22 (Moon Gemini to Cancer 11:14 p.m.) Don't believe the first thing you hear today; the report could be false. It is important not to rush to judgment, and to keep your options open. Some Virgos will have a member of the opposite sex commit him-/herself today; suddenly you are deeply involved. A response is required.

Thursday, January 23 (Moon in Cancer) There is a special softness about you today, and people may be drawn to you—some to applaud, and others to seek your counsel. Take time out to be nice. For some, a wish comes true—possibly when something that was not your problem in the first place is taken off your hands.

Friday, January 24 (Moon in Cancer) You should feel very surrounded by friends and supporters today; there is no reason to feel you must go it alone. Some will get a rather unique assignment, as well as the chance to show how clever they can be. Keep your eye on an Aquarian. The lucky number is 1.

Saturday, January 25 (Moon Cancer to Leo 8:47 a.m.) Your sales ability should be very good today, and you should put it to good use. Possibly by using an element of surprise, which is at your disposal. Somebody who's been against you recently suddenly is all for you, and it should be an excellent feeling. The lucky number is 2.

Sunday, January 26 (Moon in Leo) This full moon may be a bit unsettling for you. In some cases, it may stir up some secret fears and suspicions. There is no reason to be paranoid. Use your "funny feelings" to do something unusual in an out-of-the-way place. It could be a very romantic time. Once again, an Aquarian could be prominent in the picture.

Monday, January 27 (Moon Leo to Virgo 3:51 p.m.) Don't let a temporary delay get you down; things will soon look a lot brighter. Take this time to get a second wind and to do some soul-searching. It's important for some Virgos to remember either a special anniversary or a message of cheer owed to someone who is confined. Make it something nice.

Tuesday, January 28 (Moon in Virgo) With the moon in your sign you should be looking great and feeling the same way. Almost without your planning, you should find yourself in the right place at the right time. Take advantage of this day to ask for what you want; you have every possibility of getting it. Both in love and in business. The lucky number is 5.

Wednesday, January 29 (Moon Virgo to Libra 9:10 p.m.) You are much more able to take the initiative today than you usually are; it is the key to success now! Take advantage of this time and show both originality and the courage to walk down a new road. Some may be going through a major change in their lifestyle; the adjustment should be positive. It could involve your place of residence or your mental status.

Thursday, January 30 (Moon in Libra) Stay calm and stay confident; this should be another good day. Some will actually recoup a recent loss; others will find something they thought had been stolen. For many, an old friend turns up and is ready to do a favor. With interest. The lucky number is 7.

Friday, January 31 (Moon in Libra) Most should find themselves very appreciated—possibly even promoted as well. At least, you will have more responsibility and know that you matter. In your personal life you can make a power play. That means, if you wanted to, you can make a relationship permanent now. And feel more emotionally secure as a result.

FEBRUARY 1986

Saturday, February 1 (Moon Libra to Scorpio 1:19 a.m.) Many are in for a pleasant surprise. It could come in the form of an actual gift that someone gives you "just for being you." Tuck this away in your permanent memory book. People around you are surprisingly cooperative as well; you should respond in kind. The lucky number is 6.

Sunday, February 2 (Moon in Scorpio) Refuse to get confused today; someone may be doing it on purpose. Be very selective about what you do and who you do it with; a lot of opportunities may be presented to you. Some Virgos will have a chance to prove a major point today, but should not gloat. Be as pleasant as possible.

Monday, February 3 (Moon Scorpio to Sagittarius 4:31 a.m.) Practical issues dominate this Monday. Even though you may try to keep things on the upbeat side, it is likely that you are going to have enough to do that you really feel bogged down. Don't buckle under! In your personal life, matters of property may be very important. Realize that you can afford to relax later on.

Tuesday, February 4 (Moon in Sagittarius) Know when something is over and done with, and don't hang around too long. Stay alert for your cues. Some Virgos may get very nervous today when someone tries to intimidate them; stand up for your rights. Realize that you do not have to accept things as they are, but that you can reach higher. The lucky number is 9.

Wednesday, February 5 (Moon Sagittarius to Capricorn 7:02 a.m.) This could be an extremely emotional day—for some, that means the possibility of falling madly in love. It could be with a person, or it could be with an idea. In some cases, there will be an opportunity to correct a past mistake, and possibly to revive a relationship where you thought the fire had gone out completely.

Thursday, February 6 (Moon in Capricorn) If you thought yesterday was a wild day, wait until you see what happens today! There is a highly combustible atmosphere in effect, and you should try to use it constructively. That means you can be creative in any number of different ways—including in your love life—but you can also blow something totally out of proportion. Let a cool Aquarian or a sober Capricorn give you some advice about how to handle things.

Friday, February 7 (Moon Capricorn to Aquarius 7:35 a.m.) Your mood should be excellent, and that means you should be able to transform something you must do into something you really want to do. Today you can make a lot of fun for yourself, if you want to. The pleasure principle is emphasized in any number of ways, and you could find yourself being wined and dined. Some will get a new insight into someone they think they know well. What a surprise!

Saturday, February 8 (Moon in Aquarius) If you feel you are being tested, this time you are not imagining things. You must be alert, and take care of your own interests. Your wisest course is to stick to familiar ground, and demonstrate your willingness to go along with the crowd. Someone you thought was indifferent now indicates that he/she is interested in what you have to say. The lucky number is 4.

Sunday, February 9 (Moon Aquarius to Pisces 11:32 a.m.) In general, Virgos are keen, shrewd observers, and today someone will compliment you on these abilities. Don't hesitate to give full rein to your intellectual curiosity, because it can be satisfied now. Those who are creative will find this an excellent day to make progress in their work. For others, a Gemini or another Virgo could be an excellent and stimulating companion.

Monday, February 10 (Moon in Pisces) Don't overreact to someone who is really trying to help you. Slow down in both speech and action, and try to be as diplomatic as possible. You are going to need all the help you can get. Someone's ideas stimulate and challenge you today, but you should not let things escalate into an argument. Be as cooperative as possible.

Tuesday, February 11 (Moon Pisces to Aries 6:21 p.m.) Snooping is an activity you sometimes consider necessary; today it may really be necessary. You've got to find out what's going on behind the scenes before you can decide upon a course of action. Even if you don't go after it, a secret will come your way—and you will be relieved as a result. Once more, the focus is on interaction of others and there is the necessity to be cooperative. The lucky number is 7.

Wednesday, February 12 (Moon in Aries) Don't try to go it alone. Confer with someone who understands money and business better than you do. Your potential is very high now, and you could possibly strike it rich—but not without doing something about it. Some will have more responsibility but it is what they wanted. Someone may be after you to "do something," and you don't know what he/she really wants.

Thursday, February 13 (Moon in Aries) Many Virgos are coming to the end of a cycle, and finishing off something important. Others are wondering how to get started in a new direction; a member of the opposite sex provides excellent guidelines. Your humanitarian instinct will be stimulated today and you should act upon it. Someone really needs love and care more than you do.

Friday, February 14 (Moon Aries to Taurus 4:38 a.m.) This could be a banner Valentine's Day for many Virgos. Messages—especially from a distance—come in and relieve some of your anxious feeling about where you stand. In all ways, the emphasis is on affection today as well as spiritual insight. Many will learn a lot more about love and reality. Don't neglect to send any of your important messages.

Saturday, February 15 (Moon in Taurus) You may be a bit confused today by a lot of back and forth about who will be available when. Keep your special events calendar handy! Someone who really respects your ideas may throw you a curve by challenging one of them. Do not react in anger. Some Virgos should trust their first impressions today—as well as a Cancer, a Capricorn, or an Aquarian who offers advice. The lucky number is 2.

Sunday, February 16 (Moon Taurus to Gemini 5:17 p.m.) Many will feel very dissatisfied with the status quo now. You are right to indulge your desire and variety—as well as your curiosity about someone or something that crossed your path recently. Keep your eye on future trends, because you can make a big score by predicting them. For some, a very romantic interlude provides a lot of just the spice they are looking for.

Monday, February 17 (Moon in Gemini) Many Virgos will be delighted today when someone who has seemed a bit distant now warms up considerably. All of you can make this an excellent day to communicate with those who are difficult. There will be a chance to correct a mistake, and to say today what should have been said yesterday. Lucky you! The lucky number is 4.

Tuesday, February 18 (Moon in Gemini) Don't be embarrassed by the amount of attention you get today; a lot of people are going to be interested in what you think, say and write. One in particular—possibly a member of the opposite sex—will ask an awful lot of questions. You are wise to answer them. This is one day you can really make an impact.

Wednesday, February 19 (Moon Gemini to Cancer 7:39 a.m.) You should be able to impress higher ups today with your knowledge of things that go beyond the requirements of your job. However, for many it will be necessary to be diplomatic—and even to show that you can be gracious when you are the victor. Spend some time thinking about how you can beautify your personal environment. It could do you a lot of good. The lucky number is 6.

Thursday, February 20 (Moon in Cancer) This is a switch! What you thought was a false premise turns out to be real. When your wish comes true, thank the proper people. In many ways it is a day to be happier than you thought you could be under the circumstances. Keep your balance, because an aura of mystery is in the air. Don't tell all you know.

Friday, February 21 (Moon Cancer to Leo 3:25 p.m.) If you've got something to sell, today's the day to sell it. Your powers of persuasion should be particularly good. In some cases, it will be a member of the opposite sex who is drawn to you—amd makes no secret of his/her interest. Make the most of it! A Capricorn could be prominent in the picture.

Saturday, February 22 (Moon in Leo) If you've been looking for information, today you get it—possibly more answers than you thought were there. When the mystery is solved, it proves very advantageous for you. Most should be aware that the potential is greater than they think, and that facing a big assignment really is worth the trouble. The lucky number is 9.

Sunday, February 23 (Moon Leo to Virgo 11:58 p.m.) Stick with it today, because better things are coming. Even if something appears to be a loss, realize that it can be transformed into a gain later on. Whatever you do, insist on straight answers and do not accept evasive ones. A Leo could be very prominent.

Monday, February 24 (Moon in Virgo) This is the best full moon of the year for Virgo, occurring as it does in your own sign. Don't waste a minute, and don't fail to follow through on any of your intuitive feelings. They are most likely to be correct. You are at the peak of a cycle. Some will get involved in petty family differences, but should try to rise above them. Some apologies will be in order later on—to you, that is.

Tuesday, February 25 (Moon in Virgo) You should be riding on your moon high. Get around as much as possible, and build as many bridges as possible. Some of you will be intrigued by a very restless person—a Gemini—who seems to have the answers to how you can overcome some seemingly insurmountable barriers. Listen carefully, and take notes.

Wednesday, February 26 (Moon Virgo to Libra 4:07 a.m.) Without even trying, you come by some fascinating information about how to make the most of your assets. Don't be surprised—it's what's "coming to you." However, it is important to keep your own counsel, and not to spread the good news around. You have the inside track, and you should keep it. For many, the cash flow resumes.

Thursday, February 27 (Moon in Libra) You really want to make the right move now, and you have the energy for it. Keep your eye on the main chance, and you can achieve your goal. Many will find they have a new friend and new access to words of love and support. A Gemini, a Sagittarian, or another Virgo could play a key role today. The lucky number is 5.

Friday, February 28 (Moon Libra to Scorpio 7:06 a.m.) Don't give in to temptation today; it may come in the form of a sweet tooth. You've been very good about your diet recently, and should resolve to stick to the plan. For many of you, the money picture continues to be bright, and you even stumble upon some real bargains. There are some! The lucky number is 6.

MARCH 1986

Saturday, March 1 (Moon in Scorpio) Don't box yourself in today, but keep all your options open. Realize that somebody who makes a promise is probably sincere, but also doesn't know what he/she is talking about. Do not be confused when someone who does not have the authority gives you an order; the *real* boss may say something quite different. It is important not to be gullible now, and to insist on clear definitions by people who set down terms. Protect your own interests.

Sunday, March 2 (Moon Scorpio to Sagittarius 9:51 a.m.) Some very interesting facts surface today and give you a clearer picture of a rather murky situation. You can get an even more complete story by putting together bits of information. For many, a relationship is growing stronger. Are you ready for the additional responsibility? Keep your eye open for a money opportunity that someone casually drops.

Monday, March 3 (Moon in Sagittarius) Don't overplay your hand today, it is important to know when you've won and should quickly leave the scene. This is a rather stable day, and you should feel quite secure—particularly in financial matters. Someone will come along and untangle some red tape for you, enabling you to complete the transaction. What a relief! The lucky number is 9.

Tuesday, March 4 (Moon Sagittarius to Capricorn 12:56 p.m.) Let someone know you are willing to go back to square one and start all over again. Also let it be known that you are quite independent and do not take orders from anyone else. You can show a pioneering spirit now as well as the courage of your convictions. It will do you a lot of good to do so.

Wednesday, March 5 (Moon in Capricorn) Your emotions could easily run away with you today; try to keep your logical mind in place. When someone close to you disagrees with your choice, do not make a big issue out of it. You can be a good listener and still maintain your principles. A Cancer, a Capricorn, or an Aquarian could be a best friend today—and give you the lift you need.

Thursday, March 6 (Moon Capricorn to Aquarius 4:42 p.m.) If you make a snap decision today, you may regret it. There will be some quick changes, but that does not have to throw you off. Some may receive an invitation to travel. Others may suddenly find themselves in the midst of a "new love." It is important to keep the lines of communication open, so no matter what happens, keep on talking.

Friday, March 7 (Moon in Aquarius) Don't be too proud to get help today; this may be the only way to get the job done. Whatever you decide to do, you will find that it is necessary to review something and possibly do extra work in order to make right. Somebody who looks like a competitor—possibly a Scorpio—will prove more helpful than you can possibly imagine. The lucky number is 4.

Saturday, March 8 (Moon Aquarius to Pisces 7:48 a.m.) Someone who says he/she thinks you are just wonderful may offer advice, but you are wise to take it with a grain of salt. It is rather impractical. The way to success now is to be your own person and act in your own interest. One thing that means is getting promises in writing. Don't back down!

Sunday, March 9 (Moon in Pisces) Even though you may not like it much, you are going to have to make some kind of an adjustment today. Probably right under your own roof. It is a time when you can learn a lot about cooperation and joint efforts. For many, someone around them wants a change and makes no secret of it. Some can make things a lot better by remembering a special anniversary.

Monday, March 10 (Moon in Pisces) Now's the time to make a clean break with the past. For some, that is as simple as getting rid of unnecessary things and junk that has accumulated. For others, it will be more complicated, but ending something means beginning something else. You would do a good public relations job for yourself today. The lucky number is 7.

Tuesday, March 11 *(Moon Pisces to Aries 5:03 a.m.)* A money problem may arise today, but if you keep cool, it could be settled in your favor. A lot of pressure is indicated, as well as a lot of responsibility. However, some may discover they had assets they never even dreamed of. Keep on digging for that information—you could strike pay dirt.

Wednesday, March 12 *(Moon in Aries)* Today should have a much lighter tone, and you should be feeling more optimistic. Many can expect to meet new people now, and for some, they will be of the romantic variety. If you choose to, you can widen your personal horizons a great deal now. An Aries could be extremely helpful now.

Thursday, March 13 *(Moon Aries to Taurus 3:04 p.m.)* Don't believe everything you hear or read today; someone may be attempting to do a cover-up job. You are going to have to be very neutral now, and even possibly to walk a tightrope. Love or money could be involved. Rely on the help of a very warm person, possibly a Leo. The lucky number is 1.

Friday, March 14 *(Moon in Taurus)* The moon position is quite favorable today, particularly toward matters that involve travel and the imparting of information. For one thing, you should be able to make yourself quite clear now. Someone a bit weird really is on your side, but needs some affection from you. After the dust settles, this person can be extremely helpful. The lucky number is 2.

Saturday, March 15 *(Moon in Taurus)* Things are not quite usual today, and there could be a shakeup in the status quo. However, it should be in your favor. Both your physical and your emotional self should be quite charismatic today. If you've got something you want to sell, today's the day to sell it. Some will be delighted when a clarification makes them realize they are going in the right direction.

Sunday, March 16 (Moon Taurus to Gemini 3:23 a.m.) Now the puzzle pieces are really falling into place. You should feel secure enough to say No when you mean it. It may be a real break with tradition for you. Show that you are able to rise above petty quarrels. Someone—possibly a Scorpio or a Taurus—will find you quite fascinating now.

Monday, March 17 (Moon in Gemini) Many will renew a friendship now, and feel a lot better for it. Others will find something else to celebrate. Either way, this day looks quite positive. However, you are going to have to avoid some people who could waste your time with a lot of talk that means nothing. The evening should be lovely!

Tuesday, March 18 (Moon Gemini to Cancer 4:04 p.m.) More than one Virgo will receive a surprise gift today. In some cases, it is the result of a favor you did for someone—and almost forgot about. For many, romance is very much a part of the day and feels extremely good. Your opposite number could be a Taurus, a Libra, or a Scorpio. The lucky number is 6.

Wednesday, March 19 (Moon in Cancer) This is one of those days when a wish could actually come true. However, it might come true in a rather unusual manner. For some, it will come true learning a secret quite by accident. For others, it will be the result of finding something they thought they had lost. Whatever happens, you should feel very lucky—and be so today.

Thursday, March 20 (Moon in Cancer) Don't let anything hold you back from making a play for what you want today. Financial gain or emotional fulfillment are possible as they have not been in the recent past.

Some of you may begin to build your own private empire now. When you speak today, it will be with a silver tongue.

Friday, March 21 *(Moon Cancer to Leo 2:38 a.m.)*
Something is over and done with, and you should admit it. There is no point in brooding over the past. For some, what ends is a relationship that was draining them both emotionally and financially. You are well rid of this "security blanket." You do not have to be so self-sacrificing; it is time to be creatively selfish. The lucky number is 9.

Saturday, March 22 *(Moon in Leo)* This could be a positively fascinating day, particularly for those who dare to tread in new areas. None of you should be lonely, even if you are temporarily alone. It is an excellent time to commune with your soul. It is also a good moment to remember those who are less fortunate than you.

Sunday, March 23 *(Moon Leo to Virgo 9:39 a.m.)*
Here you go, off into Virgo moon time. That means you should be quite sure of yourself now and should even trust your hunches. Your intuitive intellect is a reliable guide. However, it is wise to stick with what you know, and to choose the bright side over the dark side. That means don't get drawn into an intrigue. A very loyal person will prove he/she deserves your love.

Monday, March 24 *(Moon in Virgo)* If you aren't careful, you could really overdo today. There will be an awful lot of demands on your time, and you may be feeling so good, you could overindulge in everything. However, everything favors your efforts today, and you are riding along with the elements of surprise and luck. Use them wisely!

Tuesday, March 25 *(Moon Virgo to Libra 1:22 p.m.)*
Your self-confidence should be firmly in place today, and you should not hesitate to ask for what you

want. Some may even be asked to make a personal appearance, and should be anything but shy. Many Virgos will be heartened when someone extends a hand and says, "I feel the same way." You have a wonderful new friend! The lucky number is 4.

Wednesday, March 26 (Moon in Libra) This full moon falls smack in your sector of money and possessions. One thing that means is that you should be able to increase your assets in some way or another. Keep your ears open for every bit of information that comes your way. Some of it could be extremely useful! Some Leos will be asked to travel or give a written report. Don't blow this golden opportunity. A Sagittarian could be helpful.

Thursday, March 27 (Moon Libra to Scorpio 3:05 p.m.) Some of you could actually be going through a change of residence or marital status. For others, the change will not be so drastic, but some kind of adjustment is definitely indicated. With your cycle still high, you should be instantly able to know what to do. Don't hesitate to ask for what you want, because you should get a positive response.

Friday, March 28 (Moon in Scorpio) There is a certain amount of confusion indicated today; it is up to you to keep things straight. Someone is seeking your counsel and wants your opinion. Be absolutely realistic and do not hold out false hopes. This is not a good day to cosign anything, and you may have to stop yourself from being too good a buddy. A Pisces is in the picture. The lucky number is 7.

Saturday, March 29 (Moon Scorpio to Sagittarius 4:20 p.m.) Go slow and don't scatter your forces today. You can easily be "all over the place." It is essential to keep a commitment, possibly one made to an older person. It is also necessary to follow through on some additional responsibility you have been given. Though there are some slight roadblocks in the way, a romantic matter is moving forward. Something happens to make your prestige greater today and you should end up happier than you were before.

Sunday, March 30 (Moon in Sagittarius) Don't take anything for granted now, and protect yourself in all the clinches. Details are more important than you think, and someone may be trying to catch you off-balance. You can disappoint them if you want. The lucky number is 9.

Monday, March 31 (Moon Sagittarius to Capricorn 6:25 p.m.) Many Virgos will have the rare opportunity to correct a past error and to have a great weight lifted off their conscience. Now you can start to rebuild in a more solid, suitable way. Someone may come to you with a problem, and you should be honest about your ability to solve it. However, you gain enlightenment through someone else's difficulty.

APRIL 1986

Tuesday, April 1 (Moon in Capricorn) The emphasis today is on the excitement of discovery; don't pass it by simply because you are preoccupied. Someone could suddenly recognize your talents, and you could be rewarded in a most substantial way. Don't ever underplay your own creative abilities. A Capricorn could play a key role in the day's activities.

Wednesday, April 2 (Moon Capricorn to Aquarius 10:11 p.m.) Once again, you should not keep your eyes on the ground but look upward for opportunity. As you complete something important, what you've been looking for suddenly comes into your hands. Once again, you are being noticed as never before. An older person will give you the benefit of his/her experience; listen patiently. The lucky number is 9.

Thursday, April 3 (Moon in Aquarius) New starts and new contacts are the order of the day. One could lead to a meaningful relationship. However, the focus is also on what needs to be done, and those who need your help. Some Virgos may feel that everybody in the world is depending on them now, but that is not quite true. Things will be different soon. The lucky number is 1.

Friday, April 4 (Moon in Aquarius) Don't hesitate to follow through on a hunch today. Sometimes you hesitate to reach beyond your current expectations. Even though you should open up in some areas, it is important to stick to the rules when it comes to your health and nutrition. Don't get bogged down in somebody else's petty quarrel; it is not worth it. A Cancer or a Capricorn could be helpful.

Saturday, April 5 (Moon Aquarius to Pisces 4:03 a.m.) Don't get bogged down in details now, it is important to see the big picture. Rather than nitpicking and analyzing, your focus now should be on bringing things and people together. For many Virgos, their most important relationship—possibly their marriage—is in a state of flux. It needn't get out of hand. Listen to a Gemini or a Sagittarian. The lucky number is 3.

Sunday, April 6 (Moon in Pisces) Suddenly you realize it's time to tear something down in order to rebuild things on a much better and stronger foundation. Don't let it overwhelm you. By checking out all the details and reading all the small print, you will find the task much easier. Don't give away something of value to someone who is not willing to give you something in return. You don't have to.

Monday, April 7 (Moon Pisces to Aries 12:12 p.m.) Get ready for a lot of change and variety. The atmosphere changes a lot and is a lot more interesting. Many will find they suddenly have a burden removed and have much greater freedom of action. Others find that someone makes a major concession, and life is suddenly a lot easier. Protect your ideas by getting them down on paper.

Tuesday, April 8 (Moon in Aries) Somebody starts talking a whole new ballgame, and you better listen. This is one change that ultimately benefits you a great deal. If you aren't afraid to dig beneath the surface, you will come up with all kinds of hidden resources. A Taurus or a Libra could be extremely helpful in making you adjust to new circumstances.

Wednesday, April 9 (Moon Aries to Taurus 10:36 p.m.) Whatever you do, do not fall for someone's story—particularly if you can see the gaping holes at first glance. However, it is not necessary to put this person down. Just be absolutely clear about what you expect. Some will be able to try out a new way of doing things with great success. The lucky number is 7.

Thursday, April 10 (Moon in Taurus) New avenues of expression are opening to you now. Don't turn down the chance to go this new route—it could prove extremely lucrative. Some will feel good when they are rewarded for past efforts they thought were totally unnoticed. Others will rejoice that a relationship is getting a lot stronger. The lucky number is 8.

Friday, April 11 (Moon in Taurus) You can learn a lot today, if you open your eyes and look at the opportunities that are presented to you. For some, the scenario includes the removal of a big problem. For others, a big lift comes when someone expresses confidence in their abilities. You may be dealing with some rather domineering people today, but you can handle them if you keep your balance and remember to keep your self-esteem intact.

Saturday, April 12 (Moon Taurus to Gemini 10:51 a.m.) A big breakthrough is possible today, and you could end up in a much better spot by the end of it. For some, opportunity will present itself in the form of a very special invitation; even if you are inclined to say No, force yourself to attend. You may have to be very direct in order to get to the heart of a matter—possibly concerning a Leo. Whatever you do, don't mince words.

Sunday, April 13 (Moon in Gemini) An almost impossible situation gets resolved in a flash—and it seems almost miraculous. Also miraculous is the enlightenment you gain from the experience. Some will find themselves the center of attention when they are asked to take on a big job in a local community project. Don't scoff at it; good things can happen as a result. The lucky number is 2.

Monday, April 14 (Moon Gemini to Cancer 11:41 p.m.) You may find yourself very much in demand now, and everybody seems to want a piece of your time. Be generous, but keep yourself intact. You may want to spend some time on your appearance—for many, that means a shopping trip. This time, try something a little different—you tend to stick to the same old thing. A Gemini or a Sagittarian could show you how to loosen up in that area. The lucky number is 3.

Tuesday, April 15 (Moon in Cancer) Don't deviate from the party line today; stick with the policies that are already in place. It is not time to be experimental. However, the cycle is extremely positive, and you could possibly win a contest. Or at least make some exciting new friends who can help you get what you want. A Taurus or a Scorpio may be among them.

Wednesday, April 16 (Moon in Cancer) Something that looks like an impersonal relationship could turn into something quite different; give it your time and attention. Also give full reign to your curiosity now, and ask as many questions about as many things as you like. No one is going to call you on it—meaning that you are not out of line. In many cases, it is important to check out source material.

Thursday, April 17 (Moon Cancer to Leo 11:10 a.m.) Somebody you gave some advice to recently lets you know that it really paid off; let him/her know you should share in the profits. Don't sell yourself short! Some Virgos will be given a token of appreciation for a recent favor they did. Even if you are not entranced with the gift, say thanks in a gracious manner. There are a lot of points to be scored in business now.

Friday, April 18 (Moon in Leo) Somebody who's been out of touch makes contact again, and you get some fascinating information. Don't be too gossipy and don't pass it on to too many people. Many Virgos will have to take a firm hold of themselves and avoid self-deceptions now. Even if you would like to believe in someone, be realistic and see him/her for what he/she really is. It may mean making a break—but in the long run it will benefit you.

Saturday, April 19 (Moon Leo to Virgo 7:24 p.m.) You should wake up today with a distinct feeling that things are on the upswing, because the moon is moving into your sign. Even if things start out quietly, you will soon be presented with an opportunity to show off how special and individual you can be. Don't blow it! For many, a delightful surprise comes in the form of a member of the opposite sex who finds you charming and makes no secret about it. You would do well to try your luck with number 8 today.

Sunday, April 20 (Moon in Virgo) Now the moon is fully moved into your sign, and you should be feeling the full effects. For many, someone who has been out of touch suddenly turns up again and a delightful reunion is the result. Others also have pleasant surprises, possibly in the form of an opportunity to ask for what they want—and get it. An Aries, a Libra, or another Virgo could be an excellent "playmate" today.

Monday, April 21 (Moon Virgo to Libra 11:50 p.m.) Stand firmly in place today and display the courage of your convictions; the more independent you are, the better it will go for you. This is the right time to take the initiative, because you can uncharacteristically go forward. Because your judgment is on target too, you can make a lot of progress. Let a charismatic Leo take you by the hand and show you how to do it.

Tuesday, April 22 (Moon in Libra) Almost by instinct, you know where the money is, and you go for it. Intuition plays a large role now, and you should trust it. For some, it will be necessary to take an inventory of personal possessions, as well as what's owed and what is owing. You can really shape up your finances now. Someone will help you, you will feel a lot more secure. The lucky number is 2.

Wednesday, April 23 (Moon in Libra) Let yourself use an element of surprise today, because it is a formidable weapon now. When you sneak up on someone or something, you will be able to take over completely. Virgos should be looking beyond the immediate now and see what the future potential is. Do not turn down any invitations you get now, because opportunity could present itself anywhere. Your prestige may be on the upswing.

Thursday, April 24 (Moon Libra to Scorpio 1:15 a.m.) You may be more aware of minor flaws than you would like to be. You will find yourself in enjoyable company, but you may find that some people fall short of your expectations. Don't be too hard on them. Someone around you may be practicing his/her salesmanship ability, and you could be the prime target. Show that you are not the patsy. The lucky number is 4.

Friday, April 25 (Moon in Scorpio) Someone you respect will tell you he/she feels the same way. However, that may present you with a problem. Do you have room for someone in your life? It is important not to box yourself in now, and to keep all your options open. The more room you give yourself, the better. The lucky number is 5.

Saturday, April 26 (Moon Scorpio to Sagittarius 1:16 a.m.) This may be one of those days when you feel you have to change something or you will lose your mind. Start with something small, like your immediate environment. Why not buy something new and attractive? You will be a lot more pleased with your surroundings, and you will feel more secure as a result. Some will be closing a major transaction. The lucky number is 6.

Sunday, April 27 (Moon in Sagittarius) If you stay alert, you will realize that you are being provided with privileged information. Remember, it is important to keep it a secret. Many will have their minds on long-range plans—possibly involving property. Others will be concerned with a relationship with an older person, possibly a parent. Realize your responsibilities, but do not let them depress you. A Pisces or another Virgo could be very helpful.

Monday, April 28 (Moon Sagittarius to Capricorn 1:14 a.m.) Things lighten up considerably today and many Virgos will find themselves feeling closer to someone than they have in a very long time. The relationship should be both warm and exciting now. However, the pressure is still on, as is the emphasis on responsibility. Check out some new methods with a Cancer or a Capricorn. The lucky number is 8.

Tuesday, April 29 (Moon in Capricorn) For many Virgos, an old friend turns up and provides a very light and bright note. For others, there is a definite stimulating of the creative juices, and you should take advantage of this free flow. All should be experiencing a turn of vitality and better health in general. If this is not the case, take your own welfare more seriously now.

Wednesday, April 30 (Moon Capricorn to Aquarius

4:06 a.m.) It's possible you are going to begin and end this day feeling rather "put upon." Unfortunately, there's lots to be done, and most of it can only be done by you. However, before you get into the "martyr mode", make an attempt to delegate some things to other people. They will be more willing to help than you suspect. If at all possible, plan some "goof off" time later on— and let the rest of the world go by.

MAY 1986

Thursday, May 1 (Moon in Aquarius) Someone who has been rather stubborn recently suddenly makes a turnover and says, "Okay, I'll go along with you." Surprising as it is, you are extremely touched and should show your appreciation. Many Virgos should realize they are not victims of circumstance, and should raise their sights a bit higher. You can do a lot better than you are doing now—the potential is there.

Friday, May 2 (Moon Aquarius to Pisces 9:30 a.m.) Once you get some practical matters out of the way, there will be smooth sailing with someone who means a lot to you. You should feel very relieved to know exactly where you stand with this person; game-playing is not your style. Some Virgos should try their wings in an independent project. Showing your willingness to do so can make a big difference. A Leo or an Aquarian could be very helpful in smoothing the path.

Saturday, May 3 (Moon in Pisces) Some of you will have to deal with the fact that what's past is past, and that you can't bring it back. In most cases, the result is positive. Some will get a real lesson in how complicated the law can be. In this or another matter, follow your hunch, because you are probably more right than the rest of them. Some minor marital problems may errupt now, but you can handle them. The lucky number is 2.

Sunday, May 4 (Moon Pisces to Aries 8:01 p.m.) You may be feeling a bit nervous and at loose ends today; try to get yourself together for constructive activity. One rewarding route to go today is in the direction of future plans—possibly travel. Others should take themselves in hand and start on a new regime to improve their physical image. The lucky number today is 3.

Monday, May 5 (Moon in Aries) If you keep your eyes and ears open, there's a lot to be learned today. Some of it may not be too palatable. Meaning that you may be disappointed in someone you thought was perfect. It should make you realize that self-reliance is the only reliable way to go. If you are asked to play second fiddle to someone, don't sell yourself short. You deserve recognition in your own right.

Tuesday, May 6 (Moon in Aries) You may get a rather puzzling message today, and you should realize that it is probably a garbled one. Wait until things get clear. Some will be delighted that a debt is easier to repay than they thought. Others will be focusing on finances, figuring out ways to make their financial security greater. Don't be afraid to make some changes in that area. The lucky number is 5.

Wednesday, May 7 (Moon Aries to Taurus 4:59 a.m.) You may have to tiptoe around someone who's feeling rather touchy today; you've had your turn. While you are busy being diplomatic, you can also get that bit of extra information that will give you the key about how to act in the present situation. There are some changes you can make that will make you look good, but actually benefit you more than others. Be shrewd!

Thursday, May 8 (Moon in Taurus) This could be a very quiet day for you. If at all possible, get away from it all and have a quiet talk with yourself. It can make all the difference in your mood. When you do interact with others, be receptive to suggestions. There is always a lot to learn. Later on, have a quiet talk with someone you love. It could be extremely positive.

Friday, May 9 (Moon Taurus to Gemini 5:26 p.m.) Today is a lot more active—both physically and mentally. Don't wait to be told what to do and how to do it, get going on your own. You have all the resources you need, and you are ready for a big breakthrough. Some will be making important new contacts now, and should not overlook any of them. You never know where opportunity is waiting.

Saturday, May 10 (Moon in Gemini) This should be a lighthearted Saturday for many Virgos. In some way or another, you are freer than in the recent past and a lot more able to "do your own thing." For some of you, that will mean getting involved in a new project in rather unfamiliar surroundings. It is good for you to broaden your vision in this way. Keep your eye on an enterprising person—possibly an Aries—who could add a lot of excitement to your life.

Sunday, May 11 (Moon in Gemini) Keep on testing yourself today; you will learn about some important capabilities you have that you were not aware of. Someone will give you more than a fair chance, and you should be grateful for the opportunity to show what you can do. Some Virgos may have to stand up for what they believe in now; don't be afraid to be a bit stubborn, because your point of view will prove to be the right one in the end. An Aquarian would be a good ally.

Monday, May 12 (Moon Gemini to Cancer 7:18 a.m.) Your intuition should be working overtime, and you should know exactly what to do and when to do it. You will be picking up all kinds of subtle vibes today and should be able to put them to good use. Don't be afraid to be a little clever and give yourself an edge. You are more than able to win friends and influence people now. The lucky number is 2.

Tuesday, May 13 (Moon in Cancer) Don't be afraid to reach out now, because you are sure of being able to grasp what you want. That could be a whole new way of doing things, and hence a whole new lease on life. Be aware that you have friends who are supportive, and who can help you make your dreams come true. Some will receive a deceptively unimportant invitation now; do not overlook it. It could be the start of something big.

Wednesday, May 14 (Moon Cancer to Leo 6:15 p.m.) Some of you have recently gone through a kind of test and today you will receive the results—they are extremely positive. All of you should realize your position is a lot stronger than you once thought, and that you are on very solid ground. In many cases, a former enemy suddenly becomes a very supportive ally—or at least a mutual participant in the current scenario. Your lucky number today is 4.

Thursday, May 15 (Moon in Leo) Don't take anything for granted now, because you could easily be fooled. It is essential to be analytical and to try to figure out what the real motives are behind the facade. Some will be experiencing some rather vague fears and apprehensions; realize that they exist only in your own mind. Get out of yourself by indulging a special interest or possibly joining a new group. If you keep your mind active, your rather jangled emotions will calm down.

Friday, May 16 (Moon in Leo) Things are beginning to look up, and you may be looking around yourself and deciding something has to be done. Let a close friend help you in your self improvement campaign. Some will get a real lift when love walks in the room—it could be spectacular. If you are asked to do something a bit less than aboveboard, think carefully before getting involved.

Saturday, May 17 (Moon Leo to Virgo 3:45 a.m.) Now you are finally out of the woods, and that black cloud lifts. Take advantage of your clear head and good feelings to take the initiative and show how sharp you can be. Something you want is easier to get than you think—so easy, it could surprise you. Trust a Pisces or another Virgo today.

Sunday, May 18 (Moon in Virgo) No matter what you choose to do, you can be particularly productive. For some, that means moving an important relationship forward. You may have to take on additional responsibility, but you are only too willing. Someone has your best interests at heart, even though he/she may not seem to; gradually you will become aware of it. Go along with this person. The lucky number is 8.

Monday, May 19 (Moon Virgo to Libra 9:41 a.m.) You are still in an up cycle, and you should not let down your efforts. In fact, many of you will be able to finish off a rather major project and get a loud round of applause for it. Don't be afraid to show your very own style and to be a lot more innovative than you usually are. In fact, an independent spirit will spark interest from someone who seems rather indifferent. The lucky number is 9.

Tuesday, May 20 (Moon in Libra) Don't be afraid to lay your cards on the table with a partner—either your spouse or your romantic interest. In fact, it is only by being frank that you can clear the air and free both of you for constructive decisions. Money is much the issue for other Virgos, and they should be able to make it stretch far enough to cover current obligations. A Leo could bring some light into your life.

Wednesday, May 21 (Moon Libra to Scorpio 12:02 p.m.) Someone lets the cat out of the bag, which works to your advantage. There's no use pretending anymore. Some Virgos will find themselves adding to their possessions or being more aware of the value of what they own. One way to achieve greater understanding now is to teach others what you know. Or to reach out in some other constructive way.

Thursday, May 22 (Moon in Scorpio) You may get the feeling that there are simply too many people involved in your life right now—and you may want to run away from all of them. However, it is important to remain in contact, to be with those who are going through rather troubled times. You can be immensely helpful and you should be. As for your own problems, a Gemini or a Sagittarian could have some excellent advice.

Friday, May 23 (Moon Scorpio to Sagittarius 11:57 a.m.) A lot of rather confusing information may come your way, and you have to be prepared to separate out the facts from the fantasies. You are able to be particularly analytical now, and you must use that ability. The full moon may add to the confusion, but it should throw only a temporary veil of mystery over what should be absolutely clear to you. A relative of someone else far away could be immensely helpful in clarifying this situation.

Saturday, May 24 (Moon in Sagittarius) Whatever you do, don't do anything which threatens your security—either financial or emotional. You could be easily preyed upon now by people who flatter you or say they desperately need your help. Look into the real motives, and try to have an open dialogue. If necessary, get things in writing. Another Virgo could be the key to the whole thing.

Sunday, May 25 (Moon Sagittarius to Capricorn 11:15 a.m.) Most will have the distinct feeling that others are rooting for them today; one person in particular may come along and extend a hand and say "Let me help." It will give you a wonderful feeling. Some Virgos will be involved in busy work, but in the end it will make them feel very constructive. The lucky number is 8.

Monday, May 26 (Moon in Capricorn) Do not believe everything you hear today. Someone may be setting you up for a reason. It is wise to keep your guard up—particularly in emotional matters. Avoid the whole thing by throwing yourself into your work coming up with some swift new way to do things. Keep your eye on a Pisces!

Tuesday, May 27 (Moon Capricorn to Aquarius noon) The pressures build up today and you may feel a little bit overloaded by responsibilities. Try to keep things in perspective today. In a relationship matter, if you don't listen very carefully, you may misunderstand a message. And it could make you unhappy unnecessarily.

Wednesday, May 28 (Moon in Aquarius) Once again, there is more to do than makes you comfortable; but you can look for a fair amount of satisfaction. In some cases, someone will let you know that your judgment is very meaningful and helpful to them. The lucky number today is 9.

Thursday, May 29 (Moon Aquarius to Pisces 3:54 p.m.) It may be getting clearer and clearer a new approach is necessary—particularly in your romantic life. The key now is to be absolutely direct and keep both your words and your thoughts as clear as a bell. If it is your work life that needs working on, the answer there is to do something that raises your self esteem; it doesn't look as if anyone else is going to do it for you right now. The lucky number today is 1.

Friday, May 30 (Moon in Pisces) You can afford to wait it out; there is no reason to rush. The agreement you seek will eventually be signed on the dotted line, so you don't have to worry. Some Virgos are going to have to steer clear of a rather erratic individual who threatens to upset what is a rather delicate balance. Do not hesitate to cut him/her off at the pass. An Aquarian would be a reliable guide.

Saturday, May 31 (Moon Pisces to Aries 11:43 p.m.) Today you should have a chance to relax and look back on the week's activities. Ignore the details, and try to get a total picture of what actually happened. Then plan a course of action. Some will be getting a rather interesting social invitation and should accept without hesitation. There is a valuable contact to be made. For best results, mix with a Gemini, a Sagittarian, or another Virgo.

JUNE 1986

Sunday, June 1 (Moon in Aries) In one situation or another, the facts are all in, and now you must come to your own verdict. Here's a clue; go in the direction where you can be sure of getting the greatest amount of support—and additional resources. It is a matter in which you definitely need a partner. The lucky number today is 1.

Monday, June 2 (Moon in Aries) Now is the time to show everyone you are strong enough to go it alone; your independence will be admired. At the same time some of you may find out the story behind the story, and the information will be very helpful. Take the financial claims of someone else with a large grain of salt.

Tuesday, June 3 (Moon Aries to Taurus 10:45 a.m.) Now's the time to diversify your interests and to stretch yourself a bit. For many, love is very much a part of the day's "business as usual"—and could include a Gemini or a Sagittarian. He/she may reveal a secret that is rather startling, but it makes you feel a lot more steady on your feet. The lucky number is 3.

Wednesday, June 4 (Moon in Taurus) You know you need some expert advice on a matter that is not your best subject. The person you seek out has a good track record, and is extremely helpful to you. Now you are ready to make a commitment and join forces with someone else toward a common goal. It's a big responsibility, but you should trust your mentor.

Thursday, June 5 (Moon Taurus to Gemini 11:26 p.m.) This is a wild day for you with lots of unusual and even downright spooky occurrences. You may get one of those rare hunches that usually prove out, and it will do so now. You spend your time in the company of a brilliant but rather unstable person, but you survive nicely. It should feel good to be out of your recent rut. You are going places! The lucky number is 5.

Friday, June 6 (Moon in Gemini) You are generally quite good at figuring out ways to get money out of people to finance your big plans. Today you are particularly creative and manage to put a pet project in the works. It may have to do with decoration of your environment or possibly enlargement of your living quarters. Some will be occupied with less creative endeavors, but even they should have a sense that what once seemed impractical now seems possible.

Saturday, June 7 (Moon in Gemini) Be cautious when you accept a proposal or offer that comes along now. The offerer, although sincere, could not know what he/she is really talking about. It is wise to keep your options open and to rely on yourself rather than on others now. A Pisces, a Gemini, or a Leo could disappoint you during this time. However, it should be an enlightening experience.

Sunday, June 8 (Moon Taurus to Cancer 12:16 p.m.) This will probably be a very busy Sunday for most Virgos; you really should take some time off and just relax, but your overactive sense of responsibility will probably not allow you to. For some, the work is not without reward—possibly financial. For others, something really creative could come out of it. Some will simply be working on their most important relationships today. The lucky number is 8.

Monday, June 9 (Moon in Cancer) This could be a very special day for some, with emotional fulfillment a reality. It may come in the form of a favor that is returned and renews your faith in people. You should be rather visible today, perhaps even more than you want to be. Your opinion will count very much.

Tuesday, June 10 (Moon in Cancer) It's important to choose quality over quantity now, even though you are going to be presented with all kinds of tantalizing things. The more selective you are, the more you will do for yourself. However, you may have to buck the crowd; don't be afraid to show your independence. Some will have to play "private eye" to get at the real root of a story.

Wednesday, June 11 (Moon Cancer to Leo 12:11 a.m.) There should be a lot of quiet time today, but if there isn't you should seek it. Prepare yourself for a much more active time to come, as your cycle moves up. Some will be feeling much freer of restrictions than in the recent past. Someone with a big problem may teach you a lesson in patience and fortitude.

Thursday, June 12 (Moon in Leo) Don't stick to one thing today; it's a wise idea to step on the grass. Without overstepping your bounds. The point is there is a lot to be learned in areas that have remained closed to you before. Someone behind the scenes is working in your behalf, and is willing to make a sacrifice for your benefit. Show that you are grateful. The lucky number is 3.

Friday, June 13 (Moon Leo to Virgo 10:18 a.m.) As the moon moves into your sign, you realize that what seems to be an impact is actually beneficial to you. You may experience a temporary postponement or delay, it lets you get your second wind. A Scorpio person is on your side, and will prove to be a valuable friend. The lucky number is 4.

Saturday, June 14 *(Moon in Virgo)* Here you go, with the moon in your sign. Now you are able to communicate freely and show how good your judgment is. Your timing should not be far behind. Creative efforts are favored today, and you should get your ideas and thoughts on paper. It is a time you can gain through the written word. Another Virgo may be prominent.

Sunday, June 15 *(Moon Virgo to Libra 5:38 p.m.)* The more diplomatic you are today, the more you will be able to accomplish of what you would rather do. A bone of contention may arise concerning decoration or remodeling; don't get sticky about it. A surprise gift might come your way, and it could be in excellent taste—however, you interpret the word. Be receptive to a relative who asks you to spend some time you would rather not spend.

Monday, June 16 *(Moon in Libra)* What appears to be a loss will boomerang in your favor; your cycle is still high, and you should not get bummed out by a temporary delay. Use the time to bring your accounts into order, and to focus on your financial situation. Someone who loves you will help you find something you lost.

Tuesday, June 17 *(Moon Libra to Scorpio 9:36 p.m.)* Don't miss any opportunity today to make something good happen for you—there is very little you cannot accomplish. For some, money suddenly becomes available; for others, a relationship gets a lot more cemented. A Capricorn or a Cancer could play an important role today.

Wednesday, June 18 *(Moon in Scorpio)* Today many will be able to complete an important project, and even be "wined and dined" as a result. Enjoy your temporary fame. Others will have other reasons to celebrate, and will feel more burdened than they have in a while. Now is "take-charge" time.

Thursday, June 19 *(Moon Scorpio to Sagittarius 10:36 p.m.)* If you try a new approach today, you will be surprised at how much cooperation you get from those around you. However, you are going to have to make it clear that you intend to continue this original way of thinking. For many, there will be a short trip in the offing and perhaps a telephone call which brings very important news. For many, it will vindicate their own views. The lucky number is 1.

Friday, June 20 *(Moon in Sagittarius)* It's important to read the small print today, and to check all the details. Someone may be trying to encroach on your territory; you do not have to allow it. Protect your safety in every way, and stick to your basic values. An older person—possibly a woman—will give you the benefit of her experience and could be extremely helpful in helping you find the money you need.

Saturday, June 21 *(Moon Sagittarius to Capricorn 10:00 p.m.)* Suddenly it will feel as if you had a lot more space—enjoy it. It's an excellent time to indulge your artistic whims and to entertain yourself. However, you still will have to work within the rules and regulations—but that is rarely difficult for you. Some will have to pull themselves back from overcommitting to others.

Sunday, June 22 *(Moon in Capricorn)* This full moon is very important to you where matters of the heart are concerned—that means any and all of your relationships. Some can expect a shakeup of the status quo; others can expect the new variety of love. A Scorpio could be extremely important in providing inspiration. A special agreement may be made before the end of the day. The lucky number is 4.

Monday, June 23 *(Moon Capricorn to Aquarius 9:50 p.m.)* Once more, love and everything connected with it dominates the scene. Some should let themselves be as creative as possible, and you may be amazed to see the results that you get. You could be a true artist—no matter what your medium. Make sure you respond positively to a very sincere request you get. A Gemini could play an outstanding role.

Tuesday, June 24 (Moon in Aquarius) Moderation is the word today, if you want to get results. You will have to stick to your last and maybe even take care of a lot of other people who depend on you. Though it may make you feel boxed in, don't let it make you overindulge in food or drink to "drown your sorrows." A Taurus or a Libra could be very helpful today.

Wednesday, June 25 (Moon in Aquarius) Take it easy today, in every sense of the word. If you overdo in any way, you are likely to string yourself out. You should also steer clear of people who simply want to waste your time and could get on your nerves. One very soft person—possibly a Pisces—would be excellent company. He/she wants you to succeed and will give you the opportunity to prove it.

Thursday, June 26 (Moon Aquarius to Pisces 12:12 a.m.) The rights of others are paramount today; you may have to give in where one of your partnerships is concerned. For many, the battleground will be their marriage or live-in status. It is wise to let others take the lead and to remain a shrewd observer. Your time will come.

Friday, June 27 (Moon in Pisces) An important transaction can be completed now—and for some of you, it will be a legal one. For everyone, you can expect the green light to flash and for a roadblock to progress to be removed. Concentrate on bettering your image, and improving your public relations position. Once again, partnerships are spotlighted.

Saturday, June 28 (Moon Pisces to Aries 6:35 a.m.) Love is definitely in the air. It could range from love of children to a hot new romance—but any way you look at it, sentiment is involved. Some will feel inclined to take a flier and speculate on one thing or another. Most will be feeling rather popular and should take advantage of every invitation that comes along. A Leo could be a lot of fun.

Sunday, June 29 (Moon in Aries) It's important to rise above petty politics today, no matter who you are dealing with. Show that you can be a bigger thinker than other people, and even a leader. Believe it or not, people are going to listen because you have special sparkle today. Follow through on a hunch you have.

Monday, June 30 (Moon Aries to Taurus 4:54 p.m.) Don't take anything for granted today; count your change in every respect. It is important to be as analytical and as picky as possible—this is one time you should be. A younger person can help you if you will let him/her. Don't let pride get in your way. The lucky number today is 3.

JULY 1986

Tuesday, July 1 (Moon in Taurus) Don't get stuck in a rut today, and insist on following a previous plan. There could be a change which you will like a lot—if you allow yourself to. Remember that someone is on your side, and that you should respond positively to his/her suggestions. Don't get overly picky about matters of food and cleanliness.

Wednesday, July 2 (Moon in Taurus) The emphasis today is on social activity of all kinds; some may be getting together with others to plan travel. Others will be dabbling in the arts in one way or another. A message that comes in from a distance is really good news, and you can use it. The lucky number is 3.

Thursday, July 3 (Moon Taurus to Gemini 5:32 a.m.) You'll feel on a lot more solid ground now, and you should be able to quickly cut through a lot of red tape and restrictions. Some will be making a definite career advance; others will be improving their prestige considerably. You do well with authority figures today. Pay attention to a Scorpio or a Taurus.

Friday, July 4 (Moon in Gemini) You should be the center of attention at whatever holiday celebration you participate in. Some of you may even be asked to make a little speech. Whatever you say, a special member of the opposite sex will show that he/she thinks you are pretty great. Don't get overly shy. The lucky number today is 5.

Saturday, July 5 (Moon Gemini to Cancer 6:19 p.m.) This is one of those days when you should get what you want fairly easily—if you are reasonably tactful about it. Don't force an issue, but feel someone out on how he/she can help you achieve some short-term goals. A Taurus could be a good buddy today, and might be an excellent person to plan a vacation with.

Sunday, July 6 (Moon in Cancer) Hopes and wishes are very much in the spotlight today. Some may even have a prophetic dream in which they see the future as it could be. However, the realization depends on you. Maintain an air of mystery today, and don't give away your hands; for many, a romantic encounter could be very important in the end. A Pisces is very key today.

Monday, July 7 (Moon in Cancer) Things seem to get on your nerves today, and the reason is you don't like the feeling that your movements are restricted. It is only temporary, and you should take advantage of this time to get some very basic stuff done. You will feel relieved and a lot less guilty about springing yourself later.

Tuesday, July 8 (Moon Cancer to Leo 5:56 a.m.) Some long-range plans come into sharp clear focus now, and you are able to virtually "see forever." Many will find that some secret fears and doubts vanish like raindrops after a sunshower. You sense that someone behind the scenes is working in your behalf, you are right. The lucky number today is 9.

Wednesday, July 9 (Moon in Leo) Show just how independent you can be, and you will gain rare insights. By daring to ask, you get the answers. For many, a sweet interlude is on the agenda—but it is a bit off the beaten path. Enjoy it without feeling guilty. A Leo or an Aquarian could be prominent.

Thursday, July 10 (Moon Leo to Virgo 3:50 p.m.) Get out there and get all the answers you need, because you will be using them soon. Some will be asked to come up with a plan, and should be ready to state their views clearly. You are well able to sell whatever you are selling today—even yourself.

Friday, July 11 (Moon in Virgo) Today you will have good reason to celebrate! A refreshing breeze should blow through your life, and you should feel invigorated and attractive. Use the special charisma you have today, and don't hesitate to play it by ear. You will do that very well. A number of people are eager to hear you and to see you.

Saturday, July 12 (Moon Virgo to Libra 11:40 p.m.) Today you are very willing to move about in the world, and it is a refreshing change of pace for you. You may be surprised that a member of the opposite sex confides his/her feelings—even some romantic notions. Take it all seriously, do not overreact. Some could really get the top spot today—or even win a contest.

Sunday, July 13 (Moon in Libra) How delightful! You discover that your money picture is brighter than you thought, and your prospects are a lot more solid. Say thanks to a family member who really wants to help, even though he/she may simply get on your nerves.

Isn't there some way in which you can satisfy this person by showing how much you need him/her? A Gemini or a Sagittarian could be a very important person today. The lucky number is 5.

Monday, July 14 (Moon in Libra) You may have to make do with whatever is at hand today; it's not a time to overspend on anything. Some will be taking stock of their personal possessions, and maybe even placing a value on them. Others could be engaged in serious talks about a change of scene—possibly even a change of residence. Listen to a Taurus or a Scorpio who knows a lot about such things.

Tuesday, July 15 (Moon Libra to Scorpio 4:58 a.m.) Some may start the day feeling very confused and rather anxious. You might do well to stay away from aggravating people today. With those you must see, make it absolutely clear that you don't want any abstract talk. Just the facts, nothing but the facts. You've got to be realistic now, and keep an open mind—without being gullible. Siblings may play an important part today.

Wednesday, July 16 (Moon in Scorpio) Now plans are taking shape, and you can transform your ideas into good working concepts. You should feel proud of yourself, and a lot more secure. There could be a change of plans, but it should not make you jittery. Enjoy the variety! You may have to dig for some information, but it is worth the search.

Thursday, July 17 (Moon Scorpio to Sagittarius 7:34 a.m.) Be sure to finish what you start today. If you feel a little hemmed in, try to look beyond the immediate—and realize that the news that you want is on the way. Some will get some kind of recognition today or have a load removed from their shoulders. It may be a financial burden that suddenly disappears. Rejoice!

Friday, July 18 (Moon in Sagittarius) Get ready for a new start, and realize that you will have one of those rare opportunities to correct a mistake you made in the past. Be gracious about admitting your error. Some should be focusing on matters of safety at home. Others should be thinking about long-term arrangements involving the family. For a very few, romance could rear its head today.

Saturday, July 19 (Moon Sagittarius to Capricorn 8:10 a.m.) Realize that you are building for security now, and you should avoid anything that smacks of sensationalism. The conservative course is the best one. Some may have to fulfill some obligations to family or friends, but it should make you feel very worthwhile, and it's as if you have a new sense of direction. What had been a barrier will no longer be an obstacle.

Sunday, July 20 (Moon in Capricorn) This is a good news day! For some, it will be their children who bring them joy. For others, pride will come from a knowledge of how much you have helped a loved one. Luck and timing are on your side today, and you could receive a very pleasant surprise. On the other hand, you could surprise someone with good results. You are extremely popular, and could get almost anything you ask for. However, be selective. The lucky number is 3.

Monday, July 21 (Moon Capricorn to Aquarius 8:17 a.m.) This full moon should stimulate your most creative instincts, as well as your romantic side. Many will feel like doing anything that feels good, and should do it with style. For many, a relationship is intensifying, and you will feel a lot more confident about it. Enjoy! A Taurus, a Leo, or a Scorpio could be intensely involved today.

Tuesday, July 22 (Moon in Aquarius) Now it's back to reality. Check on your resolutions about health and exercise. And diet as well. Catch up on a lot of things that need doing, and don't forget to remember someone via a letter or a call. You should be very much in the holiday spirit, and you may infect someone of the opposite sex with it. His/her interest is very sincere.

Wednesday, July 23 (Moon Aquarius to Pisces 9:59 a.m.) Practical matters are very much at the top of the list today, and you will have to finish some jobs that you've been neglecting lately. Or simply ignoring. On the bright side, you will find yourself involved with people who share your thinking about some important matters. It makes you realize that you are not alone, and that's a good feeling. Someone will show their appreciation in a unique manner.

Thursday, July 24 (Moon in Pisces) You'll have to be very aware of your public image today. The ball is in other people's court, and you will have to be more cooperative than they. Make sure you have all the things you have at hand, and do some fact checking in order to secure your position. Go slow, and let other people take the initiative. Don't give up anything for nothing—simply be the shrewd observer.

Friday, July 25 (Moon Pisces to Aries 3:02 p.m.) Refuse to get shaken today when someone tries to undermine your confidence; your position is very strong, and it's important that you know it. For some, they will realize that the law is on their side. Others could have a wish come true in a rather romantic way; a Cancer could be very much involved. The lucky number today is 8.

Saturday, July 26 (Moon in Aries) Something comes to light today about a financial matter; you may find out that someone's holding out on you. Some will be focusing on ways to increase income or minimize outgo. If you are very clever, you can do a lot along these lines. There are some intense feelings in the atmosphere. Many of you will feel a lot less alone than you have in the recent past.

Sunday, July 27 (Moon in Aries) Realize that something that looks totally impossible is not what it seems;

this insurmountable obstacle will soon be removed. The important thing is to ride with the tide now, and not to force any issues. Some will get a very surprising glimpse behind the scene, and realize what is really going on. The lucky number is 1.

Monday, July 28 (Moon Aries to Taurus 12:11 a.m.) Many will be focusing on higher things today. In this pensive mood, you should come to some very important conclusions about an important matter—possibly involving a relationship. Some may have to face up to the fact that something is over. Others will make a new beginning in matters of health and diet. Listen to a Capricorn.

Tuesday, July 29 (Moon in Taurus) Your mood should be lighter today, and you should even find an opportunity to show off how clever you can be. Don't use your wit at someone else's expense. Many can expect a lively exchange from a member of the opposite sex—and possibly a "happy ever after" result. It's an excellent day to splurge on something new to wear.

Wednesday, July 30 (Moon Taurus to Gemini 12:19 p.m.) Many will find themselves involved with fascinating verbal people today and will want to keep up. You may discover that you've not been doing your homework and may feel a bit at a disadvantage. Resolve to keep your mind more active. Someone—possibly a younger person—will give you a big compliment, but also make a suggestion. Listen to it carefully. The lucky number today is 4.

Thursday, July 31 (Moon in Gemini) Many will receive good news on the job; some may even get a promotion or at least added recognition. For others, travel is very much a part of the scene, and it should be exhilarating. Your best bets for fun today are a Gemini, a Sagittarian, or another Virgo.

AUGUST 1986

Friday, August 1 (Moon in Gemini) A fascinating secret may be revealed to you today, and it could be a tremendous help in your job or career. Make the most of it! Some will be making a number of good new contacts, and also should not let any possibilities escape them. Someone—possibly a Sagittarian—could help you open a door that has been shut for you till now. Things are opening up! The lucky number is 3.

Saturday, August 2 (Moon Gemini to Cancer 1:04 a.m.) Events suddenly take a turn in your favor, with the accent on romance and wishes that come true. Some could even experience what seems like pennies from heaven. If you are asked to sign anything today, hold back until you are absolutely sure of what is being expected of you. Listen to an Aquarian or a Scorpio who knows the ropes.

Sunday, August 3 (Moon in Cancer) Open up those lines of communication with someone of the opposite sex. The more receptive you are to suggestions, the better things will go between the two of you. You may not realize that someone is trying to do you a favor; don't get your back up and don't let false pride block this opportunity. A Gemini, a Sagittarian, or another Virgo could be an excellent advisor for you now.

Monday, August 4 (Moon Cancer to Leo 12:26 p.m.) Don't stray too far from the beaten path today; established procedures are the best now. Don't get involved in an intrigue, but stay in your own little world. You will be far happier there. Some will be getting some good inside tips about money and how to make more of it. The lucky number today is 6.

Tuesday, August 5 (Moon in Leo) Be very careful not to let your eyes deceive you now. You could all too easily see someone in the wrong light. Spend some time remembering people who need help more than you do at this particular time. Be as charitable as possible—and that includes with your feelings. In your work, clear the decks and get rid of what you do not need.

Wednesday, August 6 (Moon Leo to Virgo 9:44 p.m.) You may be feeling a bit overburdened today, but realize that your cycle is moving up. For some, a relationship could be a bit of a problem in its intensity. Try to keep it light now. A very sincere person deserves your sincere thanks for helping you figure out which end is up. You really need the benefit of this person's experience. The lucky number is 8.

Thursday, August 7 (Moon in Virgo) Things are much lighter and brighter today, with the moon in your sign. Some will be getting special recognition—even a kind of fame. This is a particularly good moon in Virgo time for Virgos, and you may find yourself amazed at how easily applause and praise come your way. Don't be afraid to take the initiative, knowing that your judgment is sound now.

Friday, August 8 (Moon Virgo to Libra 5:05 a.m.) Say Yes when someone asks you to pioneer a project; it will be good for you. And don't be afraid to try some new ways of doing old things. It is important to dig deep and not take surface explanations now; try to get to the heart of things. Romance could be exciting. The lucky number is 1.

Saturday, August 9 (Moon in Libra) You are being pulled in more than one direction today, and you are going to have to be very strict with yourself about which way to go. Remember that the most familiar way is usually the best way. Also do not forget those who have your best interest at heart. What appeared to be a lost cause suddenly is saved.

Sunday, August 10 (Moon in Libra) Today should feel like a relief after yesterday, because the pressure is off. For many, a family get-together will restore harmony—both in you and within your circle. Enjoy your new sense of balance, and let your sense of humor shine through. A message or call will tell you you were right all along. Enjoy the feeling!

Monday, August 11 (Moon Libra to Scorpio 10:36 a.m.) You have an irresistible urge to turn everything upside down and redo it. Your new room fever affects the whole household and everybody pitches in to refinish, refurbish, and renew. The surroundings end up being a lot brighter, and a good time is had by all. Let go of a limited viewpoint; it's time to expand your horizons.

Tuesday, August 12 (Moon in Scorpio) Today a lot of your activity is focused inward, and you actually are more comfortable alone than with others. You decide you've got to chuck some old ideas along with other debris in order to get your life on the right track. Some insights you uncover can be classified as spiritual. Take an opportunity to blow your own horn. The lucky number today is 1.

Wednesday, August 13 (Moon Scorpio to Sagittarius 2:17 p.m.) You get down to serious business today. Some time, effort, and interest you invested in the past come back to you today in the form of an excellent deal. Property may be involved. It is easy for you to decide what to do, and you are confident you made the right choice. You may need some sensitive understanding today, and may be a bit moody. Use your imagination to think your way out of the problem.

Thursday, August 14 (Moon in Sagittarius) Far away but not forgotten, someone important reenters your life today. A good chat you have with him/her makes you realize you are not alone in reassessing your life at this point. It makes you even more determined to complete your personal inventory and get your act together. In another matter, don't run yourself ragged and take a lighthearted view of the proceedings. The lucky number is 3.

Friday, August 15 *(Moon Sagittarius to Capricorn 4:22 p.m.)* The best way to advance your interest today is to take someone by surprise. Caught off-guard, he/she will be much more vulnerable to your request. You've got to be a little assertive as well, because what you are asking for is a little unorthodox. You have what it takes for follow-through, but you must be patient. Another person could lend a lot of moral support.

Saturday, August 16 *(Moon in Capricorn)* Don't be extravagant with anything today, including your energy. Take it slow and easy and concentrate on battening down the hatches for future security. Some people may not be entirely cooperative, so you may have to push a little to get at the facts you need. Romance is closer than you think, but could be delayed by your own self doubt.

Sunday, August 17 *(Moon Capricorn to Aquarius 5:44 p.m.)* You are straining against your harness today and would like to be off and running. It is frustrating to have people after you to join them in some interesting activities when you've got so many other things to do. Pace yourself today and soon you will have the time. For many, the nitty-gritty tasks they devote themselves to will save a lot of time later. The lucky number is 8.

Monday, August 18 *(Moon in Aquarius)* You've got a lot of people on your side now, but take some steps to make sure they will stay there. Patience is needed by all—including you. Don't let your enthusiasm for a project cool; spend time making initial steps and clearing the path for progress. The lucky number today is 9.

Tuesday, August 19 *(Moon Aquarius to Pisces 7:52 p.m.)* This full moon falls smack in your sector of hard work, so there is not much relief you can expect today. However, you are able to score a lot of points by being rather innovative—at least for you. Win points and surprise people by showing your original methods and how—coupled with your tidy mind—they can help you polish things off in no time at all. Later on, take some time to enjoy.

Wednesday, August 20 (Moon in Pisces) People are often drawn to you for your reasonable way of handling things. You are famous for being logical when it comes to examining all sides of the question. Today your sense of justice is rewarded by a grateful person who lets you in on some inside information that you can turn to profit. It pays to be a friendly person once in a while, doesn't it?

Thursday, August 21 (Moon in Pisces) Nobody's perfect, and wishing won't make it so. Be sure you are looking at someone in a realistic light when you assess his/her capabilities. You can still make a vast improvement in the conditions that need changing; ask people to do what they are best at and nothing more. That includes you. The lucky number is 3.

Friday, August 22 (Moon Pisces to Aries 12:27 a.m.) You may have to pull rank with someone today, even though you dislike playing the boss role. This is one time you should simply say, "Shut up and march." At least it will give you the time you need to clear your mind and look at things rationally. Too many wrong decisions are made in haste—and you of all people do not want to fall prey to that. The lucky number today is 4.

Saturday, August 23 (Moon in Aries) Today you should aim, in every sense of the word. You can afford to shoot for the moon in terms of success, but you must keep your principles just as lofty. Think in terms of everyone's rights when you take a step. It is encouraging to have the support of an enthusiastic person. The lucky number today is 5.

Sunday, August 24 (Moon Aries to Taurus 8:36 a.m.)
You may be in such an expansive mood that you might take on more than you can handle. All kinds of things are brewing in your mind and a lot of big thinking is going on. Good for you! However, take it one step at a time. Some get a real lift today when a turn of events brings something we want desperately a little closer.

Monday, August 25 (Moon in Taurus) Unlike yesterday, discretion is the order of the day. You can't afford to fool around when you are dealing with what belongs to someone else. Make sure you've got all your pins lined up before you bowl the ball—even if it means postponing a scheduled signing. Your lucky number today should be 7.

Tuesday, August 26 (Moon Taurus to Gemini 8:00 p.m.) You should be feeling very much the solid citizen, and acting the part as well. Someone is going to ask you for advice and counsel and you should soften up and give it. Many will be delighted by a present invitation that includes good food and drink. This is one time you can let your Virgo caution go by the board. Indulge!

Wednesday, August 27 (Moon in Gemini) Don't get hyperactive today, or you will get nothing done. There is a big project that someone's got under control and wants you to play a major role in. Don't hide your light under a bushel. It's the kind of job you can sink your teeth into and you should. Many will have their curiosity satisfied today, and it will be a relief. The lucky number today is 9.

Thursday, August 28 (Moon in Gemini) That's more like it! Now you are doing some really creative thinking instead of just spinning your wheels. What gets you going is a couple of pretty fascinating people who offer a challenge; good for you for not turning it down. Many will be feeling a bit scattered today because there are so many options. Choose wisely!

***Friday, August 29** (Moon Gemini to Cancer 8:40 a.m.)* You could be tempted to be a bit manipulative today when someone seems wide open to it. Resist the urge; one of your strongest points is realizing that some big people are too easily taken advantage of. Like yourself. In another area, some Virgos can be pivotal to calming down a situation that's been a bit hot. You may get a round of cheers from the people involved.

***Saturday, August 30** (Moon in Cancer)* Today you are forced to play a background role, but that generally doesn't bother you. You would just as soon lie back and watch the scenario. The group you observe has a common purpose, but today it seems to be temporarily lost. It doesn't appear that your taking an active role would help much. However, realize that you can't retire from that fray permanently.

***Sunday, August 31** (Moon Cancer to Leo 8:08 p.m.)* Now it's time for you to get into the act. Your prestige is such that you can be very effective—and net yourself more power, if you want it. Some Virgos should wait for the exactly right moment to strike, in order to make the most of the situation and come closer to what you want. What you want may be a very stimulating member of the opposite sex; realize that he/she is available.

SEPTEMBER 1986

***Monday, September 1** (Moon in Leo)* You may not know quite what to expect from a reunion today between you and a very important person in your life. In spite of your apprehension, it will all go very well—in fact, you will be surprised at how well. It feels good to be "in sync." In another matter, some Virgos are going to have to exercise patience because it is a key to winning this game. The lucky number today is 4.

***Tuesday, September 2** (Moon in Leo)* You can take everyone by surprise today when you reveal some work you've been doing in private. Your enthusiasm for your project and the ideas that are thrown at you about how you could put it to work are exciting to you, and you can't wait to get on with it. It's great to have a goal, and to know where you are going.

Wednesday, September 3 (Moon Leo to Virgo 5:06 a.m.) Now you see what all the waiting has been about recently; it pays off because you are prepared when an opportunity—a kind of test—is thrown at you. You pass with flying colors, with the moon in your sign, but also because you are well prepared. Listen to someone with a sense of flair when he or she brings up the subject of your image.

Thursday, September 4 (Moon in Virgo) You almost can't lose today by "doing what comes naturally." It's particularly nice to have things go smoothly and to feel that the world is with you, rather than against you. Try to store up some of these feelings for a less confident time—you can use them, Virgo! Make sure you look as good as you feel, and try your luck with number 7.

Friday, September 5 (Moon Virgo to Libra 11:33 a.m.) Some tips you picked up yesterday about how to improve your image give you even more charisma today, and you find it's easy to express yourself quite forcibly. Some are even able to turn a situation completely around. If you are feeling quite creative, it is no accident; indulge your taste for all things artistic today.

Saturday, September 6 (Moon in Libra) Today's a day to take stock of resources and see where you can make a good thing even better. As you put it all together you are helped by someone close to you who has your interests at heart. She (and it is probably a she) offers sound advice about stretching something so it will go further. Leave some time for simply having fun and for trying your luck with number 9.

Sunday, September 7 (Moon Libra to Scorpio 4:12 p.m.) There may be a big pull on you today, and two things could be fighting for your attention. Or two people. You are feeling rather adventurous, but you also realize the need to be practical. For now, pull in your reins and let reality dominate. When you get things in better shape there'll be plenty of time to experiment. A lively companion provides some comic relief.

Monday, September 8 (Moon in Scorpio) You love to have established routines because they make you feel comfortable. You also like it when everybody knows the part he/she is to play; that's the way you find it today. You play your role quite well by figuring out some new ways to make things safer and sounder for everyone. Before the end of the day, you get some very positive feedback, and know that you are loved.

Tuesday, September 9 (Moon Scorpio to Sagittarius 7:40 p.m.) A riddle gets solved today when you apply some creative thinking to a complex situation. You see the light and it changes your view of things totally. The problem is that others do not get it as quickly. It's up to you to explain things in a new way that everyone can understand, and react to accordingly.

Wednesday, September 10 (Moon in Sagittarius) You are feeling rather mellow today—in fact, emotionally fulfilled. For you that is. Your present mood moves you to see where you can be particularly helpful to others—something you are very good at. In some cases, the help you give may involve the purchase of something that makes life easier for everyone involved, and you will feel that the expenditure is worth it. The lucky number today is 4.

Thursday, September 11 (Moon Sagittarius to Capricorn 10:28 p.m.) A community project gets everyone pitching in and working toward a common goal—which may be making things a lot more attractive than they were. You personally get a lot of satisfaction out of it—not only the results, but the experience of rubbing shoulders with some very nice people in the process. One could be a Gemini or another Virgo.

Friday, September 12 (Moon in Capricorn) What you want now is not "Somewhere Over the Rainbow" but a real possibility. You've got to make an almost heroic effort, but you're working off a very strong base. Someone with a lot of guts is right there beside you. It's one of those cases where if you want something badly enough, you can get it. For some, sensual pleasures are the order of the day. The lucky number is 6.

Saturday, September 13 (Moon in Capricorn) This is "solid citizen day," where you appreciate your stable base of operations. It is comforting to you to have established routines so that everyone knows his or her part. You play yours very well by figuring out some new ways to make things safer and sound. Once again, many will enjoy doing things that involve a lot of pleasure; in some cases, it will be children that bring the joyous moments during the day.

Sunday, September 14 (Moon Capricorn to Aquarius 1:07 a.m.) You of all people cannot tolerate the tawdry or shoddy, and it's necessary for you to do some clearing of the decks today to eliminate what you do not want. Others may be a bit shocked at your actions, but they should know that you want nothing that isn't "perfect" and will insist on having it. Don't overwork, however, or you will get a little strung out.

Monday, September 15 (Moon in Aquarius) What you did yesterday has had a contagious effect on those around you. Suddenly you and everyone else seems a lot smarter about how to manage time, tools, and resources. Many will be pleasantly surprised when a usually difficult person suddenly gets very logical and "sees the light"—at least in your terms. Don't take advantage of the situation.

Tuesday, September 16 (Moon Aquarius to Pisces 4:27 a.m.) Back off of it today; you've been going at it pretty heavily and need some rest and recuperation time. If you are tuned into your own mechanism you will see that you need some refueling now. In any kind of a one-on-one situation, let the other person take the lead. You are better off lying back and biding your time. It's the wisest decision you could make today.

Wednesday, September 17 (Moon in Pisces) Once again, the pace is slower today, and it gives you a chance to look around at those closest to you. Their love and support is very meaningful to you and you resolve to be more sensitive to their needs. Some will have a cooperative spirit forced upon them by a mate or partner who says, "Enough already." But even these Virgos will realize that your correcting attitude comes out of loving feelings. Get away with that someone special and let others handle the children.

Thursday, September 18 (Moon Pisces to Aries 9:33 a.m.) For some Virgos, this full moon will bring a crisis in a relationship. In some cases too, it has been coming for a while—and the showdown was inevitable. Whatever your situation, try to keep cool, and not to overreact. By the time the storm clouds clear, you will both have a much clearer picture of what's going on here. Other Virgos should be particularly careful of their digestion at this time. The lucky number is 3.

Friday, September 19 (Moon in Aries) Today many of you will be able to breathe a sigh of relief and begin to look into the future with more optimism. You may even start to formulate a plan which involves getting yourself some more training in an area that fascinates you. It may be as a response to a member of the opposite sex who is very much in the picture and inspires you to think in new terms. It's an excellent day to have some fun with a Leo or an Aries who is nearby.

Saturday, September 20 (Moon Aries to Taurus 5:25 p.m.) Try to be as analytical as possible today. You may discover motives behind someone's behavior that you do not exactly approve of. The only way to combat it is to express your own ideas in a sincere, direct manner. Someone talks about a short trip and you should consider it. You could stand a change. The lucky number today is 5.

Sunday, September 21 (Moon in Taurus) There is an aura of glamour about things today. One reason may be that you gain some secret information that gives you the edge in understanding a rather strange situation. Even though you have a backstage view and have the story behind the story, keep it to yourself. You are very able to impress someone else impressive today.

Monday, September 22 (Moon in Taurus) You start out the work week full of inspiration. Keep it by your side all week long. This is one of those days when your hands, your mind, and your heart will all work together quite effectively. Spend a little time looking forward and figuring out where you go from here; if you map out a master plan now, it will serve you well in the weeks to come.

Tuesday, September 23 (Moon Taurus to Gemini 4:13 a.m.) As a general rule, you do not particularly like to experiment. However, you are very willing to, and an interesting contact tells you about a most intriguing experiment that you can try. When it pays off, you may begin to realize that it pays to diversify your interests. Agree to participate in a project you are told about today; you have a hunch it will help you, and your intuition is right.

Wednesday, September 24 (Moon in Gemini) Scrutinize every message you get today because there may be a hidden meaning. There is a high likelihood of a job promotion now—or possibly even a career change. Such things tend to unsettle you, so try not to get thrown off by whatever happens. Remember also that your reputation may hinge on your ability to be flexible now.

Thursday, September 25 *(Moon Gemini to Cancer 4:44 p.m.)* Harmony on the home front may be one of your most important goals now; realize that some adjustments will have to be made before that occurs. You can brighten up the atmosphere considerably by taking a positive attitude toward the whole thing. Later on, expect some good companionship with some good friends. The lucky number is 1.

Friday, September 26 *(Moon in Cancer)* Be willing to trust your hunches about a relationship or a friendship; something is disturbing you, and you are right to be disturbed. Look into it, but be willing to rise above petty prejudices. For some, an important decision is in the offing—face up to it and make it. The lucky number today is 2.

Saturday, September 27 *(Moon in Cancer)* Many will be feeling highly emotional today, and it is important to understand that your feelings may cloud your reason now. For some, a romantic relationship is going to require a commitment very soon. Don't get nervous! Those involved in any kind of creative work could be absolutely inspired today. The lucky number is 3.

Sunday, September 28 *(Moon Cancer to Leo 5:39 a.m.)* It's possible that you overdid yesterday and are feeling a little strung out today. Pay some attention to your health, and spend the day in watchful waiting. You may be feeling a bit at sea about how to handle the situation; some quiet meditation will bring you just the right answer. For some, it is wise to consult someone older—possibly a parent—rather than attempting to go it alone.

Monday, September 29 *(Moon in Leo)* If you can, lay back and work behind the scenes today; you can accomplish much more there and get yourself ready for a big push that's coming up soon. Keep calm and try to get as much deadwood as possible cleared away. Refuse to be intimidated by someone who tends to be a bit overbearing; you can handle him/her quite easily if you refuse to show how nervous you are about the situation. Basically, this person is a pushover.

Tuesday, September 30 (Moon Leo to Virgo 1:57 p.m.) You may start out the day a bit on the slow side, but by the middle of it you are raring to go. That's because the moon comes roaring into your sign, and you get a real burst of mental and physical energy. If you don't go overboard in the direction of helping others, you can help yourself to a big "fat piece of the pie" today. Realize that you deserve it, and go ahead and enjoy it. Virgos who don't treat themselves well once in a while can end up being rather unhappy people. Whatever you do, don't feel guilty about it.

OCTOBER 1986

Wednesday, October 1 (Moon in Virgo) As soon as you wake, you should start feeling that extra surge of energy that comes when the moon is in your sign. It doesn't necessarily mean that life will be all rosey, however; what it does mean is that you have lots of opportunities today and if you keep your eyes open you can make the most of them. One thing you should do is get up the nerve to ask someone to "pay up"; you've been waiting long enough. Try your luck with number 5 today.

Thursday, October 2 (Moon Virgo to Libra 8:03 p.m.) Once more, this is a day during which you can score a lot of points—if you are learning how to play the game. Don't get nervous when somebody asks you to "put your money where your mouth is." You should be confident enough of your own ideas to stand behind them. If you are not, go back to the drawing board and revise.

Friday, October 3 (Moon in Libra)   You may wind up the week with your mind very much on money matters. For a change, you may be thinking about where you can expand rather than where you can cut corners. In fact, some of you may feel like indulging yourself in a luxury of one sort or another. Is it really a luxury, or is it something you feel you don't deserve? Virgos should ask themselves questions like that once in a while. It can be very productive.

Saturday, October 4 (Moon Libra to Scorpio 11:35 p.m.)   You may be feeling very much in the social mode today; in fact, some of you will be entertaining in rather high style. For many Virgos a kitchen is a wonderful place to experiment; give yourself lots of latitude to do that today. It could be very good for your soul. Meanwhile, keep your eye on someone who has been acting a little strange lately. He/she may need watching.

Sunday, October 5 (Moon in Scorpio)   You may be more busy this weekend than you would like to be. A lot of coming and going is indicated, and you may find yourself getting a little strung out by the resulting confusion. Take some time out to indulge one of your favorite passions today. You do have one, don't you? If not, correct the situation immediately.

Monday, October 6 (Moon in Scorpio)   Someone with whom you have had minor differences—possibly a Scorpio—wants to make up now and you should be willing to go along with it. This is no time to split hairs over things that don't count. If you put your mind on something, you can go right to the center of it and solve a problem that's been baffling others. For you, it could mean a new start and a lot of recognition. The lucky number today is 1.

Tuesday, October 7 (Moon Scorpio to Sagittarius 1:48 a.m.)   Don't get bummed out when you find you have to wait; sometimes waiting is good for you because it makes you practice patience. Anyway, it will work out in your favor in the long run. Someone you've been making plans with tries to chicken out. You can keep this person on the hook if you really explain what you want to do and how you want to do it. Some Virgos will be saying, "Eureka, I've found it!" An Aquarian could be extremely helpful now.

Wednesday, October 8 (Moon in Sagittarius) Don't take a verbal promise someone tries to give you; get it in writing. There is no need to worry over this one. Someone who proved him-/herself a real pal in the past now reappears and indicates he/she is ready to help you again. A relationship is getting a lot more interesting and may have long-term potential. However, as serious as someone is, he may not be ready for a final decision.

Thursday, October 9 (Moon Sagittarius to Capricorn 3:52 a.m.) This is remodeling time, and you should not hesitate to completely revamp things to make them suit your own needs a lot better. Remember, you don't have to take care of anyone else except yourself right now. A younger person—or perhaps simply a livelier one than you—proves to be a marvelous companion. Don't hesitate to try your luck today; it could be good.

Friday, October 10 (Moon in Capricorn) If this starts out as a dull day, don't write it off immediately. A lot of surprise and variety are indicated. For some, there will be a real thrill of one sort or another. In many cases, it will be a surprise approach by someone you didn't think noticed at all. The lucky number is 5.

Saturday, October 11 (Moon Capricorn to Aquarius 7:45 a.m.) Slow and steady wins the race today. If you do things in spurts and don't concentrate, you will only accomplish bits and pieces—and nothing satisfying. You may be a bit weighed down by responsibility, and there may be an awful lot of people who are depending on you now. Don't let it depress you, let it make you resolve to cut through everything and have some fun later on in the day. A Taurus or a Scorpio could be very helpful now. The lucky number is 6.

Sunday, October 12 (Moon in Aquarius) Many Virgos will learn a valuable lesson today—about friendship and loyalty. Though you never believed it could happen, someone you thought had totally turned off now turns up and says, "I'll help you"; it makes your goal appear much nearer. Other Virgos are going to have to accent their resolutions about taking care of themselves. For some, it will be more difficult because they have definitely been letting themselves go. Be glad that someone close to you has come through a crisis.

Monday, October 13 (Moon Aquarius to Pisces 11:03 a.m.) You may be amazed at how much happens so fast today. You may even surprise yourself at how quickly you can get a job out of the way—and make a commitment you never thought you would make. For some, romance and love are involved. This is definitely not a halfway day—it is more like all or nothing. If you feel you need some counseling, go to someone who's been there before and knows the ropes. If you need help, it is there.

Tuesday, October 14 (Moon in Pisces) You undoubtedly sense that a break with the past is imminent. The important thing now is to learn to let go, and to stop hanging on to "security blankets" that you no longer need. In fact, in some cases your actions in trying to keep old ties tied are counterproductive. The important thing is to look toward the future. The lucky number is 9.

Wednesday, October 15 (Moon Pisces to Aries 5:13 p.m.) Once again, many of you will be coping with the fact that something has run its course—possibly a relationship. What is essential is to make a clean break, if a break is indicated. You will know what is the right thing to do from an inner feeling that tells you what will make you happy. Don't hesitate to ask someone—possibly a Leo or an Aquarian—to help you make a decision.

Thursday, October 16 (Moon in Aries) It is not the easiest time you are going through. For some it is a very emotional one. An individual from your past could return and make it seem as if an old flame can be revived; however, realize that it could also die out very quickly. Keep your basic security needs in mind at all times. Do not give up something of value for the sake of a cheap thrill. The lucky number is 2.

Friday, October 17 (Moon in Aries) During this full moon a decision that's been pending finally has to be made. For many, it will affect their marital status or at least an extremely important relationship. If you are honest with yourself, you will realize that tensions are relieved by what happens. You could be a bit psychic today and should use your powers of perception to the fullest. The lucky number is 3.

Saturday, October 18 (Moon Aries to Taurus 1:35 a.m.) In order to get back on the track, you've got to replace the old with the new. For some, making travel plans is the ideal way to fight yourself out of what might be a minor depression. For others, plunging into a course or other educational activity could be the key. If someone contacts you and says, "What's wrong?" resolve to articulate what you are feeling and what you need. There are people who are there for you.

Sunday, October 19 (Moon in Taurus) Once again, it is wise to keep in touch with those who understand you and love you. On the light side, be ready for surprises and a rather unusual experience. For some, it could be something that has been really fine up to now. For others, a new romance is a definite possibility.

Monday, October 20 (Moon Taurus to Gemini 12:15 p.m.) Now it's time for someone else to tell you what he/she needs. You may feel as if you have been a bit selfish recently—and that is possible, but understandable. Be willing to give in and make an adjustment. Also don't be surprised if you get a rather sentimental gift. The lucky number is 6.

Tuesday, October 21 (Moon in Gemini) A surprise offer comes to many today, and they should be ready to field it. Others will get congratulations when they show how superbly they can do something that others have been doing in a rather routine manner. Some Virgos will be getting a piece of confidential information that should be kept confidential. A Pisces or a Virgo may try to get it out of you. Don't give in.

Wednesday, October 22 (Moon in Gemini) You should find that being productive is a breeze today. You are charged with energy and ready to face the challenge of additional responsibility. A lot of Virgos will be feeling more financially secure when they see that there is a definite possibility of increased income. Talk it over with a Capricorn. The lucky number is 8.

Thursday, October 23 (Moon Gemini to Cancer 12:37 a.m.) Some Virgos who have been feeling rather deserted now realize that love is not only close—it's there. Others will breathe a sigh of relief when they can get rid of an unnecessary expense or a burden that was not theirs in the first place. Use your powers of persuasion today, because they should be great.

Friday, October 24 (Moon in Cancer) Many Virgos will be feeling vital, alive, and ready for anything today. Use that spirit to play the pioneer and to show that you are not afraid to branch out into new territory. A definite advance of some sort is indicated, and for many it will be in their career area. For others, there is a definite score indicated in an affair of the heart.

Saturday, October 25 (Moon Cancer to Leo 1:02 p.m.) If you think someone is on your side, you are quite right. Your hunch is very accurate, and you should follow through on it. For many, someone will be hanging around wanting to say something; it is important that you be receptive today. A long-standing wish or desire suddenly seems as if it can become an actuality. Is it really as great as you thought it would be?

Sunday, October 26 (Moon in Leo) Even though you may be feeling a bit down in the dumps, you will be rather popular today. In fact, you should definitely accept an invitation that comes your way—even if it is a last-minute one. You will be among people who share your interest and have a great deal of good will toward you. If you make the right move, you could actually win a contest of some sort.

Monday, October 27 (Moon Leo to Virgo 11:20 p.m.) This could be a rather unsettling Monday. Be ready for revisions, reviews, and unusual requests. Even if nothing very significant happens, you may be feeling some vague fears and rather uncomfortable feelings. However, don't give in to them, because "help is on the way" in the form of the moon moving into your sign. Don't pass off a contact you can make today; this individual could open doors for you.

Tuesday, October 28 (Moon in Virgo) Okay, here you go. A lot of good things will happen, even if you don't do anything. But if you do make an effort, this could be a stellar day. In fact, if you play your cards right, you could be standing in the right place at just the right moment. Show that you can be independent—and that you can think creatively. Some Virgos will have members of the opposite sex tell them they are irresistible. The lucky number today is 5.

Wednesday, October 29 (Moon in Virgo) Some rather troubled times on the home scene are now definitely over—and harmony is restored. Some of you will have a lovely reunion with a loved one who has been a bit distant recently. With your vitality making a comeback, you could be told that you look absolutely smashing! Don't be afraid to make direct appeals today for what you want. The lucky number is 6.

Thursday, October 30 (Moon Virgo to Libra 6:04 a.m.) You may be struck with the marvelous realization that you cannot only save money but actually earn more of it. Your potential is tremendous, and it is good that you are learning that now. Some Virgos will also learn a secret, and it should make them rather happy. Others will have a very important person say, "You are the one." A Pisces could play a key role.

Friday, October 31 (Moon in Libra) Happy Halloween! Since your moon cycle is high, you should have a good, fulfilling day. Some may get excellent financial news. For others, a love relationship is really firming up and you should feel a lot more confident and secure about it. Listen to a Capricorn who has something very important to say.

NOVEMBER 1986

Saturday, November 1 (Moon Libra to Scorpio 9:19 a.m.) You are going to have to be a little cautious where money is concerned; this is not the day to go on a shopping spree. You may also have to protect your interests against someone who wants something for nothing. Realize that you look like a sitting duck. Don't play the part. Many Virgos will get a surprise gift—though for some, it may be in the form of a verbal bouquet. The lucky number is 6.

Sunday, November 2 (Moon in Scorpio) For many, this could be "good news" day. The subject of the good report you get may not be momentous, but it should make you feel as if you are looking forward to something pleasant. For some, a trip is in the offing. For others, there is money coming in. In general, your responsibilities are increasing now, but you should be feeling as if you can handle them.

Monday, November 3 (Moon Scorpio to Sagittarius 10:19 a.m.) When you think about it, someone you met yesterday is more important than you thought. If you act on your thought, it will pay dividends. Many Virgos will be feeling vital, alert, alive—and loved. The object of their affection could be a Taurus, a Cancer, or a Capricorn. The lucky number today is 8.

Tuesday, November 4 (Moon in Sagittarius) By all means finish what you start now, because your mood could be a little bit irresolute today. When you complete your mission, you will feel a lot better for it. Some Virgos have the definite feeling that love is no longer a stranger. Others are feeling a lot more steady about their general security. An Aries could play a key role. The lucky number is 9.

Wednesday, November 5 (Moon Sagittarius to Capricorn 10:49 a.m.) Lucky you! You get the chance to make a new start and to wipe out a rather embarrassing mistake you made recently. Don't say you never get a chance. Some Virgos are going to lay their cards on the table with someone—either a romantic partner or a friend who has been a bit overbearing lately. A sense of purpose should be returning to your life now.

Thursday, November 6 (Moon in Capricorn) Don't be afraid to trust those "funny feelings" you have today. You may be tempted to try something new, and you should give in to that temptation. Some Virgos are going to get involved in a rather petty argument and should try to rise above it. You will find that someone is more than willing to make a concession—but just needs a way to save face. You will know just what to do at the right moment.

Friday, November 7 (Moon Capricorn to Aquarius 12:29 p.m.) Someone is going to be very frank with you today, and you should like the results. In some cases, there will be an open proposition. But it will be a sincere one. For others, popularity is on the increase, and you should sense it—and live up to it by looking rather special. A long-distance call could spell happiness for some.

Saturday, November 8 (Moon in Aquarius) Don't be afraid to say, "I goofed" and to go back to the beginning and start all over again. Even though it is a weekend, there's lots of work to be done—some of it on yourself. Think about your health. Someone very intense—possibly a Scorpio—wants your cooperation very badly and will try to get it by telling you a secret. Don't get embroiled in something you will regret!

Sunday, November 9 (Moon Aquarius to Pisces 4:30 p.m.) Diplomacy is the only way to win today. Otherwise, you will be taking an unnecessary risk and could alienate someone who really wants to be your friend. Be smart! Some Virgos should get their ideas on paper now, because they are too good to let go. A Gemini, a Sagittarian, or another Virgo could be very important people in your life today. The lucky number is 5.

Monday, November 10 (Moon in Pisces) The focus is smack on your area of relationships today—possibly your marriage or live-in arrangement. If you don't cooperate, you will find yourself in a lot of trouble. Other people feel they should take the lead now, and they should. Regard your arrangement as a "limited partnership" now. Some will have a very important fact revealed to them, and it will be advantageous.

Tuesday, November 11 (Moon Pisces to Aries 11:14 p.m.) There is a hush-hush atmosphere about this day. You sense that something is going on behind the scenes, and you are right. Some of you will be let in on it, and may even be asked to participate in a secret meeting. Don't do anything that will compromise your position later on. Keep your resolutions about diet and nutrition.

Wednesday, November 12 (Moon in Aries) By digging deep, you could uncover some information which will help you a great deal. In doing detective work, be very careful because you do not want to be caught snooping. In some ways, you are entitled to the information, but not everyone agrees with that fact. For some, a relationship is growing a lot more serious and a commitment could be in the offing.

Thursday, November 13 (Moon in Aries) What a relief! You finished off a very major project and you feel you can relax. Not so! What you find is that people are coming to you with their problems. Particularly a member of the opposite sex who wants to discuss something important; realize that this is simply a come-on. In some cases, the end result could be deep love. The lucky number is 9.

Friday, November 14 (Moon Aries to Taurus 11:14 p.m.) Today you should really be able to get your priorities in order. It falls in that sector of your chart which has to do with "higher values." Some will be receiving a call asking for advice and counsel in a rather intimate matter; only get involved if you feel you really can help. Timing and luck are on your side now, and you should not hesitate to throw your hat in the ring.

Saturday, November 15 (Moon in Taurus) Let some things slide now, and let others take the initiative. If you play your cards close to the vest, you will be in a much better position. Use this waiting time to define your goals and to realize that long-range plans can be made and that you can stick to them. Be confident! The lucky number is 2.

Sunday, November 16 (Moon Taurus to Gemini 7:26 p.m.) This full moon period should be a rather pleasant one for you, with lots of emotional fulfillment in store. Don't be afraid to take a chance on love, and to improve your chances by shaping up your image. Some will be particularly concerned about their weight, and should use this time to make some very firm resolutions. However, start your regime tomorrow.

Monday, November 17 (Moon in Gemini) You are able to clear a very important hurdle today. For many, dealings with women will have a lot to do with how the day turns out. It's easy for you to focus on details, and that is where you should put your energies today. Some may have to do a bit of ad libbing, and should try to be as creative as possible. The lucky number is 4.

Tuesday, November 18 (Moon in Gemini) For many, romance is in full bloom. Through it, you gain some kind of enlightenment and learn a very valuable lesson. Others should be ready for change of other kinds—possibly totally new experiences and sensations. Are you open to them? A special message comes in and adds spice to your life.

Wednesday, November 19 (Moon Gemini to Cancer 7:46 a.m.) Someone makes a peace offering, and you should accept it graciously. Even though you are right, don't lord it over the other person. He/she is simply trying to make amends. A Taurus, a Libra, or a Scorpio could be very important in the day's activities. As could the number 6.

Thursday, November 20 (Moon in Cancer) You are not a great one for intrigue, but it is featured today. Some of you could get involved in a rather messy situation, and perhaps should ask themselves out. Others could find that romance is very important, but a little complicated. However, your powers of persuasion are good now, and you can make a major breakthrough if you try.

Friday, November 21 (Moon Cancer to Leo 8:25 p.m.) Action and reaction—that is the order of the day. Whether it is you or the other person who takes the first step is largely a matter of personal choice. At any rate, the pressure is on today, and you may find yourself smack in the middle of some kind of crisis. Realize that differences can be settled and that a challenge need not make you feel depressed. It should make you feel great! The lucky number is 8.

Saturday, November 22 (Moon in Leo) This is one of those days you could hit the jackpot, so to speak. Not if you take a limited point of view, however. You've got to think in large terms and realize that much bigger things are ahead of you. You are no longer limited, and you should realize it. Talk it over with an active Aries, who knows what it's like. The lucky number is 9.

Sunday, November 23 (Moon in Leo) If you feel a little shaky today, it would not be surprising. That part of your chart connected with suspicions and fears is being activated. Realize that a major cycle is ending and that you are at the beginning of a brand-new period. A Leo could help you open the door.

Monday, November 24 (Moon Leo to Virgo 7:46 a.m.) What a great way to start out the workweek! Your sense of direction should be restored, and you should have a fair amount of energy. Somebody says that he/she is available for consultation, and you should take this person up on it. Your intuition is ringing true now, and you should listen to it. A loyal person says "You're the greatest," and you should believe it.

Tuesday, November 25 (Moon in Virgo) A lot of pressure is off you now, and you should have a sense of accomplishment. For many, long-term goals will be coming into sharp, clear focus. Take your popularity for granted now, and take every invitation that comes along. Someone may be talking travel, and you should enthusiastically join in the plan.

Wednesday, November 26 (Moon Virgo to Libra 3:59 p.m.) If you persist in using outmoded methods, you are going to find yourself high and dry. Try to think now and get used to new ways of doing things.

With your lunar cycle high, it should be easy for you to breeze through this day. However, if you really want to make progress, listen to that little voice that tells you what to do.

Thursday, November 27 (Moon in Libra) This should be an excellent holiday for most Virgos. Mainly because your mood should be quite upbeat, and you should be feeling accepting of everyone and everything that comes. When you open your heart, others do too—and you should know that you are cherished. However, do not get thrown off-balance when a quick change of plans occurs. If some people are late, it's not their fault. Be willing to forgive and forget.

Friday, November 28 (Moon Libra to Scorpio 8:15 p.m.) It should give most of you a great sense of satisfaction to know that the money picture is good, and that all the books are balanced, so to speak. Many of you are only happy when your accounts are straight. Some will get a pleasant surprise when they realize a family member is an ally rather than an enemy. It could be a Taurus, a Libra, or a Scorpio who delights you.

Saturday, November 29 (Moon in Scorpio) If you let your pride get in the way, you will be doing yourself a disservice. Someone really wants to help you, and you should accept it with good grace. There's nothing wrong with having someone pull strings for you. This or something similar could be the subject of private consultations many Virgos are involved in today. A Pisces may play a key role.

Sunday, November 30 (Moon Scorpio to Sagittarius 9:08 p.m.) Now you really should know where you stand. And you should like it. A dispute—possibly right under your own roof—is settled, and you should be feeling a lot less nervous as a result. Some will be doing some serious thinking about the future, and realizing some changes have to be made. The lucky number is 8.

DECEMBER 1986

Monday, December 1 (Moon in Sagittarius) Though you may have no choice but to go out, your thoughts will remain at your home base today. Matters of emotional security are uppermost in your mind. Rest assured that you can overcome what seem like great obstacles now, and come together again with someone that you love. In some cases, basic values and what things are worth are very much part of the day's mental activity. The lucky number is 7.

Tuesday, December 2 (Moon Sagittarius to Capricorn 8:26 p.m.) Someone will present you with a golden opportunity to make your money grow today; don't blow it! It's great to be cautious, but not to be totally blind. In many cases, a member of the opposite sex says, "You're the greatest." It's a pleasant surprise, but a bit unsettling as well.

Wednesday, December 3 (Moon in Capricorn) Now most of you should be willing to reach beyond what appear to be limitations. You are due for a lot greater freedom of thought and action—and you should make sure you get it. Many will be feeling so sure of themselves that they feel like taking a chance on love. Try it! And try your luck with number 9.

Thursday, December 4 (Moon Capricorn to Aquarius 8:23 p.m.) You should know where you stand, and you should know it's in a pretty good place. Your prestige may be very much on your mind. So much so that you decide that you can't waste time on anything that is not absolutely in line with the main issue. You'll catch up with pleasure pursuits later on. A partner may be disappointed.

Friday, December 5 (Moon in Aquarius) Once again you may be "all business." Take advantage of your industrious mood to streamline some of your technique so that things will go more quickly and easily in the future. Some Virgos will be able to make a great display of how special they are able to make something appear. Later on, relax and enjoy—possibly a gourmet dinner to which you are invited. However, don't throw all your resolutions about diet and health out the window. Be moderate. The lucky number is 2.

Saturday, December 6 (Moon Aquarius to Pisces 10:48 p.m.) You may be feeling a bit at loose ends today, and your forces may be rather scattered. Try to bring them together in order to see a picture as a whole and not get bogged down in petty details. Once again, you may have that nagging feeling that everybody in the world is depending on you. They aren't really.

Sunday, December 7 (Moon in Pisces) For many, a wonderful reunion with a loved one is indicated. It may have been a long time coming. Make sure you make the most of it. Other Virgos may have to toss aside some preconceived notions now and realize there is no way to handle things except to go back to square one and start all over again. Don't get discouraged!

Monday, December 8 (Moon in Pisces) Try to stay out of the spotlight today because it may tend to distract you. What you need to do is best done on your own and away from others. One person appeals for some special time with you and you should oblige, because he/she senses your mood and reacts to it. Some sort of mystery may present itself, but don't try to solve it all at once. The lucky number today is 5.

Tuesday, December 9 (Moon Pisces to Aries 4:49 a.m.) A clash of ideas could end up with a case of mutual respect between you and someone else. Many Virgos will have their minds on money matters today and in some cases the more "taxing" side. A secret meeting can lend spice, but it should not be counted on as anything permanent. A Taurus or a Libra could provide a lot of understanding.

Wednesday, December 10 (Moon in Aries) Have the courage to toss out what you don't need. The more you trim your sails, the farther you can go. Some are going to have to dig very deep for information now, and not take superficial answers. Others will gain a new understanding of someone who seems extremely shy, but really is not. A Pisces could provide excellent insight.

Thursday, December 11 (Moon Aries to Taurus 2:10 p.m.) Many Virgos will be able to save the day today by figuring out an ingenious way to get what everyone wants, within the budget. In many cases, you have someone by your side rooting for you all the way. He/she understands the challenge, and appreciates what you are able to do. This is a day when some Virgos should not hesitate to make a big step. You've got the power in your hands.

Friday, December 12 (Moon in Taurus) Once again, your self-confidence should be there when you need it. If you have a sense of your own worth, and get more familiar with your potential, there is little you cannot accomplish now. However, for some, love will be more important than money. The lucky number is 9.

Saturday, December 13 (Moon in Taurus) A bright optimistic person could come along and shake you right down to your foundation. For some, it could be love at first sight; for others, it is the beginning of a wonderful new friendship. There is someone in your circle who could help you overcome some obstacles—and some inhibitions. Listen to him/her—possibly a Leo or an Aquarian.

Sunday, December 14 (Moon Taurus to Gemini 1:41 a.m.) This could be a really fine day for you, full of excellent company and everything that goes with it. Like good food. Someone around you is going to make a special effort to make you happy; a gift could be part of the scenario. Your intuition is good now, and you should take advantage of it. The lucky number is 2.

Monday, December 15 (Moon in Gemini) Someone will approach you with an intriguing question today; your answer should be a resounding "yes." In some cases, you will be asked to take on more responsibility. You know you can do it, and you have to admit that you've been a bit bored recently. Some should relieve their boredom by going on a fashion spending spree.

Tuesday, December 16 (Moon Gemini to Cancer 2:09 p.m.) Don't let anyone throw you off-balance today; you may have to protect yourself against some form of intimidation. If it is simply that you are asked to revise something you've already done, agree wholeheartedly. This is no time for digging in your heels. During this full moon, you are going to have to protect yourself emotionally. And also remember that you have right on your side.

Wednesday, December 17 (Moon in Cancer) New prestige and a feeling that others are giving you high marks make it easy to forget past mistakes now. With a few successes under your belt, you will be finally able to begin to get some confidence that you can continue to perform well. Don't lose the feeling! And feel confident enough to make a fairly big decision.

Thursday, December 18 (Moon in Cancer) Breaking ties with past people and outworn habits is not always easy, but with a burst of energy and confidence you feel now, you are able to do it. As a result, you open doors to new opportunities—and even romance. You could sell almost anything to almost anyone today. The lucky number is 6.

Friday, December 19 (Moon Cancer to Leo 2:44 a.m.) You hope it is not a wild goose chase you set out on today; nobody seems to have the story straight and it's up to you to straighten it out. There is even a hint of mystery and a slight apprehension about what is involved. When you see the light, you get a good laugh. It's amazing what your imagination can do. Don't forget someone who is confined and needs a word of cheer.

Saturday, December 20 (Moon in Leo) What starts out looking like a totally black situation quickly does a flip-flop and ends up being a reason for celebration. Do you believe it? Quick transformations are the order of the day, as are unbelievable strokes of luck. One of them could be yours. A Cancer or a Capricorn will keep you on a steady course.

Sunday, December 21 (Moon Leo to Virgo 2:30 p.m.) Be sure to finish what you start today and realize that others are watching. If you use your intuition, you will get a rare insight and know that you are on the right track. Later on it is verified by real information. A rather "glamorous" person could take a special interest in you—and make you feel just great.

Monday, December 22 (Moon in Virgo) What a great time of year to have the moon in your sign. It should really put you in the holiday spirit. All kinds of fresh starts are indicated as are exchanges with a rather dynamic individual. This is one time you can really hold your own. You should feel quite vigorous and optimistic now—and you should remember your timing is the best. The lucky number is 1.

Tuesday, December 23 (Moon in Virgo) If there are last-minute things for the holidays that need doing, you should be able to polish them off in no time at all. And even take time out for a pleasant reunion with someone you haven't seen for a while. In some cases, a learning process is going on, and it may affect your emotional security. Even your marriage. Learn your lessons well! The lucky number is 2.

Wednesday, December 24 (Moon Virgo to Libra 12:05 a.m.) This could be a fabulous holiday for you in terms of the number of gifts you receive—and their value. However, with the moon in that area of your chart relating to personal possessions, you may have your mind a bit too much on such things. Try to get into the spiritual side of the holiday spirit. But also enjoy the popularity you have at the moment. And a compliment you receive from somebody you like.

Thursday, December 25 (Moon in Libra) Today your thoughts and your feelings come together, and it's a beautiful marriage. Your spirits should be excellent, and those around you should be feeling the same way. For some, there is a discussion of long-range prospects—and an important decision could be made. Make sure you are on the right side.

Friday, December 26 (Moon Libra to Scorpio 7:06 a.m.) You may have a little more company than you are comfortable with today. However, if you are determined to have a good time, and equally determined not to let your nerves get the better of you, you should come smiling through. Some will feel as if they are floating when the most important person in their lives expresses his/her feelings in no uncertain terms. And they are very positive. The lucky number is 5.

Saturday, December 27 (Moon in Scorpio) Things are beginning to settle down, and you may have to reconcile yourself to some kind of adjustment in your personal environment. However, once you get used to it you will love it. You may get the definite feeling that you have to pull back in terms of curbing your excellent holiday appetite. The best way is simply to pull back from the table. A Libra could be very important.

Sunday, December 28 (Moon Scorpio to Sagittarius 8:20 a.m.) Your mood improves quite dramatically, and you are virtually "bubbly" today. Show off your sense of humor—especially when you have to make a concession to someone else. It is an intelligent one, and you are right to go along with it. Your sense of guilt about someone who is waiting to hear from you could drive you to go out of your way. It is well worth the effort.

Monday, December 29 (Moon in Sagittarius) Even though you are very much in the holiday spirit, your thoughts may turn to matters of basic security. Very basic. In some cases, you may be literally taking an inventory of what you have—and what you owe. It is important not to shortchange yourself now; you might do well to get a professional appraisal of something you own. A Capricorn, a Cancer, or a Taurean could be particularly helpful in this regard. The lucky number is 8.

Tuesday, December 30 (Moon Sagittarius to Capricorn 7:54 a.m.) Yesterday's stock-taking could make you very aware that moderation is important now. Possibly necessary. Many will be embarking on a program to both affect savings and reserve resources. Others may have to make those around them understand that following the rules and regulations is not really a chore. Especially when the stakes are so high.

Wednesday, December 31 (Moon in Capricorn) For many Virgos, this could be one of the most romantic New Year's Eves in a long time. Some of you may be letting down your guard enough to let someone know how you really feel. In a very forceful manner. You are wise to put some inhibitions behind you. Enjoy a sparkling evening with a Leo, an Aquarian, or an Aries—and look forward to a marvelous year!

About This Series

This is one of a series of
Twelve Day-by-Day Astrological Guides
for the signs in 1986
by Sydney Omarr

About the Author

Born on August 5, 1926, in Philadelphia, Omarr was the only astrologer ever given full-time duty in the U.S. Army as an astrologer. He also is regarded as the most erudite astrologer of our time and the best-known, through his syndicated column (300 newspapers), and his radio and television programs (he is Merv Griffin's "resident astrologer"). Omarr has been called the most "knowledgeable astrologer since Evangeline Adams." His forecasts of Nixon's downfall, the end of World War II in mid-August of 1945, the assassination of John F. Kennedy, Roosevelt's election to a fourth term and his death in office ... these and many others ... are on record and quoted enough to be considered "legendary."

COUPON

PROF. LALLEMEND
Dept SO-8 ● POB 252
BROOKLYN, N.Y. 11204

516 Fifth Ave., NY., NY. 10036

Dear Reader,

You do not have to 'merely believe' Professor Lallemend, the renowned astrologer, because he will **PROVE** to you how he can help you make your life better!

Just fill out this form and mail it. Professor Lallemend will prepare **YOUR HOROSCOPE** and predict—without charge **TWO ESSENTIAL EVENTS IN YOUR LIFE.** You will be thoroughly convinced by the precision of the forecast and will also learn how you can gain success and inner contentment, as well as avoiding everything which can be an obstacle in the path of your happiness. You will receive his advice absolutely free of charge. All you have to do is, answer the questions below, and mail the coupon TODAY.

Please send me free of charge and without any obligation on my part my horoscope and two predictions in an unmarked envelope.

My Birthdate ....
Time .... Place ....
Please let me know as well, my lucky numbers. I enclose here a number between 0 and 9 which suddenly comes to my mind:

_____

NAME......................
ADD. ....
....
CITY......................
STATE :........ ZIP........

How well do you know yourself?

This horoscope gives you answers to these questions based on your exact time and place of birth...

How do others see you?
What is your greatest strength?
What are your life purposes?
What drives motivate you?
How do you think?
Are you a loving person?
How competitive are you?
What are your ideals?
How religious are you?
Can you take responsibility?
How creative are you?
How do you handle money?
How do you express yourself?
What career is best for you?
How will you be remembered?
Who are your real friends?
What are you hiding?

Many people are out of touch with their real selves. Some can't get ahead professionally because they are doing the wrong kind of work. Others lack self-confidence because they're trying to be someone they're not. Others are unsuccessful in love because they use the wrong approach with the wrong people. Astrology has helped hundreds of people with problems like these by showing them their real selves.

You are a unique individual. Since the world began, there has never been anyone exactly like you. Sun-sign astrology, the kind you see in newspapers and magazines, is all right as far as it goes. But it treats you as if you were just the same as millions of others who have the same Sun sign because their birthdays are close to yours. A true astrological reading of your character and personality has to be one of a kind, unlike any other. It has to be based on exact date, time, longitude and latitude of your birth. Only a big IBM computer like the one that Para Research uses can handle the trillions of possibilities.

A Unique Document Your Astral Portrait includes your complete chart with planetary positions and house cusps calculated to the nearest minute of arc, all planetary aspects with orbs and intensities, plus text explaining the meaning of:

★ Your particular combination of Sun and Moon signs.
★ Your Ascendant sign and the house position of its ruling planet. (Many computer horoscopes omit this because it requires exact birth data.)
★ The planets influencing all twelve houses in your chart.
★ Your planetary aspects.

Others Tell Us "I found the Astral Portrait to be the best horoscope I've ever read." —E.D., Los Angeles, CA
"I could not put it down until I'd read every word   It is like you've been looking over my shoulder since I arrived in this world!"—B.N.L., Redding, CA
"I recommend the Astral Portrait. It even surpasses many of the readings done by professional astrologers."
—J.B., Bristol, CT

Low Price There is no substitute for a personal conference with an astrologer, but a good astrologer charges $50 and up for a complete chart reading. Some who have rich clients get $200 and more. Your Astral Portrait is an analysis of your character written by some of the world's foremost astrologers, and you can have it not for $200 or $50 but for only $22. This is possible because the text of your Astral Portrait is already written. You pay only for the cost of putting your birth information into the computer, compiling one copy, checking it and sending it to you within two weeks.

Permanence Ordinarily, you leave as astrologer's office with only a memory. Your Astral Portrait is a thirty-five-page, fifteen-thousand-word, permanently bound book that you can read again and again for years.

Money-Back Guarantee Our guarantee is unconditional. That means you can return your Astral Portrait at any time for any reason and get a full refund of the purchase price. That means we take all the risk, not you!

You Hold the Key The secrets of your inner character and personality, your real self, are locked in the memory of the computer. You alone hold the key: your time and place of birth. Fill in the coupon below and send it to the address shown with $22. Don't put it off. Do it now while you're thinking of it. Your Astral Portrait is waiting for you.

© 1977 Para Research, Inc.

Para Research, Dept. BT, P.O. Box 61, Gloucester, Massachusetts 01930 I want to read about my real self. Please send me my Astral Portrait. I understand that if I am not completely satisfied, I can return it for a full refund. ☐ I enclose $22 plus 1.50 for shipping and handling. ☐ Charge $23.50 to my Master Card account. ☐ Charge $23.50 to my VISA account.

Card number	Good through Mo.	Day	Yr.
Mr/Ms	Birthdate Mo.	Day	Yr.
Address	Birthtime (within an hour)		AM/PM
City	Birthplace City		
State Zip	State	County	

Know in advance the changes in your life

Wouldn't it be useful to know when important events in your life are going to happen? How would you respond? What will you experience emotionally, intellectually and psychologically? And how will these experiences affect your life?

Your transits can provide valuable clues to various trends or stages of personal growth. This is especially true for the slower moving outer planets—Jupiter through Pluto. The transits for these planets are long lasting and profound in their psychological consequences. Many occur only once in a lifetime. The Astral Forecast is all about the outer planets.

This horoscope provides a reliable tool for astrological forecasting. The Astral Forecast will show you how the outer transits affect your sense of timing, that is, the times that are appropriate for you to take certain kinds of actions and inappropriate for others. This horoscope includes every significant transit to your outer planets that occurs in a twelve-month period. You can use your Astral Forecast to better understand how the outer planets affect such important life issues as career, child rearing, love, marriage and more.

For example, when Jupiter is in the first house, this transit represents a major growth cycle in your life. This is the best time for you to explore who you really are as an individual. Under this transit, you will feel more secure about yourself and the impression you make on others. Therefore, understanding yourself and your influence on others can make this transit an especially powerful and important time in your life. This is also a time for learning and gaining new experience. All this is part of your present need for personal growth, which affects not only yourself, but also the way you deal with the world as a whole. This is one time when persons and resources are likely to be drawn to you, and you should take constructive advantage of them.

You can find out in advance what your transits are going to be. But if you do it on your own, you will have to consult several astronomical tables to find the positions of each of the transiting planets every day and then compare them mathematically to the positions of the planets at the time of your birth.

There's an easier way to learn of your transits. Our IBM System/36 computer will handle all the calculations and provide you with information on all your outer transits based on your exact time and place of birth. With the Astral Forecast you not only receive the most accurate calculation of your personal transits for the next twelve months, you will also receive an extensive printout interpreting the character and significance of your individual transits.

Your Astral Forecast is the most accurate and authoritative guide to the outer transits that you can receive. It is based on the work of Robert Hand, one of America's most famous astrologers, and the author of several astrology books.

Like all Para Research horoscopes, the Astral Forecast is inexpensive. For just $16.00 you can have the same kind of advice that would otherwise cost you hundreds of dollars. This low price is possible because the astrological data is stored in our computer, and can be easily formatted and printed. Also, the mathematical calculations can be done in a matter of minutes. Your only cost is the cost of putting your personal information into the computer, producing one copy and then mailing it.

When you order your Astral Forecast, you receive an unconditional money-back guarantee. This means you can return your Astral Forecast at any time and get a full refund of the purchase price. We take all the risk.

Order your Astral Forecast today. Discover how the transits can bring energy to each part of your personality, fulfill your potential and help you gain more control over your own life.
© 1983 Para Research, Inc.

Para Research, Dept. BT, P.O. Box 61, Gloucester, Massachusetts 01930 Please send me my Astral Forecast. I understand that if I am not completely satisfied, I can return it for a full refund. ☐ I enclose $16 plus $1.50 for shipping and handling. ☐ Charge $17.50 to my MasterCard account. ☐ Charge $17.50 to my VISA account.

Card number _____ Good through Mo. _____ Day _____ Yr. _____

Mr/Ms _____ Birthdate Mo. _____ Day _____ Yr. _____

Address _____ Birthtime (within an hour) _____ AM/PM

City _____ Birthplace City _____ State _____

State _____ Zip _____ Start calendar with Mo. _____ Yr. _____

Don't Let A TERRIBLE THING HAPPEN TO YOU!

SECRET KNOWLEDGE REVEALED THAT HAS BEEN HANDED DOWN THROUGH HISTORY. TO HELP GIVE YOU A RICHER, LOVE FILLED, HAPPIER LIFE.

Will The POWER Of The OCCULT DOLL Work For YOU?

● **OCCULT SUPPLIES**—For centuries it was and still is a tradition that in Secret Ancient Rituals and Magic of Haiti, Africa, and Latin America, dolls and spells were used to carry out every purpose desired. Used for Love, Luck, Riches to gain power. These ancient rituals were rare a constant source of comfort and hope to those who pratice.

We have been making these OCCULT DOLLS and RITUALS for certain customers with Special Problems to see if they were able to help. We are happy to tell you that we feel they have been a great success. Each Doll is made of a certain color with Amulets, Charms, and Herbs sewn in. Believed to attract WHAT YOU WANT. Each Doll is handmade with Great Care by one who knows and believes. Comes with full instructions.

● **LOVE DOLL**
We feel the Most Powerful Love Occult Ritual is done with Red, and special items sewn inside. Used to bring a love back to you or get your relationship back to the love and excitement you once had we believe. Comes with special Red tipped pin, powerful instructions.
D300 . . . . 5.98

● **MONEY DRAWING DOLL**
Green Doll handmade with coins and Herbs sewn inside. We believe that Green has the power of attracting money to one in need. Strong money directions included.
D500 . . . . 5.98

● **OCCULT RITUAL HANDBOOK**
Everything you always wanted to know about Occult Rituals and Magic-songs, chants, spells for every purpose. Use of Roots, Herbs, Oils plus ceremonial rites and more. The secrets are here.
Bk120 . . . . 4.98

Triple Win BINGO BAG

Did you ever wonder why some people always win at BINGO? Do they have a secret? Now you can have your own secret! Your own BINGO BAG to carry with you.

NOW YOU CAN WIN TOO! When your numbers are called, you be the one to shout BINGO! You get Bingo Oil, Gemstone, Charm, Seal plus Green Bag and full instructions.
KK795 All 7 items 7.95

LOVE RUB

Rub on your hands or body — or on the body of the one you love. Get what you want and use it wisely.

K371-Red-Passionate Love
K372-Pink-Win love and conquer Evil
K373-Green-Money Drawing
K374-Light Blue-Power to Find a Job

3.98 Any 3 for 11.50

FOLLOW ME COLOGNE

Comes with "LUCKY FORTUNE" A Few Drops Does the Trick. To attract your love, wear this whenever you go out. Sprinkle in your draws also.

K297 Large 4 oz. size

4.98

SPIRITUAL OILS

Used by many thousands of satisfied people because the fragrance charms the senses. Try them today!

2.25 Save 77¢
Order any 3
Only 5.98

K-4 — Attraction	K-14 — Lady Luck
K-100 — Commanding	K-11 — Lodestone
K-2 — Compelling	K-112 — Lovers
K-101 — Concentration	K-113 — Lucky Money
K-102 — Crossing	K-114 — Lucky Hand
K-103 — Dragon Blood	K-9 — Money Drawing
K-18 — Fast Luck	K-7 — Power
K-104 — Finance	K-117 — Protection
K-105 — French Love	K-121 — Spirit
K-106 — Good Luck	K-8 — Success
K-107 — High Conquering	K-122 — Uncrossing
K-109 — Holy Spiritual	K-123 — Van Van
K-110 — Jinx Removing	
K-111 — King Solomon	

SPECIAL INCENSE 2.25

Save 77¢
Order any 3
Only 5.98

Burn incense to attract, to dispel wicked odors. Best incense available, attracting fragrances, satisfying results.

NUMBER IN EVERY BOX
People are used to buying incense with a number. And considering it lucky. We don't claim these numbers as such.

K-77 — Commanding	K-48 — Success
K-42 — Compelling	K-34 — Jinx Removing
K-78 — Concentration	K-84 — Lady Luck
K-97 — Crossing	K-86 — Lovers
K-80 — Dragon Blood	K-87 — Lucky Hand
K-41 — Fast Luck	K-88 — Lucky Money
K-33 — Finance	K-91 — Masters
K-81 — French Love	K-47 — Money Drawing
K-82 — Good Luck	K-39 — Power
K-83 — High Conquering	K-43 — Van Van
	K-35 — Uncrossing

Write to: ANN HOWARD DEPT.SY1 200 West Sunrise Highway, Freeport, N.Y. 11520

$5 Dollar Deposit on all C.O.D. Orders! Prepaid Orders Please Add $1.95 for Postage. FREE- Latest Catalog-Candles, Oils, Incense, Spells, More. Just Write. No claims are made. These alleged powers are gathered from writings, books, folklore & occult sources. Sold as curios.

"Next to my mother, you have been the greatest inspiration of my life."

You'll be amazed!

When you read what Marguerite Carter has to say about your life in the year ahead you'll be amazed. She delves into the most important areas of your life: romance, money, goals, and significant changes. You'll find out all the wonderful ways you can live a better life when you have your Unitology Forecast prepared for you by Marguerite Carter.

She'll help you.

Marguerite Carter has counseled thousands of enthusiastic followers around the world for decades. She has been the guiding light and helping hand for people from all walks of life: business leaders, hollywood stars and just everyday folks. There is a good reason why they seek her services year after year. They get the help they need in the most important areas of their lives!

'. . . it was amazing.'

People write all the time telling about how Marguerite Carter has helped them.

MARGUERITE CARTER

". . . it was amazing. I just can't believe it." W.C., Canada

". . . could not put it down until I read it cover to cover." M.L., Illinois.

"Without a doubt, next to my mother, you have been the greatest inspiration of my life. Many others could probably say the same thing." M.A., PA

In letter after letter people comment on the realistic guidance they've received for getting what they want from life. They've found the help they need in times of decision or resolving personal problems. These are judgments by a caring counselor, not some impersonal computer.

Hidden Opportunities

The things you want most may not be out of reach. Marguerite Carter says, "Many people are completely unaware that the opportunities for money, love or advancement are passing them by almost daily . . ." Without knowledge of when the conditions are favorable or unfavorable, the chances for success and happiness are greatly diminished.

Get your Unitology Forecast with special notations by Marguerite Carter. It will be prepared to your specific birthdate information. Remember that you will receive a full year of guidance, regardless of when your request is received, and you'll know that your forecast has come from one of the world's most highly respected astrologer-counselors.

Marguerite Carter • P.O. Box 807 • Indianapolis, Indiana 46206   O-6

☐ Yes Miss Carter, Please send me my Unitology Forecast for the year ahead. Enclosed is my remittance of $9.95 plus $1.00 for postage and handling. (First Class $1.30) Make all checks payable in U.S. funds. Allow 4 weeks for delivery.

Name _____

Address _____

City _____ State _____ Zip Code _____

Birthplace _____

Month _____ Day _____ Year _____

Place _____ Hour _____

ASTROLOGY QUESTIONNAIRE

Help us bring you even better astrology guides by filling out this survey and mailing it today.

A. Book Title (Sign): _____

B. Using the scale below how would you rate this astrological guide? (Place one rating from 0–10 in the space provided.)

Poor	Not So Good	O.K.	Good	Excellent
0 1	2 3	4 5 6	7 8	9 10

Rating

Overall Opinion of book _____

Essay On:
1. Defining Terms _____
2. Your House of The Sun _____
3. The Geometry of Relationships _____
4. Twelve Places at the Table _____
5. Moods of the Moon _____
6. Venus and Mars _____
7. Venus Sign Position Chart _____
8. Mars Sign Position Chart _____
9. The Planets as "Stars" _____
10. Astrotrivia _____
11. Sun Sign Changes _____
12. Your Sign: The Big Picture _____
13. Your Sign: Objectives and Obstacles _____
14. Pairing Off With Your Sign _____
15. Your Sign's Sex Role Dilemma _____
16. Your Sign: Female _____
17. Your Sign: Male _____
18. Your Sign: Help Wanted _____
19. How "Pure" a _____ are you? _____
20. Find Your Rising Sign _____
21. Your Sign: Astro-Outlook for '86 _____
22. 15 Months of Day-By-Day Predictions _____

C. In total about how many astrology guides have you purchased for yourself in the past 12 months?
# of books _____

D. What topics would you be interested in having Sydney Omarr write about in the 1987 Astrology Guide?

_____

_____

E. What is your education?

1( ) High School   3( ) 4 yrs college
2( ) 2 yrs college   4( ) Postgraduate

F. What is your occupation? _____

G. What is your marital status?

1( ) Single   3( ) Divorced   5( ) Widowed
2( ) Married   4( ) Separated

H. Age: _____   I. Sex: 1( ) Male
                                         2( ) Female

Please Print Name: _____

Address _____

City _____ **State** _____ **Zip** _____

Phone # ( ) _____

Thank you. Please send to New American Library, Research Dept., 1633 Broadway, New York, NY 10019